Many aspects of the internal and external workings of computers can be viewed, at different levels, as a series of communication processes. Communication complexity is the mathematical theory of such communication processes. It is also often used as an abstract model of other aspects of computation. It extends Shannon's information theory, allowing two-way communication and arbitrary processes. This book surveys this mathematical theory, concentrating on the question of how much communication is necessary for any particular process.

The first part of the book is devoted to the simple two-party model introduced by Yao in 1979, which is still the most widely studied model. The second part treats newer models, such as variable partition models, communication complexity of relations, and multiparty protocols, developed to deal with more complicated communication processes. Finally, applications of these models, including Turing machines, boolean circuits, computer networks, VLSI circuits, pseudorandomness, and data structures, are treated in the third part of the book. In particular, communication arguments are used to prove lower bounds for many problems arising in these areas.

This is an essential resource for graduate students and researchers in theoretical computer science, circuits, networks, VLSI, and information theory.

Communication Complexity

Communication Complexity

Eyal Kushilevitz

*Technion – Israel
Institute of Technology,
Haifa*

Noam Nisan

*Hebrew University,
Jerusalem*

CAMBRIDGE
UNIVERSITY PRESS

CAMBRIDGE UNIVERSITY PRESS
Cambridge, New York, Melbourne, Madrid, Cape Town, Singapore, São Paulo

Cambridge University Press
The Edinburgh Building, Cambridge CB2 2RU, UK

Published in the United States of America by Cambridge University Press, New York

www.cambridge.org
Information on this title: www.cambridge.org/9780521560672

First published 1997
This digitally printed first paperback version 2006

A catalogue record for this publication is available from the British Library

Library of Congress Cataloguing in Publication data
Kushilevitz, Eyal.
Communication complexity / Eyal Kushilevitz, Noam Nisan.
   p.   cm.
Includes bibliographical references.
ISBN 0-521-56067-5 (hardcover)
1. Boolean algebra. 2. Logic circuits. 3. Computational
complexity. I. Nisan, Noam. II. Title.   96-12840
                                                   CIP
QA10.3.K86 1996
004.6'01'5113 – dc20

ISBN-13 978-0-521-56067-2 hardback
ISBN-10 0-521-56067-5 hardback

ISBN-13 978-0-521-02983-4 paperback
ISBN-10 0-521-02983-X paperback

Contents

CONTENTS

Preface

This book surveys the mathematical field of *communication complexity*. Whereas the original motivation for studying this issue comes from computer systems and the operations they perform, the underlying issues can be neatly abstracted mathematically. This is the approach taken here.

Communication

The need for communication arises whenever two or more computers, components, systems, or humans (in general, "parties") need to jointly perform a task that none of them can perform alone. This may arise, for example, due to the lack of resources of any single party or due to the lack of data available to any single party.

In many cases, the need for communication is explicit: When we search files on a remote computer it is clear that the requests and answers are actually communicated (via electrical wires, optical cables, radio signals, etc.). In other cases, the communication taking place is more implicit: When a single computer runs a program there is some communication between the different parts of the computer, for example, between the CPU and the memory, or even among different parts of the CPU. In yet other cases, there is no real communication going on but it is still a useful abstraction. For a problem whose solution relies on several pieces of data, we can imagine that these *pieces of data* need to communicate with each other in order to solve the problem; in reality, of course, this communication will be achieved by a processor accessing them all.

Complexity

The notion of complexity is becoming more and more central in many branches of science and in particular in the study of various types of computation. In the field of *computational complexity* the central question is always "how complicated" a given problem is, rather than "what is a solution" to the problem.

The problems we will be dealing with here can all be solved trivially if unlimited communication is allowed. What we will be studying is *how much* communication is necessary to solve a given problem. The amount of communication needed is what we will call the communication complexity of the problem. We should emphasize: Communication complexity is an inherent property of a *problem*, not of any particular solution for the problem. We may design many solutions for any given problem, solutions whose efficiency may vary widely. The communication complexity is the cost of the most efficient solution for the problem.

Any study of communication complexity should be contrasted with Shannon's classical *information theory*. In information theory, the starting point is a certain communication that needs to take place; for example, one computer wishes to send certain data to another computer. Information theory then deals with the issue of how this communication can be carried out: what codes to use, how to deal with faulty communication links, what communication rates can be achieved, and so forth. In communication complexity, on the other hand, the starting point is a problem to be solved; for example, multiply two numbers, each stored on a different computer. Communication complexity then deals with *what* needs to be communicated in order to solve this problem.

This Book

The simplest mathematical scenario that captures many of the issues of communication is the two-party model suggested by Yao in 1979. This model has been quite extensively studied, is reasonably well understood, and exhibits beautiful structure. The first part of this book, Chapters 1–4, is devoted to this model.

In the second part of the book, Chapters 5–7, we look at several more complicated scenarios in which communication occurs. Each of these scenarios is intended to highlight an issue that was not dealt with by Yao's model. The models we present include those known as "variable partition models," "communication complexity of relations," and "multiparty protocols."

In the third part of the book, we demonstrate the general applicability of the notions studied in the first two parts. We present many examples of computation, in different models and settings, in which communication plays an important, usually implicit, role. In each of these examples, we use the results obtained in the study of communication complexity to prove theorems regarding the model of computation in question. Most of these applications yield *lower bounds*; that is, we prove that any solution of certain problems in the model cannot be too efficient due to the (implicit or explicit) communication needs of the problem. The models we deal with include Turing machines, boolean circuits, computer networks, VLSI circuits, data structures, pseudorandomness, and more.

The mathematical background needed for reading this book includes the material of basic courses in linear algebra, probability theory, and discrete mathematics. For the continence of the reader, we include in Appendix B some definitions and facts related to these areas. These, however, are meant to refresh the memory of a reader who have seen this material in the past and cannot serve as an introduction to any of these areas.

The reader is encouraged not to skip over the examples given throughout the book. These examples, although sometimes containing some of the more sophisticated mathematics in this book, do not just exemplify general theorems and ideas. They are an integral part of the presentation and contain a significant portion of the material.

Throughout the book we tried to provide many exercises. Some of these exercises are very simple, whereas others are quite complicated. Solutions for few of these exercises are given in Appendix C and the corresponding exercises are marked by "*" (these are typically exercises that are nontrivial and for which the solution is interesting).

At the end of each chapter we include a "Bibliographic Notes" section that gives references for the results mentioned throughout the chapter as well as pointers to further readings. In spite of our sincere efforts, it may be that some appropriate references were not included. We apologize to our colleagues for any such case. Please inform us about this as well as about any other mistakes you may find or any comments that you may have.

The Flow of Chapters

There are several ways to use this book. The obvious one is to read it from the beginning to the end. This may be the best way for those readers who are interested in a thorough understanding of the area. It is also possible to read this book in an "application-driven" manner. You should read Chapter 1 first and then proceed by focusing on an application

To read . . .	read first . . .
Sections 8.1 and 8.3	Chapter 7
Section 8.2	Chapter 3
Section 9.1	Chapter 7
Sections 9.2 and 9.3	Section 4.3
Chapter 10	Chapter 5
Section 10.4	Chapter 2
Section 10.5	Section 4.2
Section 11.1	Chapter 7
Section 11.2	Chapter 3 and Chapter 7
Section 11.3	Chapter 6
Sections 12.3 and 12.4	Chapter 7
Section 13.1	Section 3.4
Section 13.2	Section 4.4
Section 13.3	Section 3.5

Figure 0.1: Organization

from the third part of the book and reading from Chapters 2–7 only the material that is needed by the application. Figure 0.1 summarizes what material is needed by each application.

This book may be used in a graduate course in several ways. A general course in concrete computational complexity may include only the material in Chapter 1 and an application or two (for example, for Turing machines or decision trees). A course devoted to communication complexity may cover all of Chapters 1, 2, and 3 and a significant portion of the rest of the book.

Acknowledgments

We have greatly benefited by many, many discussions with several of our colleagues. It is very clear to us that this book has been deeply influenced by them, and we sincerely wish to thank all of them. In particular, we thank Laci Babai, Peter Bro Miltersen, Benny Chor, Thomas Feder, Oded Goldreich, Johan Håstad, Russell Impagliazzo, Mauricio Karchmer, Richard Karp, Ilan Kremer, Nati Linial, Yishay Mansour, Moni Naor, Ilan Newman, Rafi Ostrovsky, Michael Rabin, Dana Ron, Steven Rudich, Muli Safra, Mike Sipser, Jiri Sgall, Madhu Sudan, Mario Szegedy, Amnon Ta-Shma, Umesh Vazirani, and Avi Wigderson.

The first author thanks Benny Chor for introducing him to the area of communication complexity (back in 1989). The second author thanks Avi Wigderson for being a constant source of ideas and knowledge. We wish to thank Jiri Sgall and Daniel Lewin for reading an early version of this book and for giving us many useful comments and suggestions. We thank Amos Beimel, who was forced to listen (and verify) some proofs and ideas from this book. We also thank our editor, Lauren Cowles, for sharing with us her experience and for giving us advice.

We have been helped by several existing manuscripts: Richard Karp's lecture notes on concrete complexity, Laci Lovasz's survey of Communication Complexity, T. Lengauer's survey on VLSI theory, and Benny Chor's personal notes, which served as the basis for Section 4.6.

The first step toward writing this book was taken when the second author presented a series of lectures on communication complexity at a workshop organized by Pierre McKenzie and Denny Thérien and held in Barbados in the winter of 1993. We thank Pierre and Denny for suggesting communication complexity as a worthwhile topic. The material in this book has been presented by the first author at class given in the Technion in the fall of 1994. We thank the students in this class and the Teaching Assistant, Amos Beimel, for their feedback. In particular, some of the solutions (and exercises) are based on their excellent homework.

Eyal Kushilevitz, Dept. of Computer Science, Technion, Haifa 32000, Israel.
e-mail: eyalk@cs.technion.ac.il
http://www.cs.technion.ac.il/~eyalk

Noam Nisan, Dept. of Computer Science, Hebrew University, Jerusalem, Israel.
e-mail: noam@cs.huji.ac.il.
http://www.cs.huji.ac.il/~noam

PART ONE

Two-Party Communication Complexity

CHAPTER 1

Basics

The general communication problem may be described in the following terms: A system must perform some task that depends on information distributed among the different parts of the system (called *processors*, *parties*, or *players*). The players thus need to communicate with each other in order to perform the task. Yao's model of communication complexity, which is the subject of this chapter, is the simplest scenario in which such a situation occurs. Yao's model makes the following simplifying assumptions:

- There are only two parts in the system.
- Each part of the system gets a fixed part of the input information.
- The only resource we care about is communication.
- The task is the computation of some prespecified function of the input.

These assumptions help us concentrate on the core issue of communication. Despite its apparent simplicity, this is a very rich model that exhibits a nice structure and in which issues such as randomization and nondeterminism, among others, can be studied. We can also translate our understanding of this model to many other scenarios in which communication is a key issue.

1.1. The Model

Let X, Y, Z be arbitrary finite sets and let $f : X \times Y \to Z$ be an arbitrary function. There are two players, Alice and Bob, who wish to evaluate $f(x, y)$, for some inputs $x \in X$ and $y \in Y$. The difficulty is that Alice only knows x and Bob only knows y. Thus, to evaluate the function, they will need to communicate with each other. The communication will be carried out according to some fixed protocol $\mathcal{P}$ (which depends only on f). The protocol consists of the players sending bits to each other until the value of f can be determined.

At each stage, the protocol $\mathcal{P}$ (for the function f) must determine whether the run terminates; if the run has terminated, the protocol must specify the answer given by the protocol (that is, $f(x, y)$); and if the run has not terminated, the protocol must specify which player sends a bit of communication next. This information must depend solely on the bits communicated so far during this run of the protocol, because this is the only knowledge common to both Alice and Bob. In addition, if it is Alice's turn to speak (that is, to communicate a bit), the protocol must specify what she sends; this depends on the communication so far as well as on x, the input visible to Alice. Similarly, if it is Bob's turn to speak, the protocol must specify what he sends; this depends on the communication so far and on y, his input.

We are only interested in the amount of communication between Alice and Bob, and we wish to ignore the question of the internal computations each of them makes. Thus, we allow Bob and Alice to have unlimited computational power. The cost of a protocol $\mathcal{P}$ on input (x, y) is the number of bits communicated by $\mathcal{P}$ on input (x, y). The cost of a protocol $\mathcal{P}$ is the *worst* case (that is, maximal) cost of $\mathcal{P}$ over all inputs (x, y). The complexity of f is the minimum cost of a protocol that computes f.

To formalize this model from the players' point of view, we could define functions specifying who speaks at each point (for example, $NEXT: \{0, 1\}^* \rightarrow \{Alice, Bob\}$), what they say, when they stop speaking, and what the answer is. Since we do not want to run the protocol but to analyze it, the following formalization, from the protocol designer's point of view, will be more convenient:

Definition 1.1: *A protocol $\mathcal{P}$ over domain $X \times Y$ with range Z is a binary tree where each internal node v is labeled either by a function $a_v: X \rightarrow \{0, 1\}$ or by a function $b_v: Y \rightarrow \{0, 1\}$, and each leaf is labeled with an element $z \in Z$.*

The value of the protocol $\mathcal{P}$ on input (x, y) is the label of the leaf reached by starting from the root, and walking on the tree. At each internal node v labeled by a_v walking left if $a_v(x) = 0$ and right if $a_v(x) = 1$, and at each internal node labeled by b_v walking left if $b_v(y) = 0$ and right if $b_v(y) = 1$. The cost of the protocol $\mathcal{P}$ on input (x, y) is the length of the path taken on input (x, y). The cost of the protocol $\mathcal{P}$ is the height of the tree.

Intuitively, each internal node v labeled by a function a_v corresponds to a bit sent by Alice (the bit being $a_v(x)$) and each internal node v labeled by b_v corresponds to a bit sent by Bob. Figure 1.1 shows a protocol tree for some (Boolean) function f defined on $X \times Y$ for $X = \{x, x', x'', x'''\}$ and $Y = \{y, y', y'', y'''\}$. The function f computed by this protocol appears in Figure 1.2. For example, on input (x'', y) the path followed by the protocol is the rightmost path of the tree. The value computed by the protocol is therefore 0. Also note that the value of the function a_4 on x and x' may be arbitrary. This is because $a_1(x) = a_1(x') = 0$ and therefore input pairs in which the value given to Alice is either x or x' take the left edge going from the root and hence a_4 will never be evaluated for such inputs.

Definition 1.2: *For a function $f: X \times Y \rightarrow Z$, the (deterministic) communication complexity of f is the minimum cost of $\mathcal{P}$, over all protocols $\mathcal{P}$ that compute f. We denote the (deterministic) communication complexity of f by $D(f)$.*

Sometimes we consider slight variations of this model. For example, in our model the value of the protocol must be evident solely from the communication exchanged

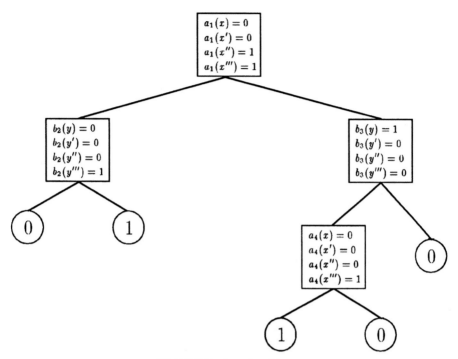

$$a_1(x) = 0$$
$$a_1(x') = 0$$
$$a_1(x'') = 1$$
$$a_1(x''') = 1$$

$$b_2(y) = 0$$
$$b_2(y') = 0$$
$$b_2(y'') = 0$$
$$b_2(y''') = 1$$

$$b_3(y) = 1$$
$$b_3(y') = 0$$
$$b_3(y'') = 0$$
$$b_3(y''') = 0$$

0   1

$$a_4(x) = 0$$
$$a_4(x') = 0$$
$$a_4(x'') = 0$$
$$a_4(x''') = 1$$

0

1   0

Figure 1.1: A protocol tree

	y	y'	y''	y'''
x	0	0	0	1
x'	0	0	0	1
x''	0	0	0	0
x'''	0	1	1	1

Figure 1.2: The function f computed by the protocol of Figure 1.1

by the parties (this is implicit in the definition by the requirement that the protocol terminates only at leaves where the output is uniquely defined). We may relax this by requiring that only one of the parties knows the answer. This changes the complexity by at most $\log_2 |Z|$. In our model, the order of communication between the two parties is arbitrary. We may require that Alice and Bob each send one bit in her/his turn. This changes the complexity by at most a factor of two.

The simplest way for Alice and Bob to evaluate a function f is for one of the players, say Alice, to send all her input to Bob (requiring $\log_2 |X|$ bits using an appropriate encoding), for Bob to compute $f(x, y)$ privately (with his unlimited computational power), and then for Bob to send the answer back to Alice ($\log_2 |Z|$ more bits). We thus have:

Proposition 1.3: *For every function* $f : X \times Y \to Z$,

$$D(f) \leq \log_2 |X| + \log_2 |Z|.$$

▶ **Example 1.4:** Alice and Bob hold subsets $x, y \subseteq \{1, \ldots, n\}$ respectively and they wish to compute MAX(x, y), the maximal number in $x \cup y$. For this, Alice sends to Bob the maximal number in x ($\log n$ bits). Bob compares this value with the maximal number in y and sends the larger of them as the output ($\log n$ bits). Therefore, $D(\text{MAX}) \leq 2 \log n$.

Exercise 1.5: Alice and Bob hold subsets $x, y \subseteq \{1, \ldots, n\}$, respectively, and they wish to compute AVG(x, y), which is defined as the average number in the multiset $x \cup y$. Prove that $D(\text{AVG}) = O(\log n)$. (Note that the average need not be an integer.)

In many cases more clever protocols can be designed.

▶ **Example 1.6:** Alice and Bob hold subsets $x, y \subseteq \{1, \ldots, n\}$, respectively. MED$(x, y)$ is defined to be the median of the multiset $x \cup y$ (if $x \cup y$ contains an even number $t = 2k$ of (not necessarily distinct) elements, then the median is defined as (say) the k-th smallest element). By Proposition 1.3, $D(\text{MED}) \leq n + \log_2 n$ (observe that a subset of $\{1, \ldots, n\}$ can be represented using an n-bit string).

A better protocol for MED may proceed using binary search as follows: At each stage Alice and Bob have an interval $[i, j]$ in which the median may still lie. They halve the interval by deciding whether the median is above or below $k = (i + j)/2$. This is done by Alice sending to Bob the number of elements in x that lie above k and the number that lie below k ($O(\log n)$ bits). Bob can now decide whether the median lies above or below k, and he sends this information to Alice (1 bit). This protocol has $O(\log n)$ stages and each requires $O(\log n)$ bits of communication, so $D(\text{MED}) = O(\log^2 n)$.

Exercise 1.7*: Give an $O(\log n)$ bit protocol for MED.

Exercise 1.8*: Given any graph G on n vertices, we define the following "clique vs. independent set" problem with respect to G: Alice receives as an input C, which is a clique in G (a set of vertices with an edge between any two of them). Bob receives as an input I, which is an independent set in G (a set of vertices with no edges between them). The function $\text{CIS}_G(C, I)$ is defined as the size of $C \cap I$ (observe that this size is either 0 or 1). Prove that $D(\text{CIS}_G) = O(\log^2 n)$, for all G. (A lower bound better than $\Omega(\log n)$ is not known for any G.)

As these examples show, Yao's communication complexity model is quite powerful and allows the design of "clever" protocols. Our main concern will be proving lower bounds on communication complexity: Given a function f, we would like to prove that in any protocol that computes f at least a certain number of bits must be exchanged. For functions with a large range, the following trivial lower bound is often useful.

Exercise 1.9: Show that for every function $f : X \times Y \to Z$, $D(f) \geq \log_2 |\text{Range}(f)|$, where $\text{Range}(f)$ is the set of all $z \in Z$ for which there exists a pair $(x, y) \in X \times Y$ such that $f(x, y) = z$. Conclude that for the function MED the upper bound of Exercise 1.7 is tight (up to a constant).

For the case we are mostly concerned with, that is *Boolean* functions $f : X \times Y \to \{0, 1\}$, this bound only says that $D(f) \geq 1$ and is therefore useless.

From this point on, unless explicitly stated, we always assume $Z = \{0, 1\}$. Most of the techniques we present easily extend to the nonboolean case. In other cases, bounds can be obtained by considering the functions $f_i(x, y)$, the i-th bit of $f(x, y)$, instead of considering f. These functions are Boolean, hence our techniques can be applied. Also, in the Boolean case, we will often not insist that the output be clear from the communication because with a $+1$ increase in the communication complexity this property can be achieved.

1.2. Rectangles

The success in proving good lower bounds on the communication complexity of various functions comes from the *combinatorial* view we take on protocols. The idea is to view protocols as a way to partition the space of all possible input pairs, $X \times Y$, into sets such that for all input pairs in the same set the same communication is sent during the execution of the protocol. In the terminology of protocol trees this means that the inputs in each set are those inputs that reach a certain leaf. Then, we show that these sets of inputs are restricted to have a very special structure. This restriction is imposed by the fact that Alice sees only x and Bob sees only y. This leads to the introduction of the most fundamental element in the combinatorics of protocols – the *(combinatorial) rectangle*.

Definition 1.10: *Let P be a protocol and v be a node of the protocol tree. R_v is the set of inputs (x, y) that reach node v.*

It immediately follows that:

Proposition 1.11: *If L is the set of leaves of a protocol P, then $\{R_\ell\}_{\ell \in L}$ is a partition of $X \times Y$.*

The structure of the sets R_ℓ (and more generally the sets R_v) is not at all arbitrary. The study of this structure is at the center of our approach to communication complexity.

Definition 1.12: *A combinatorial rectangle (in short, a rectangle) in $X \times Y$ is a subset $R \subseteq X \times Y$ such that $R = A \times B$ for some $A \subseteq X$ and $B \subseteq Y$.*

An equivalent definition is given by the following proposition.

Proposition 1.13: $R \subseteq X \times Y$ *is a rectangle if and only if*

$$(x_1, y_1) \in R \text{ and } (x_2, y_2) \in R \Rightarrow (x_1, y_2) \in R.$$

— 7 —

PROOF:

Only if: Assume R is a rectangle, that is $R = A \times B$. If $(x_1, y_1) \in R$, then $x_1 \in A$. Similarly, because $(x_2, y_2) \in R$, then $y_2 \in B$. It follows that $(x_1, y_2) \in A \times B = R$.

If: Define the sets

$$A = \{x \mid \text{exists } y \text{ such that } (x, y) \in R\}$$

and

$$B = \{y \mid \text{exists } x \text{ such that } (x, y) \in R\}.$$

We claim that $R = A \times B$. The inclusion $R \subseteq A \times B$ is clear from the definition of A and B ($(x, y) \in R$ implies $x \in A$ and $y \in B$ hence $(x, y) \in A \times B$). To show that $A \times B \subseteq R$, consider $(x, y) \in A \times B$. Since $x \in A$ there exists y' such that $(x, y') \in R$. Similarly, because $y \in B$ there exists x' such that $(x', y) \in R$. Using the assumption this implies $(x, y) \in R$. □

The connection between rectangles and communication complexity is given by the following proposition:

Proposition 1.14: *For every protocol $\mathcal{P}$ and leaf ℓ in it, R_ℓ is a rectangle.*

PROOF: We will prove by induction on the depth of v that R_v is a rectangle. For the root, it is clear that $R_{root} = X \times Y$, which is a rectangle. Otherwise, let w be the parent of v and assume, without loss of generality, that v is the left son of w and that in w Alice speaks (that is, w is labeled with a function $a_w : X \to \{0, 1\}$). Then

$$R_v = R_w \cap \{(x, y) \mid a_w(x) = 0\}.$$

By the induction hypothesis, $R_w = A_w \times B_w$, and thus

$$R_v = (A_w \cap \{x \mid a_w(x) = 0\}) \times B_w$$

which is a rectangle. □

Note that the proof shows that all the sets R_v are rectangles and not only those corresponding to leaves of the tree. It may be instructive to see another proof of this proposition using the second definition of a rectangle, given by Proposition 1.13.

PROOF: Assume $(x_1, y_1) \in R_\ell$ and $(x_2, y_2) \in R_\ell$, we will show that also $(x_1, y_2) \in R_\ell$, that is, we will show that on input (x_1, y_2) the protocol will behave the same as on (x_1, y_1) and (x_2, y_2). We will follow the communication performed (that is, the path taken) on input (x_1, y_2) and show that it never deviates from the path to ℓ. If we have reached a node v on the path in which Alice speaks, then because she cannot distinguish between (x_1, y_2) and (x_1, y_1) (in both cases, she evaluates $a_v(x_1)$) she will behave the same on both inputs. Thus, on (x_1, y_2) we will also move toward ℓ. If we have reached a node v in which Bob speaks then because Bob cannot distinguish between (x_1, y_2) and (x_2, y_2) he will behave the same on both inputs, that is, again we will move toward ℓ. □

	000	001	010	011	100	101	110	111
000	0	1	1	0	1	0	0	0
001	1	0	0	0	0	0	0	1
010	1	0	0	0	1	0	0	0
011	0	0	!	0	0	0	0	1
100	1	0	0	0	1	0	0	1
101	1	1	1	0	0	0	1	1
110	0	0	0	0	1	0	0	0
111	0	1	1	0	1	1	0	1

Figure 1.3: A 0-monochromatic rectangle

In both proofs the reason R_ℓ is a rectangle is that Alice and Bob each know only one of the inputs x and y. The second proof is in fact a "cut-and-paste" argument: We take the way Alice behaves out of the communication on (x_1, y_1), and the way Bob behaves out of the communication on (x_2, y_2), and we put them together to get the communication on (x_1, y_2). This kind of argument is found in many other proofs, especially those that deal with crossing sequences. Indeed, as is shown in Part III of this book, in many cases we can reprove results that were initially proved with crossing sequences using communication complexity. The new proofs do not repeat the cut-and-paste argument, thus abstracting away these types of arguments.

If a protocol $\mathcal{P}$ computes a function f then for every leaf ℓ of $\mathcal{P}$, all inputs $(x, y) \in R_\ell$ must have the same value of f, the value with which ℓ is labeled.

Definition 1.15: *A subset $R \subseteq X \times Y$ is called f-monochromatic (in short, monochromatic) if f is fixed on R.*

Figure 1.3 shows an example of a monochromatic rectangle, where the rows correspond to $X = \{0, 1\}^3$, the columns correspond to $Y = \{0, 1\}^3$, and the rectangle $R = A \times B$ is defined by $A = \{001, 010, 100, 110\}$ and $B = \{001, 010, 011, 101, 110\}$. We emphasize that, although in many figures it will be convenient to draw the rectangles as having adjacent rows and columns, the definition does *not* require this. This section can now be summarized by:

Lemma 1.16: *Any protocol $\mathcal{P}$ for a function f induces a partition of $X \times Y$ into f-monochromatic rectangles. The number of rectangles is the number of leaves of $\mathcal{P}$.*

Figure 1.4 shows the partition of the space of inputs $X \times Y$ by the protocol of Figure 1.1 (for the function f given in Figure 1.2).

Corollary 1.17: *If any partition of $X \times Y$ into f-monochromatic rectangles requires at least t rectangles, then $D(f) \geq \log_2 t$.*

PROOF: By Lemma 1.16, the leaves of any protocol for f induce a partition of $X \times Y$ into f-monochromatic rectangles. Hence, by the assumption, any such protocol must

	y	y'	y''	y'''
x	0	0	0	1
x'	0	0	0	1
x''	0	0	0	0
x'''	0	1	1	1

Figure 1.4: The function f computed by the protocol of Figure 1.1

have at least t leaves and thus the depth of its tree (since the tree is binary) is at least $\log_2 t$. $\qquad\qquad\square$

This corollary gives a strategy for proving lower bounds on the communication complexity of a function f: prove lower bounds on the number of rectangles in any partition of $X \times Y$ into f-monochromatic rectangles. In the next sections we present several techniques for doing this.

Exercise 1.18: Let $X = Y = \{1, \ldots, n\}$. A geometric rectangle is a set of the form $\{(x,y) \mid x_{min} \le x \le x_{max}, y_{min} \le y \le y_{max}\}$, for some values $x_{min}, x_{max}, y_{min}$, and y_{max} in $\{1, \ldots, n\}$. A *comparison protocol* is a one in which at each node v, if Alice needs to transmit a bit then this bit is the result of comparing her input x with some value θ_v (that is, $a_v(x)$ is 0 if $x < \theta_v$ and 1 if $x \ge \theta_v$). Similarly, at each node v where Bob speaks he sends the result of comparing his input y with some value θ_v. Prove that every comparison protocol for computing a function f partitions the space $X \times Y$ into f-monochromatic geometric rectangles.

1.3. Fooling Sets and Rectangle Size

Our first lower bound technique is called the "fooling set" technique. It says that if we exhibit a large set of input pairs such that no two of them can be in a single monochromatic rectangle, this implies that the number of monochromatic rectangles is large. The idea is to use the fact that each protocol partitions the space $X \times Y$ into monochromatic rectangles (Lemma 1.16), together with the property of rectangles given by Proposition 1.13 (see Figure 1.5). These together imply that if two input pairs (x_1, y_1) and (x_2, y_2) are in the same monochromatic rectangle induced by a given protocol $\mathcal{P}$, then the value of f on both of them is some z, and that the two input pairs (x_1, y_2)

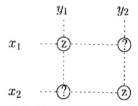

Figure 1.5: The rectangle's property

and (x_2, y_1) must also be in the same monochromatic rectangle. In particular, f has the same value z on both of (x_1, y_2) and (x_2, y_1). In other words, if the value of f on either (x_1, y_2) or (x_2, y_1) is not z, then (x_1, y_1) and (x_2, y_2) cannot be in the same rectangle. This is formalized by the following definition and lemma.

Definition 1.19: *Let $f : X \times Y \to \{0, 1\}$. A set $S \subset X \times Y$ is called a* fooling set *(for f) if there exists a value $z \in \{0, 1\}$ such that*

- *For every $(x, y) \in S$, $f(x, y) = z$.*
- *For every two distinct pairs (x_1, y_1) and (x_2, y_2) in S, either $f(x_1, y_2) \neq z$ or $f(x_2, y_1) \neq z$.*

Lemma 1.20: *If f has a fooling set S of size t, then $D(f) \geq \log_2 t$.*

PROOF: It is enough to prove that no monochromatic rectangle contains more than one element of S. Assume that a rectangle R contains two distinct pairs (x_1, y_1) and (x_2, y_2) that belong to S. By Proposition 1.13, it must also contain (x_1, y_2) and (x_2, y_1). However, since S is a fooling set, the value of f on both (x_1, y_1) and (x_2, y_2) is z, whereas on at least one of (x_1, y_2) and (x_2, y_1) the value of f is different than z. It follows that R is not monochromatic. Therefore, at least t rectangles are needed to cover S, and the lemma follows by Corollary 1.17. □

The above bound is obtained by considering a fooling set that contains only points of $X \times Y$ whose f-value is some $z \in \{0, 1\}$. In fact, we get a lower bound on the number of z-rectangles. To improve the lower bound, we can obtain such a bound for both the 0-rectangles and the 1-rectangles. The total number of rectangles needed in a partition is at least the sum of these two numbers. Despite the simplicity of the fooling set technique, it gives tight bounds for several interesting functions.

▶ **Example 1.21:** Alice and Bob each hold an n-bit string, $x, y \in \{0, 1\}^n$. The equality function, EQ(x, y), is defined to be 1 if $x = y$ and 0 otherwise. A fooling set of size 2^n is

$$S = \{(\alpha, \alpha) \mid \alpha \in \{0, 1\}^n\}$$

(because for every α, EQ$(\alpha, \alpha) = 1$, whereas for every $\alpha \neq \beta$, EQ$(\alpha, \beta) = 0$). It follows that $D(\text{EQ}) \geq n$. By also counting 0-rectangles, we conclude $D(\text{EQ}) \geq n + 1$. Finally, recall that $D(f) \leq n + 1$ for every function $f : \{0, 1\}^n \times \{0, 1\}^n \to \{0, 1\}$ (by Proposition 1.3). Therefore, $D(\text{EQ}) = n + 1$.

Exercise 1.22: Alice and Bob each hold an n-bit integer $0 \leq x, y < 2^n$. The "greater than" function, GT(x, y), is defined to be 1 iff $x > y$. Prove that $D(\text{GT}) = n + 1$.

▶ **Example 1.23:** Alice and Bob each hold a subset of $\{1, \ldots, n\}$ (x and y, respectively). The disjointness function, DISJ(x, y), is defined to be 1 iff $x \cap y = \emptyset$. A fooling set of size 2^n is given by

$$S = \{(A, \bar{A}) \mid A \subseteq \{1, \ldots, n\}\}$$

(without loss of generality, for $A \neq B$ there exists an element a such that $a \in A, a \notin B$; hence $A \cap \bar{B} \neq \emptyset$). It follows that $D(\text{DISJ}) \geq n$. Once again, by also counting 0-rectangles we conclude $D(\text{DISJ}) = n + 1$.

The fooling set technique is a special case of a more general technique for proving lower bounds on the communication complexity. The idea is to prove that the "size" of every monochromatic rectangle is small, implying that many monochromatic rectangles are needed in any partition of $X \times Y$. Naturally, the "size" measure can be chosen to our advantage, and in general we can use any probability distribution as a size measure.

Proposition 1.24: *Let μ be a probability distribution of $X \times Y$. If any f-monochromatic rectangle R has measure $\mu(R) \leq \delta$, then $D(f) \geq \log_2 1/\delta$.*

PROOF: Since $\mu(X \times Y) = 1$, there must be at least $1/\delta$ rectangles in any f-monochromatic partition of $X \times Y$. Thus, the bound follows from Corollary 1.17. □

To see that the fooling set technique is indeed a special case of Proposition 1.24, we consider any fooling set S of size t and define a probability distribution μ as follows: $\mu(x, y) = 0$ for $(x, y) \notin S$ and $\mu(x, y) = 1/t$ for $(x, y) \in S$. What we have shown in the proof of Lemma 1.20 is that every monochromatic rectangle R can contain at most one element of the fooling set and thus has measure $\mu(R) \leq 1/t$. Another special case is obtained by looking at the actual size of the f-monochromatic rectangles. If we can prove that all monochromatic rectangles are of size smaller than k, then the number of rectangles is at least $|X||Y|/k$ and hence $D(f) \geq \log |X| + \log |Y| - \log k$. To see that this is also a special case of Proposition 1.24, consider the uniform distribution $\mu(x, y) = 1/|X||Y|$. The above property guarantees that every monochromatic rectangle R has measure $\mu(R) \leq k/|X||Y|$. A slight variant of this argument can be obtained by considering only the inputs for which $f(x, y) = 0$. This is done in Example 1.25.

▶ **Example 1.25:** Alice and Bob each hold an n-bit string, $x, y \in \{0, 1\}^n$. The inner-product function, IP, is defined by $\text{IP}(x, y) = \sum_{i=1}^{n} x_i y_i \pmod{2}$. That is, $\text{IP}(x, y)$ is just the inner product $\langle x, y \rangle$ modulo 2. We will show that any 0-monochromatic rectangle covers at most 2^n of the input pairs (out of about $2^{2n}/2$ 0s). Thus, if μ is the uniform distribution on the 0s of the function then, for all rectangles R, $\mu(R) \leq 2^{-(n-1)}$. This implies, by Proposition 1.24, that $D(\text{IP}) \geq n - 1$.

Let $R = A \times B$ be any 0-rectangle. First, we replace A by $A' = span(A)$ and B by $B' = span(B)$, where $span(C)$ denotes the linear span, over the vector space Z_2^n, of vectors in the set C. The extended rectangle $A' \times B'$ may have larger area but since the inner product satisfies

$$\langle a + a', b + b' \rangle = \langle a, b \rangle + \langle a, b' \rangle + \langle a', b \rangle + \langle a', b' \rangle$$

then $A' \times B'$ is still 0-monochromatic. Finally, since A' and B' are orthogonal subspaces of Z_2^n, then by linear algebra the sum of $dim(A')$ and $dim(B')$ is at most n, the dimension of the whole space. Therefore, the size of the rectangle is bounded by $|A'||B'| = 2^{dim(A')}2^{dim(B')} \leq 2^n$.

Exercise 1.26: Prove that the size of any 1-monochromatic rectangle of the DISJ function (Example 1.23) is at most 2^n. Conclude that $D(\text{DISJ}) = \Omega(n)$.

1.4. Rank Lower Bound

In this section we present a very different lower bound technique. This technique also gives a lower bound on communication complexity by giving a lower bound on the number of monochromatic rectangles in any partition of $X \times Y$, but it does so in an *algebraic* way. This allows us later to use algebraic tools for proving communication complexity lower bounds. To this end, we associate with every function $f : X \times Y \to \{0, 1\}$ a matrix M_f of dimensions $|X| \times |Y|$. The rows of M_f are indexed by the elements of X and the columns by the elements of Y. The (x, y) entry of M_f is simply defined as $f(x, y)$. For example, Figure 1.6 shows the matrix M_{EQ} corresponding to the equality function EQ (Example 1.21). This matrix is simply the identity matrix. The following algebraic property of the matrix M_f is useful for proving lower bounds on the communication complexity of f.

Definition 1.27: $rank(f)$ is the linear rank of the matrix M_f over the field of reals.

Lemma 1.28: For any function $f : X \times Y \to \{0, 1\}$,

$$D(f) \geq \log_2 rank(f).$$

PROOF: Let $\mathcal{P}$ be a protocol for f and let L_1 be the set of leaves of $\mathcal{P}$ in which the output is 1. For each leaf $\ell \in L_1$, define a matrix M_ℓ by $M_\ell(x, y) = 1$ for $(x, y) \in R_\ell$ and $M_\ell(x, y) = 0$ for $(x, y) \notin R_\ell$, where R_ℓ is the rectangle of all inputs reaching the

	000	001	010	011	100	101	110	111
000	1	0	0	0	0	0	0	0
001	0	1	0	0	0	0	0	0
010	0	0	1	0	0	0	0	0
011	0	0	0	1	0	0	0	0
100	0	0	0	0	1	0	0	0
101	0	0	0	0	0	1	0	0
110	0	0	0	0	0	0	1	0
111	0	0	0	0	0	0	0	1

Figure 1.6: The matrix M_{EQ}

13

leaf ℓ. With this notation, observe that every (x, y) for which $f(x, y) = 0$ is 0 in all the matrices M_ℓ, whereas every (x, y) for which $f(x, y) = 1$ is 1 in a single such matrix. In other words,

$$M_f = \sum_{\ell \in L_1} M_\ell.$$

By the properties of the rank, we have

$$\text{rank}(M_f) \le \sum_{\ell \in L_1} \text{rank}(M_\ell).$$

Finally, $\text{rank}(M_\ell) = 1$ so $\text{rank}(M_f) \le |L_1| \le |L|$. In particular, $\mathcal{P}$ must have at least $\text{rank}(f)$ leaves and the lemma follows by Corollary 1.17. $\square$

Note that the above proof actually gives a lower bound on the number of 1-rectangles. By switching the role of 1 and 0 (that is, looking at the function $not(f)$), we also get a lower bound on the number of 0-rectangles in any partition. Also, observe that the ranks of the matrices M_f and $M_{not(f)}$ differ by at most 1, since $M_{not(f)} = J - M_f$, where J is the all-1 matrix (whose rank is 1). Therefore, Lemma 1.28 implies that

$$D(f) \ge \log_2(2\text{rank}(f) - 1).$$

▶ **Example 1.29:** As noted, the matrix M_{EQ} corresponding to the function EQ is simply the identity matrix, for which $\text{rank}(M_{\text{EQ}}) = 2^n$ and hence $D(\text{EQ}) \ge n$. Next, consider the inner product function IP (as in Example 1.25). The rank of M_{IP} seems at first difficult to analyze. Luckily, the matrix $N = (M_{\text{IP}})^2$ has a simple form: the (y, y') entry of N is simply $\sum_{z \in \{0,1\}^n} \langle y, z \rangle \cdot \langle z, y' \rangle$, which is exactly the number of zs for which $\langle y, z \rangle = \langle z, y' \rangle = 1$. By the properties of the inner product, N is a diagonal matrix with the value 2^{n-1} on the diagonal and the value 2^{n-2} off the diagonal (except for the first row and first column, which are identically 0). Thus, N has almost full $(2^n - 1)$ rank and so is M_{IP} (this is because for two matrices A and B, $\text{rank}(AB) \le \min(\text{rank}(A), \text{rank}(B))$). It follows that $D(\text{IP}) \ge n$.

Exercise 1.30: In the previous section, we proved (using the fooling set technique) that the communication complexity of each of the functions EQ, GT, and DISJ is $n + 1$. Prove these facts using a rank argument.

Exercise 1.31: Let $f: X \times Y \to \{0,1\}$ be a Boolean function.

- Prove that if f is such that all the rows of M_f are distinct, then $D(f) \ge \log \log |X|$.
- Prove that $D(f) \le \text{rank}(f) + 1$.

1.5. Bibliographic Notes

The first motivation for studying communication complexity was the AT^2 lower bound for VLSI of [Thompson 1979] (see Section 8.3). The two-party communication complexity model, as presented here, was first defined and discussed in the seminal paper

[Yao 1979]. Yao identified central notions such as *rectangles* and *covers* as well as several of the examples used commonly in the study of communication complexity (for example, EQ, GT, and DISJ). Example 1.6 and Exercise 1.7 are due to M. Karchmer (private communication). A different $O(\log^2 n)$ solution to the median problem of Example 1.6 can be derived from [Rodeh 1982]. Exercise 1.8 appears in [Yannakakis 1988]. The notion of *Fooling set* is implicit in [Yao 1979] and appears in the work of [Lipton and Sedgewick 1981]. The terminology we use follows that in [Karp 1986]. The *rank lower bound* was discovered by [Mehlhorn and Schmidt 1982].

Further results related to these notions appear in Chapter 2. See the bibliographic notes in that chapter for additional references. We also refer the reader to the surveys of [Lovász 1989] and [Lengauer 1990].

More on Covers

In Chapter 1 we saw that every communication protocol induces a partition of the space of possible inputs into monochromatic rectangles and learned of two lower bound techniques for the number of rectangles in such a partition. In this section we study how closely these combinatorial measures relate to communication complexity and to each other.

2.1. Covers and Nondeterminism

Although every protocol induces a partition of $X \times Y$ into f-monochromatic rectangles, simple examples show that the opposite is not true. In Figure 2.1, a partition of $X \times Y$ into monochromatic rectangles is given that do not correspond to any protocol. To see this, consider any protocol $\mathcal{P}$ for computing the corresponding function f. Since the function is not constant, there must be a first player who sends a message that is not constant. Suppose that this player is Alice. Since the messages that Alice sends on x, x' and x'' are not all the same, there are two possibilities: (1) her messages on x and x' are different. In this case the rectangle $\{x, x'\} \times \{y\}$ is not a monochromatic rectangle induced by the protocol $\mathcal{P}$; or (2) her messages on x' and x'' are different. In this case the rectangle $\{x', x''\} \times \{y''\}$ is not a monochromatic rectangle induced by the protocol $\mathcal{P}$. Similarly, if Bob is the first player to send a nonconstant message, then this message is inconsistent with either the rectangle $\{x\} \times \{y', y''\}$ or with the rectangle $\{x''\} \times \{y, y'\}$.

   A natural question is therefore: How good are lower bound techniques for communication complexity that use lower bounds on the number of monochromatic rectangles in partitions of the space $X \times Y$ and ignore the additional restriction that these partitions should correspond to some protocol? All of the techniques presented so far are of this type. On the other hand, we are also interested in relaxing the need to *partition* the space $X \times Y$ into f-monochromatic rectangles by allowing *covering* of this space (that is, allowing intersections between rectangles). Coverings are more convenient combinatorial objects than partitions. In addition, there is a natural notion of *nondeterministic*

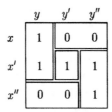

Figure 2.1: A partition that does not correspond to any protocol

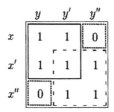

Figure 2.2: An overlapping cover

protocols that correspond to coverings. Again, simple examples show that sometimes it is easier to cover a space than to partition it. Consider, for example, the function presented in Figure 2.2. In this case, the space $X \times Y$ can be covered by 4 monochromatic rectangles (the pair (x', y') belongs to 2 rectangles) and it can be verified that to *partition* the space at least 5 monochromatic rectangles are needed. The fooling set method, for example, actually gives the same lower bounds even if we allow for covering the space (and do not restrict ourselves to partitions). Again, this raises the question of how good can this technique be.

To study these issues, we make the following definitions:

Definition 2.1: *Let* $f : X \times Y \to \{0, 1\}$ *be a function.*

1. *The* protocol partition number *of* f, $C^P(f)$, *is the smallest number of leaves in a protocol tree for* f.

2. *The* partition number *of* f, $C^D(f)$, *is the smallest number of monochromatic rectangles in a partition (that is, a disjoint cover) of* $X \times Y$.

3. *The* cover number *of* f, $C(f)$, *is the smallest number of monochromatic rectangles needed to cover* $X \times Y$ *(possibly with intersections).*

4. *For* $z \in \{0, 1\}$, $C^z(f)$ *is the number of monochromatic rectangles needed to cover (possibly with intersections) the* z-*inputs of* f.

The following properties should be obvious:

Proposition 2.2: *For all* $f : X \times Y \to \{0, 1\}$:

1. $C(f) \le C^D(f) \le C^P(f) \le 2^{D(f)}$.

2. $C(f) = C^0(f) + C^1(f)$.

---— 17 —---

The measure $C^z(f)$ has a natural interpretation in terms of the *nondeterministic communication complexity of* f. Assume that an all powerful prover, who sees x and y, is trying to convince Alice and Bob that "$f(x, y) = z$." If $f(x, y) \neq z$, then Alice and Bob must be able to detect that the proof is wrong no matter what the prover says, but if indeed $f(x, y) = z$, then the prover must be able to convince Alice and Bob. For example, a prover who wishes to convince Alice and Bob that two n-bit strings x and y are different, can do so by providing them with an index i such that $x_i \neq y_i$. Then, Alice and Bob can easily check the correctness of the proof by exchanging these two bits. If $x \neq y$, then there is a proof (that is, an index i) that would convince Alice and Bob that indeed this is the case, whereas if $x = y$, then no such proof exists. We claim that the amount of communication (including the "proof" and the bits exchanged by Alice and Bob in order to verify the "proof") in the most efficient proof system, denoted by $N^z(f)$, is essentially $\log_2 C^z(f)$. Why is this so? On one hand, any cover of the z-inputs gives a proof system where a "proof" is a name of a rectangle $S \times T$ in the cover in which the input (x, y) resides; the number of bits required is $\log_2$ of the number of rectangles. Alice and Bob can convince themselves that "$f(x, y) = z$" if Alice checks (and tells Bob) that $x \in S$ and Bob checks that $y \in T$. On the other hand, consider any proof system using at most b bits. As in the deterministic case, the set of inputs corresponding to a specific communication in which Alice and Bob are convinced is a z-monochromatic rectangle. Since for every (x, y) such that $f(x, y) = z$ there must be an appropriate proof, the set of rectangles corresponding to all possible communications is a cover of the z-inputs of f and there are at most 2^b such rectangles. Since we do not require a single proof for each (x, y), the rectangles may indeed overlap each other. This definition can be further extended to allow proving $f(x, y) = z$ for both the case where $f(x, y) = 0$ and the case where $f(x, y) = 1$. The complexity in this case is denoted by $N(f)$.

Nondeterminism need not be defined as a proof system but may also be defined as a two-party protocol in which Alice and Bob are allowed to take nondeterministic steps. The reader is encouraged to formalize in both different ways the notion of nondeterministic communication complexity and transform Definition 2.3 below into a lemma claiming the equivalence of these definitions. Since we will be interested mainly in the combinatorial properties of nondeterministic protocols, the formal definitions of the measures $C^z(f)$ and $C(f)$ are enough for our purposes.

Definition 2.3: *The nondeterministic communication complexity of a Boolean function* f *is* $N^1(f) = \log_2 C^1(f)$. *The co-nondeterministic communication complexity of* f *is* $N^0(f) = \log_2 C^0(f)$. *Also,* $N(f) = \log_2 C(f)$.

By looking more closely into the two techniques for lower bounds introduced in the previous chapter, we see that the lower bounds actually obtained are:

Lemma 2.4: *For* $f : X \times Y \rightarrow \{0, 1\}$:

1. $C^D(f) \geq 2 \operatorname{rank}(f) - 1$.

2. Let μ be a probability distribution on the z-inputs of f for some $z \in \{0, 1\}$. If every z-monochromatic rectangle R has measure $\mu(R) \leq \delta$, then $C^z(f) \geq 1/\delta$. (In particular, this implies that the fooling set method can be used to prove lower bounds on $C^z(f)$.)

The first thing we can settle is the relationship between deterministic and nondeterministic communication complexity.

▶ **Example 2.5:** We have already seen in Example 1.21 that $D(\text{EQ}) = n + 1$. In fact, the same proof also shows that $N^1(\text{EQ}) = n$. On the other hand, we can show that $\log_2 n \leq N^0(\text{EQ}) \leq \log_2 n + 1$. A proof that $x \neq y$ is simply an index i of a bit in which x and y differ (i.e, $x_i \neq y_i$). Such a proof requires $\log_2 n$ bits to specify the index i and another bit to specify whether $x_i = 1$ and $y_i = 0$, or $x_i = 0$ and $y_i = 1$ (alternatively, this can be viewed as a cover of the 0-inputs using $2n$ rectangles). This argument supplies an upper bound. The lower bound follows from the following exercise.

Exercise 2.6: Prove that for all $f : X \times Y \to \{0, 1\}$ and $z \in \{0, 1\}$, $D(f) \leq C^z(f) + 1$.

Thus, by the above example and exercise, we see that the gap between deterministic and nondeterministic communication complexity may be exponential but not more than this.

Exercise 2.7: Show that both $N^0(\text{GT})$ and $N^1(\text{GT})$ are at least n.

2.2. Communication Complexity Versus Protocol Cover

It is possible that a certain protocol induces a small number of rectangles, yet requires the players to exchange a large number of bits (in the worst case). In other words, the protocol tree is deep but has a small number of leaves. The following lemma shows that $D(f) = \Theta(\log C^P(f))$. Thus the protocol partition number of a function determines, essentially completely, the communication complexity of the function.

Lemma 2.8: $\log_2 C^P(f) \leq D(f) \leq 2 \log_{3/2} C^P(f)$.

PROOF: The lower bound on $D(f)$ is trivial (see Proposition 2.2) so we shall prove the upper bound. The basic idea is that a protocol with a certain number of leaves can be converted into a "balanced" protocol in which the depth is about the logarithm of the number of leaves.

Consider a protocol for f with t leaves. It is a simple combinatorial fact that in a binary tree with t leaves there exists an internal node v, such that t_v, the number of leaves in the subtree rooted at v, satisfies $t/3 < t_v \leq 2t/3$. To see this, we start at the root of the tree and keep going to the child u that has more than $2t/3$ leaves in its subtree. When we cannot continue anymore then we are at a node u, which has a son with the desired property. Let R_v be the rectangle of inputs arriving at v in the protocol. The new protocol for f goes as follows:

1. Alice and Bob determine whether $(x, y) \in R_v$. This requires two bits of communication.

2. If $(x, y) \in R_v$, Alice and Bob recursively solve f in the rectangle R_v, for which they have a protocol with t_v leaves.

3. If $(x, y) \notin R_v$, Alice and Bob recursively solve f' on $X \times Y$, where $f' = f$ outside R_v and is 0 in R_v. By taking the original protocol for f and replacing the subtree rooted at v by a 0-leaf, we get a protocol for f' with $t - t_v + 1$ leaves.

For the correctness, computing f' in the third step (instead of f) makes no difference since the inputs (x, y) in R_v never reach this step. By the property of v, in both cases (whether $(x, y) \notin R_v$ or not) there is a protocol with at most $2t/3$ leaves. Therefore, the recurrence relation we get for $D(t)$, the depth in this transformation starting with a t-leaf protocol, is $D(t) \le 2 + D(2t/3)$. Obviously, $D(1) = 0$, so solving the recurrence gives $D(t) \le 2 \log_{3/2} t$. By taking $t = C^P(f)$, the lemma follows. $\qquad \square$

Exercise 2.9: Improve the constant in the above upper bound to $D(f) \le 3 \log_2 C^P(f)$. Hint: find a node v that splits the tree into three parts, each of them with at most $t/2$ nodes.

2.3. Determinism Versus Nondeterminism

We have already seen that $D(f) = \Theta(\log C^P(f))$ and, on the other hand, that $D(f)$ may be exponentially larger than $\log C^1(f)$. We still have to figure out the exact relation between $D(f)$ and the measures $C^D(f)$ and $C(f)$. Proposition 2.2 states that $D(f) \ge \log C^D(f)$. It is not known whether this is always tight.

Open Problem 2.10: Is $D(f) = O(\log C^D(f))$?

The following theorem implies that if there is a gap between $D(f)$ and $O(\log C^D(f))$ it cannot be too large. In fact, even the gap between $D(f)$ and $N(f)$ $(= \log C(f))$ is not very large:

Theorem 2.11: *For every function* $f : X \times Y \to \{0, 1\}$,

$$D(f) = O(N^0(f)N^1(f)).$$

We provide two proofs of this central theorem. The first is algorithmic, whereas the second is more combinatorial. Both proofs rely on the following simple property of rectangles: Let $R = S \times T$ be a 0-monochromatic rectangle and $R' = S' \times T'$ be a 1-monochromatic rectangle. Then, either R and R' do not intersect in rows (that is, $S \cap S' = \emptyset$) or R and R' do not intersect in columns (that is, $T \cap T' = \emptyset$). Otherwise, there exist $x \in S \cap S'$ and $y \in T \cap T'$ such that the pair (x, y) belongs to both R and R'. However, $(x, y) \in R$ implies $f(x, y) = 0$, whereas $(x, y) \in R'$ implies $f(x, y) = 1$ – a contradiction.

PROOF (ALGORITHMIC VERSION): We describe a protocol for Alice and Bob. The idea is that Alice and Bob search for a 0-rectangle that contains the input (x, y). If they fail, they conclude that $f(x, y) = 1$. In each phase of the protocol the players exchange $\log C^1(f) + O(1)$ bits and they reduce the number of 0-rectangles that are "alive" (that is, which may include (x, y)) by a factor of 2 (initially all 0-rectangles are alive). Hence, there are at most $\log C^0(f)$ phases. In each phase the players do the following:

1. Alice considers the 0-monochromatic rectangles that are still alive.
   If there are no such rectangles she outputs $f(x, y) = 1$.
   Otherwise, she looks for a 1-rectangle Q that contains the row x and that intersects in rows with at most half of the 0-rectangles that are alive. If she finds such a rectangle Q, she sends its name to Bob and the phase is completed (the 0-rectangles that remain alive are those that intersect in rows with Q). Otherwise, she tells Bob that there is no such rectangle.

2. Bob looks for a 1-rectangle Q that contains the column y and that intersects in columns with at most half of the 0-rectangles that are alive. Again, if such a rectangle Q exists, then Bob sends its name to Alice and the phase is completed (the 0-rectangles that remain alive are those that intersect in columns with Q). Otherwise, Bob outputs $f(x, y) = 0$.

Each phase reduces the number of 0-rectangles that are alive by a factor of 2, while using $\log C^1(f) + O(1)$ bits of communication, hence giving the required complexity. For the correctness, if (x, y) belongs to some 0-rectangle R, then R remains alive during the whole protocol. Therefore, if no 0-rectangle is alive, then $f(x, y) = 1$. On the other hand, if neither Alice nor Bob finds a 1-rectangle to announce during a phase, this implies $f(x, y) = 0$. This is because if (x, y) is in a 1-rectangle then, by the above property, either this rectangle intersects in rows at most half of the 0-rectangles, or it intersects in columns at most half of the 0-rectangles. Therefore, either Alice or Bob should be able to find a Q as needed. □

PROOF (COMBINATORIAL VERSION): Let $L(k, \ell)$ denote the maximum of $C^P(g)$ over all Boolean functions g such that $C^1(g) \leq k$ and $C^0(g) \leq \ell$. Consider the optimal cover for f. Let $R = S \times T$ be a 0-monochromatic rectangle in this cover. By the above-mentioned property we can assume, without loss of generality, that at least half of the 1-monochromatic rectangles $R' = S' \times T'$ in the cover do not intersect R in rows; that is, $S' \cap S = \emptyset$. (Otherwise, replace Alice by Bob and S by T in the rest of the proof.)

A protocol for f will proceed as follows: First Alice tells Bob whether $x \in S$. If $x \in S$ then they proceed by recursively solving f on the domain $S \times Y$. On this domain f has a 1-cover with at most $k/2$ rectangles (those R' such that $S' \cap S \neq \emptyset$). If $x \notin S$ then they recursively solve f on the domain $\bar{S} \times Y$. On this domain f has a 0-cover with at most $\ell - 1$ rectangles (the original cover without R). We thus get the recurrence $L(k, \ell) \leq L(k/2, \ell) + L(k, \ell - 1)$, which implies, by induction on k and ℓ (together with $L(k, 0) = L(0, \ell) = 1$), that $L(k, \ell) \leq (\ell + 1)^{\log k}$. Therefore, $C^P(f) \leq (C^0(f) + 1)^{\log C^1(f)}$. The proof follows since $D(f) = O(\log C^P(f))$ (Lemma 2.8). □

Obviously, this theorem implies that $D(f) = O((N(f))^2)$, which in turn implies $D(f) = O((\log C^D(f))^2)$. This theorem also means that, while one of $N^0(f)$ and $N^1(f)$ can be exponentially smaller than $D(f)$, it cannot be the case that both $N^0(f)$ and $N^1(f)$ are much smaller than $D(f)$. The following example shows that this theorem is the best possible on the connection between $D(f)$ and $N(f)$.

▶ **Example 2.12:** Alice and Bob hold inputs x and y (respectively), each of which is a subset of $\{1, \ldots, n\}$ of size k (for some fixed $0 \le k \le n/2$). The k-disjointness function, $\mathrm{DISJ}_k(x, y)$, is defined to be 1 iff $x \cap y = \emptyset$ (obviously, for $k > n/2$ the function becomes constant). Note that the size of X (and of Y) is $m = \binom{n}{k}$. We will analyze both the deterministic and nondeterministic communication complexity of the function DISJ_k, proving that there is a large gap between them.

We start by analyzing the nondeterministic communication complexity of the function DISJ_k. Clearly, $N^0(\mathrm{DISJ}_k) \le \log n$, because a proof that two sets x and y intersect is simply a name of an element in the intersection. We show that $N^1(\mathrm{DISJ}_k) = O(k + \log \log n)$, by building an appropriate 1-cover using the probabilistic method. Choose a set $S \subseteq \{1, \ldots, n\}$ at random (each i is in S with probability $1/2$). The set

$$R_S = \{x \mid x \subseteq S, |x| = k\} \times \{y \mid y \subseteq \bar{S}, |y| = k\}$$

is obviously a 1-rectangle. For each input (x, y) such that $x \cap y = \emptyset$ (and each is of size k), $\Pr_S[(x, y) \in R_S] = 2^{-2k}$. Thus, if we choose $t = 2^{2k} \ln(m^2)$ random rectangles, we get a collection of t rectangles for which the probability that (x, y) is not covered is $(1 - \frac{1}{2^{2k}})^t < 1/m^2$. Since there are less than m^2 such inputs, this implies that the probability that there exists a 1-input that is not covered is less than 1. Alternatively, with a positive probability such a random cover covers every 1-input. Hence, a cover of size t exists and $N^1(\mathrm{DISJ}_k) = O(\log t) = O(k + \log \log n)$.

Now we analyze the deterministic communication complexity of DISJ_k. We use the rank lower bound to prove that $D(\mathrm{DISJ}_k) \ge \log_2 m$. For this, consider the matrix D_k^n associated with the function. Denote by $\vec{x}$ the row of the matrix corresponding to the set x. We prove, by induction on n and k, that D_k^n has full rank. It is true in the base cases D_0^n (this is a 1×1 matrix whose single entry is 1) and D_k^{2k} (each set is disjoint only to its complement so this is a diagonal matrix). For the induction step, let X_1 be the set of rows $\vec{x}$ of D_k^n for which the corresponding set x does not contain the element n, and let X_2 be the set of rows that contain n. Similarly, Y_2 and Y_1 are the columns whose sets contain or do not contain (respectively) the element n. Note that $X_1 \times Y_1$ is simply D_k^{n-1} and that $X_2 \times Y_2$ is the 0 matrix. We apply a linear transformation on D_k^n (which can only decrease the rank). This transformation changes only the rows of X_2 so as to get in $X_2 \times Y_1$ the 0-matrix and in $X_2 \times Y_2$ the matrix D_{k-1}^{n-1} (see Figure 2.3). By induction hypothesis, both D_k^{n-1} and D_{k-1}^{n-1} have full rank, so the matrix D_k^n also has full rank.

It remains to describe the linear transformation. Consider any set $x \in X_2$. It can be written as $x = x' \cup \{n\}$, where x' is a set of size $k - 1$. We replace the row $\vec{x}$ by a row $\hat{x}$ as follows:

$$\hat{x} = \frac{1}{n - 2k + 1} \cdot \vec{v}_x - \frac{n - 2k}{n - 2k + 1} \cdot \vec{x} \quad \text{where } \vec{v}_x = \sum_{z : x' \subseteq z, |z| = k} \vec{z}.$$

We first need to show that for all $y \in Y_1$, $\hat{x}[y] = 0$ (that is, the y-th entry of $\hat{x}$ contains 0). There are two cases:

- If $\vec{x}[y] = 0$, this means that x intersects y. Since y does not contain n, then x' already intersects y, and hence each set z containing it intersects y. That is, for each such z, $\vec{z}[y] = 0$ and therefore $\vec{v}_x[y] = 0$. In this case $\hat{x}[y] = 0 - 0 = 0$.

22

	Y_1	Y_2
X_1	D_k^{n-1}	?
X_2	?	0

$\Longrightarrow$

	Y_1	Y_2
X_1	D_k^{n-1}	?
X_2	0	D_{k-1}^{n-1}

Figure 2.3: The matrix D_k^n before the linear transformation (left) and after the linear transformation (right)

- If $\vec{x}[y] = 1$, this means that y and x (and certainly x') are disjoint. The sets z (of size k) that contain x' and are disjoint from y are exactly those whose k-th element was not chosen from $x \cup y$. There are $n - 2k$ such sets and hence $\vec{v}_x[y] = n - 2k$. In this case $\hat{x}[y] = \frac{n-2k}{n-2k+1} - \frac{n-2k}{n-2k+1} = 0$.

Next, consider $y \in Y_2$. Such y can be written as $y = y' \cup \{n\}$. We will show that $\hat{x}[y] = \text{DISJ}_{k-1}(x', y')$ (as noted, in this case, $\vec{x}[y] = 0$). Again, there are two cases:

- If x' and y' intersect then so do z and y', for all z containing x'. Hence $\vec{v}_x[y] = 0$. So $\hat{x}[y] = 0 - 0 = 0$.
- If x' and y' are disjoint then the number of zs containing x' and disjoint from y' (certainly those that are disjoint from y and y' are the same since we consider only zs that do not contain n) is exactly $n - 2k + 1$ (since this time $x \cup y$ contains only $2k - 1$ elements). In this case $\hat{x}[y] = \frac{n-2k+1}{n-2k+1} - 0 = 1$.

Let $k = \log_2 n$. The above lower bound (together with the trivial upper bound in which Alice sends x to Bob using $\log m$ bits) shows that $D(\text{DISJ}_k) = \theta(\log^2 n)$. We also showed that $N(\text{DISJ}_k) = O(\log n)$ (Theorem 2.11 shows that in fact $N(\text{DISJ}_k) = \theta(\log n)$). To conclude, this example shows that for certain functions the gap between the deterministic communication complexity and the nondeterministic communication complexity may be quadratic.

Another example exhibiting this gap appears in Example 4.5.

Exercise 2.13: Recall the definition of geometric rectangles given in Exercise 1.18. Let f be any function for which $X \times Y$ can be covered by t f-monochromatic *geometric* rectangles (possibly with overlaps). Prove that $D(f) = O(\log t)$.

2.4. Rectangle Size and Covers

We have seen two lower bound techniques so far: the *rectangle size technique* in which we try to give an upper bound on the "size" of any monochromatic rectangle, and the *rank technique* in which we try to give a lower bound on the rank of the associated matrix. In this section we study the tightness of the rectangle size technique, whereas in Section 2.5 we deal with the tightness of the rank technique. Recall that to use the rectangle size technique we define some probability distribution μ on, say, the 1-inputs of f. We then look at max $\mu(R)$, where R ranges over all 1-monochromatic rectangles, and conclude (by Lemma 2.4) that $C^1(f) \geq 1/\max \mu(R)$.

Definition 2.14: *Let μ be a probability distribution on the 1s of f. The μ-rectangle size bound of f, $B_\mu(f)$, is $B_\mu(f) = 1/\max_R \mu(R)$, where R ranges over all 1-monochromatic rectangles. The rectangle size bound of f, $B_*^1(f)$, is the maximum bound achievable this way, that is $B_*^1(f) = \max_\mu B_\mu(f)$, where μ ranges over all probability distributions over the 1s of f.*

Since (the second part of) Lemma 2.4 holds for every probability distribution μ, it immediately follows that $B_*^1(f)$ gives a lower bound on the nondeterministic communication complexity of f.

Proposition 2.15: $C^1(f) \geq B_*^1(f)$, *and thus* $N^1(f) \geq \log_2 B_*^1(f)$.

It turns out that this bound is nearly tight.

Theorem 2.16: *For any function $f : \{0, 1\}^n \times \{0, 1\}^n \to \{0, 1\}$, $C^1(f) \leq \ln(2)\, 2n B_*^1(f)$, and thus $N^1(f) \leq \log_2 B_*^1(f) + \log_2 n + O(1)$.*

PROOF: We adaptively build a cover for the 1s of f, by adding in the i-th step a 1-monochromatic rectangle R_i to the cover. Let μ_i be the uniform distribution on the 1s of f that were not covered during the first $i - 1$ steps. Let R_i be the largest 1-monochromatic rectangle according to this distribution; that is, R_i is a rectangle of size max $\mu_i(R) = 1/B_{\mu_i}(f) \geq 1/B_*^1(f)$. Add R_i to the cover and continue (unless all the 1s of f are already covered).

Let us see how large this cover is. Let n_i be the number of 1s not covered after the first i rectangles have been chosen. By the choice of R_i, $n_{i+1}/n_i \leq 1 - 1/B_*^1(f)$. This is because during the i-th step we choose the largest rectangle according to a distribution μ_i that is *uniform* on n_i entries and the size of this rectangle was at least $1/B_*^1(f)$ of these n_i entries. Since $n_0 \leq 2^{2n}$ we have $n_i \leq 2^{2n}(1 - 1/B_*^1(f))^i$. Thus for $i > \ln(2^{2n})B_*^1(f)$, we have $n_i < 1$, and thus all the 1s of f must be covered by then. Therefore, $C^1(f) \leq \ln(2)2n B_*^1(f)$. $\qquad\square$

This bound is essentially tight:

▶ **Example 2.17:** Let NE$(x, y) = not\,($EQ$(x, y))$. That is, the nonequality function, NE, is 1 iff the two strings x and y are *not equal*. We have already seen in Example 2.5 that $N^1($NE$) = \log_2 n + 1$ (in the terminology of covers $C^1($NE$) = 2n$, which is obtained by defining for each index i and a bit b a rectangle $R_{i,b}$ of all pairs (x, y) in which x_i equals b and y_i equals the complement of b). On the other hand, we claim that $B_*^1($NE$) \leq 4$.

To see this, let μ be any distribution on the 1s of NE. We will show that there exists a rectangle R such that $\mu(R) \geq 1/4$. Hence $B_\mu(\text{NE}) \leq 4$ and because this holds for *all* distributions, then $B_*^1(f) \leq 4$. Consider a monochromatic rectangle chosen at random as follows: choose a random n-bit string r, and a random bit b. Let

$$R_{r,b} = \{x \mid \langle x, r \rangle = b\} \times \{y \mid \langle y, r \rangle \neq b\}.$$

Clearly, $R_{r,b}$ is a 1-monochromatic rectangle. By the properties of the inner product, for any fixed (x, y) such that $x \neq y$, $\Pr_{r,b}[(x, y) \in R_{r,b}] = 1/4$. Now consider $\mathrm{E}_{r,b}[\mu(R_{r,b})]$. If we show that this expectation is at least $1/4$, then there exists a rectangle $R_{r,b}$ for which $\mu(R_{r,b}) \geq 1/4$, as desired. Denote by $Z_{r,b}(x, y)$ a random variable that gets the value $\mu(x, y)$ if $(x, y) \in R_{r,b}$ and 0 otherwise. We can write $\mathrm{E}_{r,b}[\mu(R_{r,b})] = \mathrm{E}_{r,b}[\sum_{x \neq y} Z_{r,b}(x, y)]$, which by linearity of the expectation equals $\sum_{x \neq y} \mathrm{E}_{r,b}[Z_{r,b}(x, y)]$. By the above, $\mathrm{E}_{r,b}[Z_{r,b}(x, y)] = \frac{1}{4}\mu(x, y)$. Hence,

$$\mathrm{E}_{r,b}[\mu(R_{r,b})] = \sum_{x \neq y} \frac{1}{4}\mu(x, y) = \frac{1}{4}\sum_{x \neq y} \mu(x, y) = 1/4.$$

We may also ask whether the *fooling set* method (which is a special case of the rectangle size method) always suffices. The answer is no:

Exercise 2.18*: Show that most functions $f: \{0,1\}^n \times \{0,1\}^n \to \{0,1\}$ satisfy $N^1(f) = \Omega(n)$, and yet the size of the largest fooling set for f is $O(n)$. (An explicit example of a function with these properties is given in Example 4.16.)

2.5. On Rank and Covers

We now turn our attention to the rank lower bound which states that $D(f) \geq \log \text{rank}(f)$ (in fact, in Lemma 2.4 we have already observed that the rank lower bound actually gives a lower bound on the partition number, $C^D(f)$). The best upper bound known is $D(f) \leq \text{rank}(f) + 1$ (Exercise 1.31). The gap between these two bounds is huge. The following example shows that, for certain functions f, the deterministic communication complexity can be significantly larger than $\log \text{rank}(f)$.

▶ **Example 2.19:** Let h_1 be the following polynomial in 3 Boolean variables

$$h_1(z_1, z_2, z_3) = z_1 + z_2 + z_3 - z_1 z_2 - z_1 z_3 - z_2 z_3.$$

This polynomial is a (symmetric) Boolean function that gives 1 iff one or two of its input are 1s. We now recursively define a function h_k on 3^k variables by

$$h_k(z_1, \ldots, z_{3^k})$$
$$= h_1(h_{k-1}(z_1, \ldots, z_{3^{k-1}}), h_{k-1}(z_{3^{k-1}+1}, \ldots, z_{2 \cdot 3^{k-1}}), h_{k-1}(z_{2 \cdot 3^{k-1}+1}, \ldots, z_{3^k})).$$

The following properties of h_k are easily proved by induction on k: (1) The number of terms in this polynomial is bounded by $6^{2^k - 1}$. (2) h_k is a Boolean function (on Boolean z_is); moreover, if all the 3^k input variables are 0, then h_k gives the value 0 and if exactly one input variable is 1, then h_k gives the value 1. We now use these polynomials to construct the desired Boolean function f. Assume that $n = 3^k$ for some k. For $x, y \in \{0, 1\}^n$ we define $f(x, y) = h_k(x_1 y_1, \ldots, x_n y_n)$.

To prove that $D(f) = \Omega(n)$, consider the disjointness function DISJ. We have already showed that the communication complexity of this function (that is, of deciding whether two sets x and y are disjoint or not) is $\Omega(n)$. In Section 4.6 we will prove a much stronger property: *any* function g such that $g(x, y) = 0$ when $x \cap y = \emptyset$ and $g(x, y) = 1$ when $|x \cap y| = 1$ satisfies $D(g) = \Omega(n)$. By property (2), f is such a function (transform the sets x and y into their characteristic vectors and observe that intersection occurs iff $x_i y_i = 1$) and hence $D(f) = \Omega(n)$. On the other hand, let

$$h_k(z_1, \ldots, z_n) = a_1 T_1 + a_2 T_2 + \cdots + a_s T_s$$

be the representation of h_k as a polynomial of s terms. For a term T_i, let R_i be the set of all inputs (x, y) that satisfy the term T_i (that is, if $T_i = z_{i_1} z_{i_2} \cdots z_{i_l}$ then R_i is the set of all inputs (x, y) where $x_{i_1} = y_{i_1} = 1, \ldots, x_{i_l} = y_{i_l} = 1$). Clearly, R_i is a rectangle. Let M_i be a matrix whose (x, y) entry is a_i if (x, y) is in R_i and 0 otherwise. Then, $\text{rank}(M_i) = 1$. Moreover, $M_f = \sum_{i=1}^s M_i$, which implies that $\text{rank}(M_f) \le \sum_{i=1}^s \text{rank}(M_i) = s$. By property (1),

$$\log \text{rank}(M_f) \le \log s = O(2^k) = O\left(n^{1/\log_2 3}\right) = O(n^{0.631\ldots}).$$

This is significantly smaller than the communication complexity of f, which is, as shown, $\Omega(n)$.

We can state the following open problem.

Open Problem 2.20: Does $D(f) = (\log \text{rank}(f))^{O(1)}$, for all $f: X \times Y \to \{0, 1\}$?

Any improvement of either the lower bound for the gap (Example 2.19) or the upper bound (Exercise 1.31) seems interesting. It is known that to give a positive answer it suffices to show that either $N^0(f)$ or $N^1(f)$ equals $(\log \text{rank}(f))^{O(1)}$:

Exercise 2.21: Show that $D(f) = O(N^0(f) \log \text{rank}(f))$. Hint: Look at the proof of Theorem 2.11 (Combinatorial Version). Similarly, $D(f) = O(N^1(f) \log \text{rank}(f))$.

In fact, to give a positive answer to the above open problem, it suffices to show that every low rank matrix has a large monochromatic rectangle:

Exercise 2.22: Let Mono(f) denote the fraction of M_f's entries covered by the largest monochromatic rectangle of f. Show that if for every function f, $\log(1/\text{Mono}(f)) = (\log \text{rank}(f))^{O(1)}$ then Open Problem 2.20 gets a positive answer. Hint: Look at the proof of Theorem 2.11 (Combinatorial Version).

The next exercise shows that several possible extensions of Open Problem 2.20 are false:

Exercise 2.23:

- Let INTER: $\{0, 1\}^n \times \{0, 1\}^n \rightarrow \{0, 1, \ldots, n\}$ be the function that counts the number entries in which $x_i = y_i = 1$ (think of x and y as sets, then INTER(x, y) is the size of their intersection). Show that the rank of M_{INTER} is n. Conclude that for nonboolean functions the gap between $D(f)$ and log rank(f) may be exponential.

- Show that the rank of M_{IP} over $GF(2)$ is n. Conclude that if we consider rank over finite fields (instead of the reals) the gap between $D(f)$ and log rank(f) may be exponential.

Hint: In both cases present the matrix as a product of two matrices.

2.6. Bibliographic Notes

Nondeterministic communication complexity was defined by [Lipton and Sedgewick 1981]. The two types of definitions of nondeterministic protocols, as a proof system and as a protocol in which the players may take nondeterministic steps, correspond to the two possible definitions of the class *NP* in computational complexity. Nondeterministic communication complexity was extensively studied by [Aho et al. 1983]. In particular they proved a weaker version of Theorem 2.11. This theorem was later strengthened to its current form by [Halstenberg and Reischuk 1988a]. The tightness of the theorem was proved by [Fürer 1987] (see also [Mehlhorn and Schmidt 1982, Itai 1991]), using the function that appears in Example 4.13. The example given here (that is, the function DISJ$_k$, Example 2.12) is due to [Razborov 1990b]. The fact that the matrix corresponding to DISJ$_k$ has full rank follows from the Ray–Chaudhury–Wilson Theorem (see [Babai and Frankl 1988]). The proof given here is completely different; it is based on homework of the students in the communication complexity class given at the Technion in 1994 by the first author.

Lemma 2.8 is a folklore fact. It was found independently by several people and, to the best of our knowledge, it was never published. Exercise 2.9 was suggested by J. Sgall. The best known answer with respect to Open Problem 2.10 is given by [Kushilevitz, Linial, and Ostrovsky 1996], where a small gap between $D(f)$ and log $C^D(f)$ is shown.

The results of Section 2.4 are due to [Karchmer, Kushilevitz, and Nisan 1992a]. The proof of Theorem 2.16 is really a special case of a more general result of Lovász regarding the relation between the fractional cover number of a hypergraph and its cover number [Lovász 1975].

As mentioned, the rank lower bound was presented in [Mehlhorn and Schmidt 1982]. Increasing gaps between this lower bound and the communication complexity were demonstrated by [Alon and Seymour 1989, Razborov 1992] and [Raz and Spieker 1993]. The current gap (Example 2.19) is due to [Nisan and Widgerson 1994]. This was slightly improved by Kushilevitz (unpublished). Interesting examples of using the rank lower bound for matrices of a certain type are given by [Lovász and Saks 1988, Björner, Karlander, and Lindström 1992], and in [Faigle, Schrader, and Turan 1992].

Further aspects of nondeterministic communication complexity were studied in the work of [Dolev and Feder 1989, Fleischer 1989, Karchmer et al. 1992b].

CHAPTER 3

Randomization

In the basic model of communication complexity, Alice and Bob were all powerful, but deterministic. This means that in any stage, when one of the players needs to communicate a bit, the value of this bit is a deterministic function of the player's input and the communication so far. In this chapter, we study what happens when Alice and Bob are allowed to act in a randomized fashion. That is, the players are also allowed to "toss coins" during the execution of the protocol and take into account the outcome of the coin tosses when deciding what messages to send. This implies that the communication on a given input (x, y) is not fixed anymore but instead it becomes a random variable. Similarly, the output computed by a randomized protocol on input (x, y) is also a random variable. As a result, the success of a randomized protocol can be defined in several ways. The first possibility, which is more conservative (sometimes called *Las-Vegas* protocols), is to consider only protocols that always output the correct value $f(x, y)$. The more liberal possibility is to allow protocols that may err, but for every input (x, y) are guaranteed to compute the correct value $f(x, y)$ with high probability (sometimes called *Monte-Carlo* protocols). Similarly, the cost of a randomized protocol can also be defined in several ways. We can either analyze the worst case behavior of the protocol, or we can analyze the average case behavior.

3.1. Basic Definitions

As previously, Alice and Bob get x and y, respectively, as inputs. The twist is that Alice and Bob are also allowed to flip a random coin. Formally, Alice has access to a random string r_A of some arbitrary length, and similarly Bob has access to a random string r_B. These two strings are chosen independently, according to some probability distribution. When we look at the tree defining the protocol, then Alice's nodes are labeled by arbitrary functions of x and r_A, and Bob's nodes are labeled by arbitrary functions of y and r_B. As before, every combination of x, y, r_A, and r_B determines a leaf of the protocol tree where some value z is defined as the output of the protocol on (x, y). It is possible that for a certain input (x, y), with different choices of r_A and r_B, the protocol outputs different values. Hence, when randomization is allowed, protocols may err. The following definition gives the types of errors we consider:

Definition 3.1: *Let P be a randomized protocol. All the probabilities below are over the random choices of r_A and r_B.*

- *P computes a function f with* zero error – *if for every (x, y),*

$$\Pr[P(x, y) = f(x, y)] = 1.$$

- *P computes a function f with ε-error – if for every (x, y),*

$$\Pr[P(x, y) = f(x, y)] \geq 1 - \varepsilon.$$

- *P computes a function f with* one-sided ε-error – *if for every (x, y) such that $f(x, y) = 0$,*

$$\Pr[P(x, y) = 0] = 1,$$

and for every (x, y) such that $f(x, y) = 1$,

$$\Pr[P(x, y) = 1] \geq 1 - \varepsilon.$$

Randomization not only allows us to get different values in different executions of the protocol but also allows the number of bits exchanged to vary in different executions on the same (x, y) (with different random strings r_A and r_B). Hence, in the case of randomized protocols, there are two natural choices for the definition of the running time of the protocol on a given input (x, y). We can measure the running time with respect to the *worst* random strings or with respect to the *average* random strings:

Definition 3.2: *The* worst case running time *of a randomized protocol P on input (x, y) is the maximum number of bits communicated for any choice of the random strings, r_A and r_B. The* worst case cost *of P is the maximum, over all inputs (x, y), of the worst case running time of P on (x, y).*

The average case running time *of a randomized protocol P on input (x, y) is the expected number of bits communicated (or, equivalently, depth of leaves) over all choices of the random strings, r_A and r_B. The* average case cost *of P is the maximum, over all inputs (x, y), of the average case running time of P on (x, y).*

The only distribution is on the random strings r_A and r_B and hence we can talk about the average number of bits exchanged for some fixed input (x, y). We cannot talk about an "average input" since we have not yet defined a probability distribution on inputs. We will consider such a variant in Section 3.4.

The three different types of errors lead naturally to three complexity measures. In each case, the complexity is the cost of the "best" protocol that meets the error requirement. We choose the notion of "cost" to be either worst case or average case according to the type of error we allow:

Definition 3.3: *Let $f: X \times Y \rightarrow \{0, 1\}$ be a function. We consider the following complexity measures for f.*

- $R_0(f)$ *is the minimum average case cost of a randomized protocol that computes f with zero error.*

- *For $0 < \varepsilon < 1/2$, $R_\varepsilon(f)$ is the minimum worst case cost of a randomized protocol that computes f with error ε. We denote $R(f) = R_{1/3}(f)$.*

- *For $0 < \varepsilon < 1$, $R_\varepsilon^1(f)$ is the minimum worst case cost of a randomized protocol that computes f with one-sided error ε. We denote $R^1(f) = R_{1/2}^1(f)$.*

The reader may get annoyed by the fact that we use worst case cost for protocols that allow error and average case cost for zero error protocols. In general, the worst case measure is more convenient to work with. For protocols with error, the complexity remains the same to within a multiplicative constant whether we use the worst case measure or the average case measure. More precisely, given a protocol $\mathcal{P}$ that makes an error $\varepsilon/2$ and the average number of bits exchanged is t, it can be modified as follows: execute $\mathcal{P}$ as long as at most $2t/\varepsilon$ bits are exchanged. If the protocol finishes, use its output; otherwise, output 0. By a simple counting argument, the probability that in $\mathcal{P}$ more than $2t/\varepsilon$ bits are exchanged is at most $\varepsilon/2$. Hence the error made by the modified protocol can be at most ε and the number of bits exchanged in the *worst case* is now $2t/\varepsilon$. (Also observe that if the original protocol makes a one-sided error, then so does the modified protocol.) Therefore, for protocols with errors we use the more convenient worst case cost. On the other hand, for zero error protocols, using the worst case cost gives exactly the deterministic communication complexity, because a deterministic protocol will simply fix some values for r_A and r_B and proceed. Therefore, for zero error protocols, the only interesting cost is the average case cost.

Exercise 3.4: The following are basic properties of the definitions given above:

- For $0 < \varepsilon \leq \varepsilon' < 1/2$, $R_\varepsilon(f) \leq O(\log_{\varepsilon'} \varepsilon \cdot R_{\varepsilon'}(f))$. Conclude that the error probability can be reduced with a small penalty in the communication complexity. Hint: Start by proving the same relation with respect to $R^1(f)$. Then use Chernoff inequality to generalize your proof for $R(f)$.

- $R_\varepsilon(f) \leq R_\varepsilon^1(f) \leq O(\log \varepsilon^{-1}) R_0(f)$.

- $R_0(f) = O(\max[R^1(f), R^1(not(f))])$.

The following randomized protocol is an important example of the power of randomness.

▶ **Example 3.5:** Consider the equality function EQ. Denote the input of Alice by $a = a_0 a_1 \cdots a_{n-1}$, and the input of Bob by $b = b_0 b_1 \cdots b_{n-1}$. We think of these inputs as two polynomials over the field $GF[p]$ where $n^2 < p < 2n^2$ is a prime (theorems regarding the density of primes guarantee the existence of such p). That is,

$$A(x) = a_0 + a_1 x + \cdots + a_{n-1} x^{n-1} \quad (\text{mod } p)$$

and

$$B(x) = b_0 + b_1 x + \cdots + b_{n-1} x^{n-1} \quad (\text{mod } p).$$

Alice picks at random a number t in $GF[p]$ and sends Bob the values t and $A(t)$. Bob outputs 1 if $A(t) = B(t)$ and 0 otherwise. The number of bits exchanged is $O(\log p) = O(\log n)$. For the correctness, note first that if $a = b$ then $A(t) = B(t)$ for all t, so the output is always 1. If $a \neq b$ we have two distinct polynomials A and B of degree $n - 1$. Such polynomials can be equal on at most $n - 1$ (out of p) elements of the field (since their difference is a non-zero polynomial of degree at most $n - 1$, which may have at most $n - 1$ roots). Hence the probability of error is at most $(n - 1)/p \leq n/n^2 = 1/n$.

We have thus shown $R(\text{EQ}) = O(\log n)$, and in fact, $R_{1/n}(\text{EQ}) = O(\log n)$, and even more, $R^1_{1/n}(\text{NE}) = O(\log n)$. In contrast, recall that $D(\text{NE}) = D(\text{EQ}) = n + 1$ (Example 1.21).

Exercise 3.6: Prove that the following protocol for EQ achieves similar performance. Alice and Bob view their inputs a and b as n-bit integers (between 1 and 2^n). Alice chooses a prime number p at random among the first n^2 primes. She sends both p and $a \bmod p$ to Bob. Bob checks whether $a \bmod p = b \bmod p$, and if so he outputs 1, otherwise he outputs 0.

3.2. Randomization Versus Determinism

How different can randomized complexity be from deterministic complexity? What kind of lower bounds can we prove for randomized complexity? Randomization without error, or even with one-sided error, cannot be stronger than nondeterminism. This is because in a nondeterministic protocol the players may simply "guess" the random choices leading to accepting paths. We thus have:

Proposition 3.7: *For every $0 \leq \varepsilon < 1$, $R^1_\varepsilon(f) \geq N^1(f)$.*

A similar argument shows that $R_0(f) \geq N(f)$ (the players can "guess" the random choices for which the computation ends within at most the average cost). In particular (by Theorem 2.11), this implies that $R_0(f)$ may only be quadratically smaller than $D(f)$. Below we will give an example (Example 3.16) showing that this gap may be achieved. Example 3.5 above shows that for $R^1(f)$ and $R(f)$ the gap from the deterministic complexity may be exponential. Proposition 3.7 (together with Exercise 2.6) implies that no larger gap is possible for the one-sided complexity, $R^1(f)$. The following lemma shows that the same is true for $R(f)$.

Lemma 3.8: $R(f) = \Omega(\log D(f))$.

PROOF: We will prove a somewhat more delicate statement:

$$D(f) \leq 2^{R_\varepsilon(f)} \cdot \left(\log \left(\frac{1}{2} - \varepsilon \right)^{-1} + R_\varepsilon(f) \right).$$

For this, we present a deterministic simulation of a given randomized protocol $\mathcal{P}$. For each leaf ℓ of the protocol $\mathcal{P}$, Alice will send Bob the value p_ℓ^A, which is the probability (over the choices of r_A) that, given her input x, she indeed responds according to the path leading to this leaf. Bob can then compute privately p_ℓ^B, the probability (over the choices of r_B) that, given his input y, he follows the path leading to the leaf ℓ. He can then compute $p_\ell = p_\ell^A \cdot p_\ell^B$, which is the probability of reaching the leaf ℓ. Because the players do this computation for each of the $2^{R_\varepsilon(f)}$ leaves (and because each leaf determines a single value, 0 or 1, as the output), Bob can check which of the values (0 or 1) has probability of at least $1 - \varepsilon$ and this is the correct value $f(x, y)$.

The difficulty is that this simulation requires sending *real* numbers (the probabilities). However, these real numbers need only be transmitted with precision of $k = \log(\frac{1}{2} - \varepsilon)^{-1} + R_\varepsilon(f)$ bits. This guarantees that the value sent for each p_ℓ^A is different from the true value by at most $2^{-k} = (\frac{1}{2} - \varepsilon)/2^{R_\varepsilon(f)}$. This implies that p_ℓ, computed by Bob, is at most $(\frac{1}{2} - \varepsilon)/2^{R_\varepsilon(f)}$, far from the true value (since $p_\ell^B \leq 1$). Hence the total error, over all the leaves ℓ, is at most $\frac{1}{2} - \varepsilon$. Therefore it suffices that Bob checks which of the values (0 or 1) has probability of more than $1/2$ and this is the correct value $f(x, y)$. $\qquad\square$

▶ **Example 3.9:** We can now completely analyze the randomized complexity of EQ and NE.

1. $R^1(\text{EQ}) = \Theta(n)$, $R_0(\text{EQ}) = R_0(\text{NE}) = \Theta(n)$. These lower bounds follow from Proposition 3.7 and the nondeterministic lower bounds for EQ.
2. $R(\text{EQ}) = R(\text{NE}) = \Theta(\log n)$, $R^1(\text{NE}) = \Theta(\log n)$. The upper bounds were derived above, and the lower bounds follow from the deterministic lower bounds for EQ and Lemma 3.8.

Exercise 3.10: Show that $R(\text{GT}) = O(\log^2 n)$. In contrast, by Exercise 2.7, both $N^0(\text{GT})$ and $N^1(\text{GT})$ (and thus also $R^1(\text{GT})$) are linear. (See Exercise 3.18 for an improvement of this result.)

We do not have any technique that gives us better lower bounds for randomized complexity than for nondeterministic complexity.

Open Problem 3.11: Is $R_0(f) = O(N(f))$, for every Boolean function f? (Clearly the gap can be at most quadratic since even $D(f) = O(N(f)^2)$.) How about $R^1(f) = O(N^1(f))$?

3.3. Public Coin Versus Private Coin

In our definition of randomized protocols, each party has its own random coin to flip. Alice cannot see Bob's coin flips and vice versa. We could have allowed them to have a "public" coin, so that both Alice and Bob see the results of a single series of random coin flips. More formally, there exists a common random string r (chosen according to some probability distribution Π), and in the protocol tree Alice's communication corresponds to functions of x and r and Bob's communication corresponds to functions of y and r. Alternatively, this can be viewed as a distribution, $\{P_r\}_{r\in\Pi}$, of deterministic protocols.

Alice and Bob choose together a string r (according to the probability distribution Π, and independently of x and y) and then follow the deterministic protocol P_r.

Definition 3.12: *A (randomized) public coin protocol is a probability distribution over deterministic protocols. The* success probability *of a public coin protocol on input (x, y) is the probability of choosing a (deterministic) protocol, according to the probability distribution Π, that computes $f(x, y)$ correctly. We add a superscript "pub" to the notations to indicate public coin protocols. For example, $R_\varepsilon^{pub}(f)$ is the minimum cost of a public coin protocol that computes f with an error of at most ε (for every input (x, y)).*

Note that, for example, $R_\varepsilon^{pub}(f) \leq R_\varepsilon(f)$. This is because a private coin protocol can be simulated by a public coin protocol where the public random string r is the concatenation of the random strings r_A and r_B needed by Alice and Bob (each is chosen according to the appropriate distribution and independently of the other).

▶ **Example 3.13:** The following is a public coin protocol for the function NE: Alice and Bob jointly choose a random n-bit string r. Alice computes the inner product $b = \langle x, r \rangle$ and transmits it (a single bit) to Bob. Bob checks whether $b = \langle y, r \rangle$ and outputs "equal" if so and "not equal" otherwise. Clearly, if $x = y$ the output is always "equal." On the other hand, if $x \neq y$, then by the properties of the inner product,

$$\Pr_r[\langle x, r \rangle \neq \langle y, r \rangle] = 1/2,$$

and thus Bob outputs "not equal" with probability $1/2$. By repeating this procedure twice (with two independent rs) and deciding "equal" only if the inner product is equal in both of them, the error probability is reduced to $\frac{1}{4} < \frac{1}{3}$. We have thus shown $R^{pub}(\text{NE}) = R^{pub}(\text{EQ}) = O(1)$, and even $R^{1,pub}(\text{NE}) = O(1)$.

This example shows that the gap between $D(f)$ and $R^{pub}(f)$ may be arbitrarily large. Also, because we know that with private coin the equality function, EQ, requires $\Omega(\log n)$ bits we see that public coin can be better than a private coin. It turns out that this is as good as they get. That is, any public coin protocol can be transformed into a private coin one with a small penalty in the error and a small additive penalty in the communication complexity. Formally,

Theorem 3.14: *Let $f: \{0, 1\}^n \times \{0, 1\}^n \to \{0, 1\}$ be a function. For every $\delta > 0$ and every $\varepsilon > 0$, $R_{\varepsilon+\delta}(f) \leq R_\varepsilon^{pub}(f) + O(\log n + \log \delta^{-1})$.*

PROOF: It is sufficient to prove that any public coin protocol $\mathcal{P}$, using any number of random bits, can be transformed into another public coin protocol, $\mathcal{P}'$, with the same communication complexity that uses only $O(\log n + \log \delta^{-1})$ random bits, while increasing the error by only δ. The proof then follows because Alice can simply flip that many random coins by herself, send the random coin flips to Bob, and then the two players proceed as in $\mathcal{P}'$.

Let $Z(x, y, r)$ be a random variable that gets the value 1 if the answer that $\mathcal{P}$ gives on input (x, y) and random string r is wrong (that is, different than $f(x, y)$) and 0 otherwise. Because $\mathcal{P}$ computes f with ε error we have $E_{r \in \Pi}[Z(x, y, r)] \leq \varepsilon$, for all (x, y). We will build a new protocol, which uses fewer random bits, using the probabilistic method. Let t be a parameter (to be fixed) and $r_1, \ldots, r_t$ be t strings. For such strings, define a protocol $\mathcal{P}_{r_1, \ldots, r_t}$ as follows: Alice and Bob choose $1 \leq i \leq t$ uniformly at random and then proceed as in $\mathcal{P}$ with r_i as their common random string. We now show that there exist strings $r_1, \ldots, r_t$ such that $E_i[Z(x, y, r_i)] \leq \varepsilon + \delta$, for all (x, y). For this choice of strings the protocol $\mathcal{P}_{r_1, \ldots, r_t}$ is the desired protocol. To do so, we choose the t values $r_1, \ldots, r_t$ at random (according to the probability distribution Π). Consider a particular input pair (x, y) and compute the probability that $E_i[Z(x, y, r_i)] > \varepsilon + \delta$ (where i in this expectation is uniformly distributed). This is exactly the probability that $\frac{1}{t} \sum_{i=1}^{t} Z(x, y, r_i) > \varepsilon + \delta$. By the Chernoff inequality, since $E_r[Z(x, y, r)] \leq \varepsilon$, we get

$$\Pr_{r_1, \ldots, r_t} \left[\left(\frac{1}{t} \sum_{i=1}^{t} Z(x, y, r_i) - \varepsilon \right) > \delta \right] \leq 2e^{-2\delta^2 t}.$$

By choosing $t = O(n/\delta^2)$, this is smaller than 2^{-2n}. Thus, for a random choice of $r_1, \ldots, r_t$ the probability that for *some* input (x, y), $E_i[Z(x, y, r_i)] > \varepsilon + \delta$ is smaller than $2^{2n} \cdot 2^{-2n} = 1$. This implies that there exists a choice of $r_1, \ldots, r_t$ where for *every* (x, y) the error of the protocol $\mathcal{P}_{r_1, \ldots, r_t}$ is at most $\varepsilon + \delta$. Finally, note that the number of random bits used by the protocol $\mathcal{P}_{r_1, \ldots, r_t}$ is $\log t = O(\log n + \log \delta^{-1})$ and that the communication complexity is bounded by the communication complexity of $\mathcal{P}$. $\square$

A very similar theorem holds for one-sided protocols. The case of zero error protocols is slightly different:

Exercise 3.15: Show that $R_0(f) = O(R_0^{pub}(f) + \log n)$.

The following example shows that sometimes it is much easier to provide public coin protocols than private ones.

▶ **Example 3.16:** Recall the function DISJ$_k$ from Example 2.12, whose deterministic communication complexity is $\log \binom{n}{k}$. We provide an $O(k)$ bit protocol using a public coin. This implies that (using a private coin) $R(\text{DISJ}_k) = O(k + \log n)$. Let x be Alice's set and y be Bob's set.

The public coin flips will denote a sequence of random subsets $S_1, S_2, \ldots$ of $\{1, \ldots, n\}$. The two players maintain an index i of the "current set" in the sequence that always increases (initially $i = 0$). In each iteration of the protocol Alice finds the first i in the sequence (with i greater than the index of the current set) such that S_i contains the set x and sends Bob the distance from the current set to i. Bob then replaces y by $y \cap S_i$. Then, Bob finds the first $j > i$ in the sequence such that S_j contains (the new) y and sends the distance from i to j to Alice. Alice now replaces x by $x \cap S_j$. They continue with this procedure until either x or y becomes empty – in this case they announce "disjoint," or else until more than ck bits have been communicated (for some constant c) – in this case they announce "not disjoint."

It is easy to verify that if x and y were disjoint originally, then they remain so during the protocol. On the other hand, if x and y intersect originally, then their intersection belongs to both x and y during the whole protocol. Hence, it follows that for intersecting (x, y) the protocol never errs. To analyze the protocol for disjoint (x, y), we note that the expected size of y (and x) is halved in every iteration (since x and y are disjoint, the fact that $x \subseteq S_i$ has no influence on y's elements; that is, every element of y belongs to S_i with probability $1/2$). Because the probability that a random S_i contains a certain set of size s is exactly 2^{-s}, it follows that the expected number of bits communicated by Alice (respectively Bob) when x (respectively y) is of size s is $O(s)$ (the expected number of sets before the next S_i that contains a certain set of size s is exactly 2^s. However, the expected number of bits communicated is *not exactly* s). Thus, the expected number of bits that should be exchanged before x or y become empty is $O(k)$. As discussed in Section 3.1, by multiplying this number of bits by $1/\varepsilon$ we can guarantee that the protocol always stops within $O(k/\varepsilon)$ bits (which is $O(k)$ for fixed ε) and errs with probability at most ε. Hence, $R^{pub}(\text{DISJ}_k) = O(k)$.

Exercise 3.17: The above protocol has one-sided error. Modify this protocol to prove that $R_0^{pub}(\text{DISJ}_k)$ and hence $R_0(\text{DISJ}_k)$ are $O(k + \log n)$. Conclude (by substituting $k = O(\log n)$) that the gap between deterministic and zero error randomized communication complexity may be quadratic (by Section 3.2, this is the maximal possible gap).

Exercise 3.18*: Prove that $R^{pub}(\text{GT}) = O(\log n)$. Conclude that $R(\text{GT}) = O(\log n)$, improving over Exercise 3.10. (An easier task is to prove that $R^{pub}(\text{GT}) = O(\log n \log \log n)$, which is already an improvement over Exercise 3.10.)

3.4. Distributional Complexity

In this section we present a technique that provides lower bounds for randomized protocols that are allowed two-sided error. For this purpose, we present a model of distributional communication complexity in which we consider a probability distribution over the *inputs*. This is in opposition to the model of randomized protocols, in which we have only considered a probability space on the random choices by the players and we considered worst case inputs.

Definition 3.19: *Let μ be a probability distribution on $X \times Y$. The (μ, ε)-distributional communication complexity of f, $D_\varepsilon^\mu(f)$, is the cost of the best deterministic protocol that gives the correct answer for f on at least a $1 - \varepsilon$ fraction of all inputs in $X \times Y$, weighted by μ.*

For example, $D_{1/4}^{uniform}(\text{GT}) \leq 2$: Alice sends Bob x_1, the most significant bit of x, and Bob, by comparing x_1 with y_1 can compute the correct answer for at least $3/4$ of the input pairs (that is, if $x_1 \neq y_1$, then the number that starts with "1" is the larger, whereas if $x_1 = y_1$, Bob decides that, say, $\text{GT}(x, y) = 0$; that is, y is larger). As can be seen in Figure 3.1 (for the case $n = 3$), the protocol partitions $\{0, 1\}^n \times \{0, 1\}^n$ into four rectangles. Two of them (the lower left and the upper right) are monochromatic

	000	001	010	011	100	101	110	111
000	0	0	0	0	0	0	0	0
001	1	0	0	0	0	0	0	0
010	1	1	0	0	0	0	0	0
011	1	1	1	0	0	0	0	0
100	1	1	1	1	0	0	0	0
101	1	1	1	1	1	0	0	0
110	1	1	1	1	1	1	0	0
111	1	1	1	1	1	1	1	0

Figure 3.1: A protocol for the "greater than" function, GT, with low distributional communication complexity

with respect to GT and so the output of the protocol is always correct. The other two are not monochromatic, and so the protocol is wrong for every pair (x, y) in these two rectangles for which $GT(x, y) = 1$.

In the next section we will see a lower bound technique for distributional communication complexity. It is easy to see that for every probability distribution μ, the measure $D_\varepsilon^\mu(f)$ provides a lower bound on $R_\varepsilon(f)$. It turns out that such bounds completely suffice to characterize the public coin complexity.

Theorem 3.20: $R_\varepsilon^{pub}(f) = \max_\mu D_\varepsilon^\mu(f)$.

PROOF: The $\geq$ direction is simple: the randomized protocol is correct for *every* input with probability $\geq 1 - \varepsilon$. Therefore, for each μ, the randomized protocol is correct with probability $\geq 1 - \varepsilon$, where the probability is taken over both the public coin flips and the random input. It follows by a counting argument, that for some fixed choice of the public coin flips, a probability of success larger than $1 - \varepsilon$ is achieved, where this time the probability is taken only over the inputs.

For the $\leq$ direction, let $c = \max_\mu D_\varepsilon^\mu(f)$. Consider a two-player zero-sum game as follows. Player 1 chooses a deterministic c-bit communication protocol $\mathcal{P}$. Player 2 chooses an arbitrary input $(x, y) \in X \times Y$ (neither player knows the particular choice of the other player). The payoff for Player 1 is 1 if $\mathcal{P}(x, y) = f(x, y)$ and 0 otherwise. Using this terminology, the fact that for every μ, the distributional communication complexity, $D_\varepsilon^\mu(f)$, is at most c means that for every randomized (or "mixed") strategy of Player 2 (which is just a probability distribution μ on $X \times Y$), Player 1 can obtain payoff $1 - \varepsilon$. We can now use the min–max theorem of zero-sum games, which says that in such a case Player 1 also has a randomized strategy that provides the same payoff for *every* choice of Player 2. Such a randomized strategy is a distribution on c-bit deterministic protocols (that is, a randomized protocol with a public coin) that is correct on every input with probability $\geq 1 - \varepsilon$. $\square$

Exercise 3.21: Show that a similar connection holds for zero error randomized complexity. That is, for a distribution μ, denote by $D_0^\mu(f)$ the expected communication used by a deterministic protocol for f (expectation taken over all inputs, weighted by μ). Prove that $R_0^{pub}(f) = \max_\mu D_0^\mu(f)$.

Based on the above theorem (and exercise) a possible way of proving lower bounds on *randomized* communication complexity is by choosing a "convenient" probability distribution μ and proving lower bounds on the *distributional* communication complexity with respect to μ.

▶ **Example 3.22:** Consider the function DISJ (Example 1.23). In Section 4.6 we will prove that there exist two sets of inputs $A \subseteq \text{DISJ}^{-1}(1)$ and $B \subseteq \text{DISJ}^{-1}(0)$, a probability distribution μ, and positive constants α and δ such that (1) $\mu(A) = 3/4$, and (2) for every rectangle R, $\mu(R \cap B) \geq \alpha \cdot \mu(R \cap A) - 2^{-\delta n}$. In words, we have a lower bound on the weight of B-elements in every rectangle as a function of the weight of A-elements (in particular, only rectangles in which $\mu(R \cap A)$ is very small may be 1-monochromatic).

We use this to prove $D_\varepsilon^\mu(\text{DISJ}) \geq \delta n - O(1)$ for sufficiently small ε. Suppose $D_\varepsilon^\mu(\text{DISJ}) = k$. Then, the appropriate protocol induces a partition of $\{0, 1\}^n \times \{0, 1\}^n$ into (at most) 2^k rectangles. Let $R_1, \ldots, R_t$ ($t \leq 2^k$) be those rectangles in which the protocol announces "1" as the output. Because we allow at most ε error, and because we assumed $\mu(A) = 3/4$, we get $\mu(\bigcup_{i=1}^t (R_i \cap A)) \geq \frac{3}{4} - \varepsilon$. On the other hand, for each element of B that appears in these rectangles we make a mistake. Hence, the error of the protocol is at least

$$\mu\left(\bigcup_{i=1}^t (R_i \cap B)\right) \geq \sum_{i=1}^t (\alpha \cdot \mu(R_i \cap A) - 2^{-\delta n}) \geq \alpha \cdot \left(\frac{3}{4} - \varepsilon\right) - 2^{k-\delta n}.$$

However, by assumptions, the error of the protocol is at most ε. Combining these two facts, $\alpha \cdot (\frac{3}{4} - \varepsilon) - 2^{k-\delta n} \leq \varepsilon$, which implies, for small enough ε, that $k \geq \delta n - O(1)$.

Open Problem 3.23: How far can the best lower bound obtained using this technique be from the true randomized complexity?

Distributions in which x and y are chosen *independently* are sometimes of interest:

Definition 3.24: A distribution μ over $X \times Y$ is called rectangular (or a product distribution) if for some distributions μ_X over X and μ_Y over Y, $\mu(x, y) = \mu_X(x) \cdot \mu_Y(y)$. Denote $R^{[]}(f) = \max_\mu D^\mu(f)$, where the maximum is taken over all rectangular distributions μ.

In the proof of Theorem 3.20 it is important that μ may range over *all* distributions over $X \times Y$. Indeed, the following exercise shows that the theorem does not hold for rectangular distributions.

Exercise 3.25: Prove that $R^{[]}(\text{DISJ}) = O(\sqrt{n} \log n)$. Contrast this result with the fact that $R(\text{DISJ}) = \Theta(n)$ (Example 3.22). For the uniform distribution (which is rectangular), show that $D^{uniform}(\text{DISJ}) = \Theta(\sqrt{n})$.

Open Problem 3.26: Is $R(f) = (R^{[]}(f))^{O(1)}$?

3.5. Discrepancy

The most natural method to prove lower bounds for D_ε^μ is by giving upper bounds for the size of rectangles that are "almost" monochromatic. An extreme case of this method would be to show, for a certain function f, that every large enough rectangle must be almost completely balanced between 1s of the function and 0s of the function. In such a case we can use only "small" rectangles and hence need "many" rectangles. This can be thought of as a generalization of the rectangle size method (Section 1.3), where now protocols can make mistakes but they are still deterministic. We start with a definition:

Definition 3.27: *Let $f: X \times Y \to \{0, 1\}$ be a function, R be any rectangle, and μ be a probability distribution on $X \times Y$. Denote*

$$Disc_\mu(R, f)$$
$$= \left| \Pr_\mu[f(x, y) = 0 \text{ and } (x, y) \in R] - \Pr_\mu[f(x, y) = 1 \text{ and } (x, y) \in R] \right|.$$

The discrepancy of f *according to μ is*

$$Disc_\mu(f) = \max_R Disc_\mu(R, f),$$

where the maximum is taken over all rectangles R.

Note that for every *monochromatic* rectangle $R, Disc_\mu(R, f) = \mu(R)$. The definition becomes more interesting for nonmonochromatic rectangles. Consider the function of Figure 3.2, and let μ be the uniform distribution on $\{0, 1\}^3 \times \{0, 1\}^3$. That is, every input (x, y) has weight $\mu(x, y) = 1/64$. The rectangle R shown in the figure has 29 0-entries (whose weight is therefore 29/64) and seven 1-entries (whose weight is therefore 7/64). Hence, $Disc_\mu(R, f) = 22/64$.

Bounds on the discrepancy turn out to be strong enough to give lower bounds for D_ε^μ, even when ε is very close to $1/2$.

Proposition 3.28: *For every function $f: X \times Y \to \{0, 1\}$, every probability distribution μ on $X \times Y$, and every $\varepsilon \geq 0$, $D_{\frac{1}{2}-\varepsilon}^\mu(f) \geq \log_2(2\varepsilon/Disc_\mu(f))$.*

	000	001	010	011	100	101	110	111
000	0	1	1	0	1	0	0	0
001	1	0	0	0	0	0	0	1
010	1	0	0	0	1	0	0	0
011	0	0	1	0	0	0	0	1
100	1	0	0	0	1	0	0	1
101	1	1	1	0	0	0	1	1
110	0	0	0	0	1	0	0	0
111	0	1	1	0	1	1	0	1

Figure 3.2: A rectangle with large discrepancy

PROOF: Let $\mathcal{P}$ be a protocol using c bits of communication attempting to compute f, which is correct with probability at least $1/2 + \varepsilon$. We can now write

$$2\varepsilon \leq \Pr_{\mu}[\mathcal{P}(x, y) = f(x, y)] - \Pr_{\mu}[\mathcal{P}(x, y) \neq f(x, y)]$$

$$= \sum_{\ell} \Big(\Pr_{\mu}[\mathcal{P}(x, y) = f(x, y) \text{ and } (x, y) \in R_\ell]$$

$$- \Pr_{\mu}[\mathcal{P}(x, y) \neq f(x, y) \text{ and } (x, y) \in R_\ell] \Big)$$

where the summation is over all leaves ℓ of the protocol. Since for each leaf a specific output (0 or 1) is given, we can bound this expression from above by

$$\sum_{\ell} \left| \Pr_{\mu}[f(x, y) = 0 \text{ and } (x, y) \in R_\ell] - \Pr_{\mu}[f(x, y) = 1 \text{ and } (x, y) \in R_\ell] \right|.$$

Since for each ℓ, R_ℓ is a rectangle, each of these (at most) 2^c terms is bounded from above by $Disc_\mu(f)$. Thus, we get $2^c Disc_\mu(f) \geq 2\varepsilon$, which implies $c \geq \log(2\varepsilon/Disc_\mu(f))$, as claimed. □

We are now ready to use the technique. In Exercise 3.31 you are asked to prove that, for a *random* function, the distributional communication complexity is at least $n - O(\log(1/\varepsilon))$. The next example shows a similar bound for an explicit function.

▶ **Example 3.29:** Consider again the inner product function, IP (Example 1.25). We will show that $Disc_{uniform}(\text{IP}) = 2^{-n/2}$, and hence $D_{\frac{1}{2}-\varepsilon}^{uniform}(\text{IP}) \geq n/2 - \log(1/\varepsilon)$, and thus $R_{\frac{1}{2}-\varepsilon}^{pub}(\text{IP}) \geq n/2 - \log(1/\varepsilon)$.

Let H be a $2^n \times 2^n$ matrix where $H(x, y) = 1$ if $\langle x, y \rangle = 0$, and $H(x, y) = -1$ otherwise. The first observation is that $HH^T = 2^n I$, where I is the identity matrix. This is because the (x, y) entry of the matrix HH^T is (by definition of matrix multiplication) $\sum_z H(x, z) \cdot H(z, y)$. By the properties of the inner product, if $x = y$, then $H(x, z) = H(z, y)$, therefore each of the summands equals 1 and the sum is 2^n. On the other hand, if $x \neq y$, then for $1/2$ of the zs $H(x, z) = H(z, y)$ (in which case the summand is 1) and for $1/2$ of the zs $H(x, z) \neq H(z, y)$ (in which case the summand is -1). Therefore in this case the sum is 0. Using this observation, the *norm* of H satisfies $\|H\| = \sqrt{2^n}$, since for all vectors v, $vHH^T = 2^n v$ and hence 2^n is the only eigenvalue of HH^T. Consider a rectangle $S \times T$ in H. Note that

$$Disc_{uniform}(S \times T, \text{IP}) = \frac{\left| \sum_{x \in S, y \in T} H(x, y) \right|}{2^{2n}} = \frac{|\vec{1}_S \cdot H \cdot \vec{1}_T|}{2^{2n}},$$

where $\vec{1}_S$ and $\vec{1}_T$ are the characteristic vectors of S and T, respectively. This we can bound from above by the product of the norms, $\|\vec{1}_S\| \cdot \|H\| \cdot \|\vec{1}_T\| = \sqrt{|S|}\sqrt{2^n}\sqrt{|T|}$. Finally, because $|S|, |T| \leq 2^n$, we get

$$Disc_{uniform}(\text{IP}) = \max_{S,T} Disc_{uniform}(S \times T, \text{IP}) \leq \frac{\sqrt{2^{3n}}}{2^{2n}} = 2^{-n/2},$$

as desired.

Exercise 3.30: Prove that in fact, $R_{\frac{1}{2}-\varepsilon}(\text{IP}) \geq n - O(\log(1/\varepsilon))$.

Exercise 3.31: Prove that for "most" Boolean functions $D_{\frac{1}{2}-\varepsilon}^{uniform}(f) = n - O(\log\frac{1}{\varepsilon})$. That is, only an exponentially small fraction of the functions have better complexity. Hint: Pick a function at random and compute the probability that it has a "large," "almost monochromatic" rectangle.

Exercise 3.32: Let $Disc(f) = \min_{\mu} Disc_{\mu}(f)$.

- Prove that $Disc(\text{DISJ}) \geq 1/(2n+1)$.

- Prove that for every function f, $R^{pub}(f) \leq (1/Disc(f))^{O(1)}$. Hint: Use the distributional complexity.

The above exercise shows that the discrepancy technique sometimes gives only very poor bounds. Particularly, for the disjointness function, DISJ, it gives only a logarithmic lower bound, whereas Example 3.22 shows that in fact the randomized communication complexity of DISJ is linear. The only other lower bound technique known for two-sided error randomized complexity is the method used in Example 3.22, which is essentially a generalization of the technique of giving an upper bound on the discrepancy.

3.6. Bibliographic Notes

Randomized communication complexity was also defined in the seminal paper [Yao 1979]. The $O(\log n)$ randomized protocol for EQ (the version given in Exercise 3.6) was found by Rabin and Yao. The randomized communication complexity of the GT function was studied by Nisan and Safra, see in [Nisan 1993]. Example 3.16 is due to Håstad and Wigderson (private communication). Open Problem 3.11 was suggested in [Beame and Lawry 1992].

The relations between the public coin model of randomized protocols and the private coin model were studied by [Newman 1991]. The relations between the number of random bits used by randomized protocols and their communication complexity are studied in [Canetti and Goldreich 1990, Fleischer, Jung, and Melhorn 1990]

The relations between distributional complexity and randomized complexity, are a general phenomena exhibited by [Yao 1983], based on von-Neumann's min–max theorem of game theory (see, for example, [Owen 1982]). The distributional communication complexity of the inner product function, IP, was studied by [Chor and Goldreich 1985], improving on a result of [Vazirani 1985]. The proof presented here (in Example 3.29) is similar to the proof in [Chor and Goldreich 1985] (see also [Babai, Frankl, and Simon 1986]), which is based on a lemma by Lindsey. The proof does not hold only for the function IP, but it can be extended to any function f whose corresponding matrix is a so-called *Hadamard* matrix. The distributional (and randomized) communication complexity of the disjointness function (Example 3.22) was first handled by [Babai et al. 1986]. Their result was improved by [Kalyanasundaram and Schnitger 1987]. A simplified proof was presented by [Razborov 1990a] (see Section 4.6). Exercise 3.25 is due to [Babai et al. 1986].

An "unbounded" version of randomized communication complexity, with a weaker success requirement, was considered by [Paturi and Simon 1984] and [Alon, Frankl, and Rödl 1985]. The "unbounded" model exhibits a different behavior than the model described here as, for example, the communication complexity of the function EQ is $O(1)$ in the "unbounded" model in opposition to $\Theta(\log n)$ in the standard (private coin) model.

CHAPTER 4

Advanced Topics

In this chapter we consider several, more advanced, topics related to the two-party communication model.

4.1. Direct Sum

The direct-sum problem is the following: Alice gets two inputs $x_f \in X_f$ and $x_g \in X_g$. Bob gets two inputs $y_f \in Y_f$ and $y_g \in Y_g$. They wish to compute both $f(x_f, y_f)$ and $g(x_g, y_g)$. The obvious solution would be for Alice and Bob to use the best protocol for f to compute the first value, $f(x_f, y_f)$, and the best protocol for g to compute the second value, $g(x_g, y_g)$. We stress that the two subproblems are totally independent. Thus one would tend to conjecture that nothing better than the obvious solution can be done: Alice and Bob cannot "save" any communication over the obvious protocol. As we shall see, in some cases and for some measures of complexity, this intuition is wrong.

Denote by $D(f, g)$ the (deterministic) communication complexity of this computation. Similarly, we define all other complexity measures such as $R(f, g)$, $N(f, g)$, and so forth. We also use the notation $D(f^\ell)$ as the (deterministic) communication complexity of computing f on ℓ instances; that is, computing $f(x_1, y_1)$, $f(x_2, y_2)$, ..., $f(x_\ell, y_\ell)$.

Open Problem 4.1: Can $D(f,g)$ be smaller than $D(f) + D(g)$? How much smaller can it be? How much smaller can $D(f^\ell)$ be compared to $\ell \cdot D(f)$?

In some cases we are not interested in computing both f and g but rather some function of the two. For example, consider the function $f \wedge g[(x_f, x_g), (y_f, y_g)] = f(x_f, y_f) \wedge g(x_g, y_g)$. Obviously $D(f \wedge g) \leq D(f, g)$. Again, we can ask:

Open Problem 4.2: Can $D(f \wedge g)$ be smaller than $D(f) + D(g)$? How much smaller?

These problems try to attack a very basic question about the model of communication complexity: Can we solve two problems in this model simultaneously in a way that is better than to solve each of the two problems separately? In other words, does the model behave as our intuition suggests it should, or does it have some surprising phenomena?

We present several results that handle questions of this type relative to several of the complexity measures introduced in the previous chapters. (For additional results see Lemma 4.60 and Example 4.61) We start by showing that, for randomized communication complexity, Alice and Bob can indeed "save." In contrast, we show that for nondeterministic communication complexity, Alice and Bob cannot "save" too much (but can still "save a little"). The most interesting case, the deterministic communication complexity, remains wide open.

4.1.1. The Randomized Case

In the randomized case we can present a function f such that the complexity of computing f^ℓ is significantly smaller than the obvious. Let us first remark that we require a randomized protocol for f^ℓ to be correct with probability $2/3$ *simultaneously* on all ℓ instances. This may eliminate the possibility of computing f^ℓ simply by executing the best randomized protocol for f on each of the ℓ instances (as this only guarantees that for each instance there is a probability of at least $2/3$ to compute the correct answer).

▶ **Example 4.3:** Consider the equality function. By Example 3.9, $R(\text{EQ}) = \Theta(\log n)$. We present a protocol for EQ^ℓ that does much better than $\ell \cdot \log n$.

The protocol is obtained by considering first the public coin model. Example 3.13 gives an $O(1)$ public coin protocol that errs with probability at most $1/3$ if $x \neq y$ and is always correct if $x = y$. If the protocol is repeated $\log 3\ell$ times then it computes the equality function with $O(\log \ell)$ bits and error of at most $1/3\ell$. Repeating this process for each of the ℓ instances, we can compute EQ^ℓ, in the public coin model, with $O(\ell \log \ell)$ bits and probability of making even a single error of at most $1/3$. Finally, by Theorem 3.14 (and observing that for the proof of this theorem f need not be Boolean), the cost of transforming this protocol to the private coin model is an additive factor of $O(\log(\ell n))$, since ℓn is the total size of the input. All together, $R(\text{EQ}^\ell) = O(\ell \log \ell + \log n)$. For example, for $\ell = \log n$, we get

$$R(\text{EQ}^{\log n}) = O(\log n \log \log n) \ll (\log n) \cdot R(\text{EQ}) = \Theta(\log^2 n).$$

This type of saving comes in handy when we are given a single problem that contains many instances of EQ. In fact, sometimes additional saving is possible when we do not require all the different answers, but rather only a single answer that depends on them. Such an example is given next:

▶ **Example 4.4:** Consider the list-nonequality function $\text{LNE}_{\ell,k}(x, y)$: Alice views her input x (an $n = \ell k$ bit string) as consisting of ℓ blocks $x^1, \ldots, x^\ell$ of k bits each. Bob views his input y in a similar way. $\text{LNE}_{\ell,k}(x, y) = 1$ if and only if $x^j \neq y^j$ for all j. By using the protocol of Example 4.3 to compute all equalities, we get that $R(\text{LNE}_{\ell,k}) = O(\ell \log \ell + \log k)$. We now improve over this bound and show that $R(\text{LNE}_{\ell,k}) = O(\ell + \log k)$. Again, it suffices to prove $R^{pub}(\text{LNE}_{\ell,k}) = O(\ell)$. For this, Alice and Bob use the following protocol:

- Let $j = 1$.
- While $j \leq \ell$ do at most 4ℓ times:
  Alice and Bob choose (without any communication) a random string $r \in \{0, 1\}^k$. They compare the inner product of r with x^j and y^j. If $\langle x^j, r \rangle \neq \langle y^j, r \rangle$, then certainly $x^j \neq y^j$ and they proceed to the next block by setting $j = j + 1$. Otherwise, if $\langle x^j, r \rangle = \langle y^j, r \rangle$ they do nothing (so in the next iteration they will compare again the j-th blocks).
- If all blocks were compared (that is, $j > \ell$) the output is 1. Otherwise, the output is 0.

Since there are at most 4ℓ iterations and two bits are exchanged in each iteration, the complexity of this protocol is $O(\ell)$ bits. Clearly, if there is a block j_0 such that $x^{j_0} = y^{j_0}$, then for all r, $\langle x^{j_0}, r \rangle = \langle y^{j_0}, r \rangle$. Hence, j never exceeds j_0 and the protocol always outputs the correct answer (that is, 0). If no such block exists, the probability that Alice and Bob will not eliminate all blocks is the probability that in 4ℓ independent trials, with probability $1/2$ of success in each of them, Alice and Bob will have less then ℓ successes. This probability is $\sum_{i=0}^{\ell-1} \binom{4\ell}{i}/2^{4\ell}$, which is exponentially small.

The above protocol has one-sided error. With slightly more efforts we can give a zero error protocol for LNE.

▶ **Example 4.5:** Consider again the list-nonequality function LNE. We now show that also $R_0(\text{LNE}_{\ell,k}) = O(\ell + k)$. In Example 4.13 we show that $D(\text{LNE}_{\ell,k}) = \Omega(k\ell)$. Thus, for the choice of $\ell = k = \sqrt{n}$ this gives the largest gap possible between deterministic communication complexity and zero error randomized communication complexity (see Section 3.2).

To see that $R_0(\text{LNE}) = O(\ell + k)$, we consider first the public coin model and then, using Exercise 3.15, transform the protocol to the private coin model with an additive factor of $O(\log(\ell k))$ to the complexity. The protocol is a modification of the protocol given in Example 4.4 in which we eliminate the possibility of error by adding a verification for the equality of x^j and y^j at the end. More precisely, Alice and Bob do the following block by block (they stop if they find a block in which $x^j = y^j$). They exchange the inner product of x^j and y^j with a random vector $r \in \{0, 1\}^k$ (from the public random string). If $\langle x^j, r \rangle \neq \langle y^j, r \rangle$, then $x^j \neq y^j$ so Alice and Bob proceed to the next block. If $\langle x^j, r \rangle = \langle y^j, r \rangle$, they repeat this with another random string. If after k times all inner products are equal they simply exchange the blocks x^j and y^j themselves. They output 0 if $x^j = y^j$. If $x^j \neq y^j$, they proceed to the next j. The correctness of the protocol is obvious. For the complexity of the protocol, note that if $x^j = y^j$, then $O(k)$ bits are exchanged. However, this is done at most once (for the first such j). On the other hand, when $x^j \neq y^j$ the probability that $\langle x^j, r \rangle = \langle y^j, r \rangle$ is $1/2$ at each test. Hence, the expected number of bits exchanged for such a block is $\sum_{i=1}^{k} \frac{1}{2^i} 2i + \frac{1}{2^k} 2k = O(1)$, since $\sum_{i=1}^{\infty} \frac{i}{2^i} = 2$. By linearity of expectation, these blocks contribute $O(\ell)$ bits to the complexity.

The question of what are the largest possible gaps in randomized communication complexity remains open for all the different measures. For example,

Open Problem 4.6: Does there exist f such that $R^{\mathrm{pub}}(f^\ell) < \ell \cdot R^{\mathrm{pub}}(f)$? How big can the gap be?

Exercise 4.6a: Show that $R^{\mathrm{pub}}(f^\ell) = O(\ell \cdot \log \ell \cdot R^{\mathrm{pub}}(f))$, for all f

4.1.2. The Nondeterministic Case

In this subsection we consider nondeterministic communication complexity. We show that in the nondeterministic case the complexity of (f, g) cannot be much smaller than the sum of the complexities. We will concentrate on the measure N^1, but similar results hold also for the measures N^0 and N.

Recall the definitions of the μ-rectangle size bound, $B_\mu(f)$, and of the rectangle size bound, $B_*^1(f)$ (Definition 2.14). The key tool that we need is the following property of the measure B_*^1:

Lemma 4.7: $B_*^1(f \wedge g) \geq B_*^1(f) \cdot B_*^1(g)$.

PROOF: Let μ_f be the distribution that gives the maximum for $B_*^1(f)$ and similarly let μ_g be the distribution that gives the maximum for $B_*^1(g)$. That is, for every 1-monochromatic rectangle R of f, $\mu_f(R) \leq 1/B_*^1(f)$ and for every 1-monochromatic rectangle R' of g, $\mu_g(R') \leq 1/B_*^1(g)$. Define a distribution μ on the 1s of $f \wedge g$ by:

$$\mu((x_f, x_g), (y_f, y_g)) = \mu_f(x_f, y_f) \cdot \mu_g(x_g, y_g)$$

Note that μ is indeed a probability distribution. Now, consider a 1-monochromatic rectangle R of $f \wedge g$. Let R_f be the projection of R on f's input. That is,

$$R_f = \{(x_f, y_f) : \exists (x_g, y_g) \text{ such that } ((x_f, x_g), (y_f, y_g)) \in R\}.$$

Similarly, let R_g be defined as

$$R_g = \{(x_g, y_g) : \exists (x_f, y_f) \text{ such that } ((x_f, x_g), (y_f, y_g)) \in R\}.$$

Because R is a rectangle, then so are R_f and R_g. Moreover, because R is 1-monochromatic with respect to $f \wedge g$, then so are R_f with respect to f and R_g with respect to g. Also, $R \subseteq R_f \times R_g$ and hence $\mu(R) \leq \mu(R_f \times R_g)$. By the definition of μ, $\mu(R_f \times R_g)$ is equal to $\mu_f(R_f) \cdot \mu_g(R_g)$, which is at most $1/(B_*^1(f)B_*^1(g))$. We have shown that there exists a probability distribution μ such that, for every 1-monochromatic rectangle R of $f \wedge g$, $\mu(R) \leq 1/(B_*^1(f)B_*^1(g))$. This implies, by definition, that $B_*^1(f \wedge g) \geq B_\mu(f \wedge g) \geq B_*^1(f)B_*^1(g)$. □

Exercise 4.8: Lemma 4.7 only states the property that we need for our purposes. In this exercise we take a more complete view on the measure B_*^1.

1. Express B_*^1 as a linear program. Use the duality theorem of linear programming to write its *dual* program.
Use the dual program to solve the next two parts of this exercise.

2. Prove that $B_*^1(f \wedge g) = B_*^1(f)B_*^1(g)$ (that is, Lemma 4.7 holds with equality).

3. Prove that $\log B_*^1(f) \leq R^{1,\mathsf{pub}}(f) + O(1)$ (recall that $R^{1,\mathsf{pub}}(f)$ is the complexity of computing f using a public coin protocol that makes a one-sided error).

Corollary 4.9: *For all Boolean functions* $f, g : \{0, 1\}^n \times \{0, 1\}^n \to \{0, 1\}$,

- $N^1(f \wedge g) \geq N^1(f) + N^1(g) - 2\log n - O(1)$.
- $N^1(\wedge_{j=1}^{\ell} f) \geq \ell(N^1(f) - \log n - O(1))$.

PROOF: Combining Proposition 2.15, Theorem 2.16, and Lemma 4.7 we get:

$$N^1(f \wedge g) \geq \log B_*^1(f \wedge g) \geq \log B_*^1(f) + \log B_*^1(g)$$
$$\geq N^1(f) + N^1(g) - 2\log n - O(1).$$

Similarly,

$$N^1(\wedge_{j=1}^{\ell} f) \geq \log B_*^1(\wedge_{j=1}^{\ell} f) \geq \log(B_*^1(f))^{\ell}$$
$$= \ell \log B_*^1(f) \geq \ell(N^1(f) - \log n - O(1)),$$

as desired. □

▶ **Example 4.10:** Consider the NE function. We know that $N^1(\mathrm{NE}) = \log n + 1$ (Example 2.17). By Example 2.17, $B_*^1(\mathrm{NE}) \leq 4$ (alternatively, recall that $R^{1,pub}(\mathrm{NE}) = O(1)$ (Example 3.13) and use Exercise 4.8). By Exercise 4.8, $B_*^1(\wedge_{j=1}^{\ell}\mathrm{NE}) \leq 4^{\ell}$, which implies, by Theorem 2.16, $N^1(\wedge_{j=1}^{\ell}\mathrm{NE}) = O(\ell + \log n)$ (compared to $\ell \cdot N^1(\mathrm{NE}) = O(\ell \log n)$). Therefore, the $O(\log n)$ term in Corollary 4.9 is necessary.

4.1.3. The Deterministic Case

In the previous subsections, we showed that for some functions f, the randomized communication complexity of f^{ℓ} or the nondeterministic communication complexity of f^{ℓ} may be smaller than ℓ times the corresponding complexity of f, but that the gap in the case of nondeterministic communication complexity cannot be too large. In order to prove a similar result for the deterministic case we need, for some function f, to prove an upper bound on $D(f^{\ell})$ and to prove a lower bound on $D(f)$. Some bounds on the gap can be obtained by results we have already seen.

Exercise 4.11: Prove that for all Boolean functions f,

$$D(f^{\ell}) = \Omega(\ell(\sqrt{D(f)} - \log n - O(1))).$$

Hint: Use Corollary 4.9 to prove that $N(f^{\ell}) \geq \ell(N(f) - \log n - O(1))$. Then, use the connection between nondeterministic communication complexity and deterministic communication complexity.

Let us consider what techniques might be used to obtain such a gap. What was shown in Section 4.1.2 is that if the lower bound on $D(f)$ was proved using the rectangle size bound, $B_*^1(f)$, then because

$$D(f^\ell) \geq D\big(\wedge_{j=1}^\ell f\big) \geq N^1\big(\wedge_{j=1}^\ell f\big) \geq \log B_*^1\big(\wedge_{j=1}^\ell f\big) \geq \log\big(B_*^1(f)\big)^\ell$$
$$= \ell \log\big(B_*^1(f)\big)$$

any protocol for $D(f^\ell)$ has complexity that is ℓ times the lower bound for $D(f)$. The same reasoning excludes using the rectangle size bound on the 0-rectangles.

The second lower bound technique we have for proving lower bounds on $D(f)$ is by using the rank of M_f (see Sections 1.4 and 2.5). However, the following exercise shows that if the lower bound for $D(f)$ is proved using the rank method then, again, $D(f^\ell)$ is at least ℓ times larger than this lower bound.

Exercise 4.12: Show that $\mathrm{rank}(f \wedge g) = \mathrm{rank}(f)\mathrm{rank}(g)$. Hint: Use the Kronecker product.

The following example shows how to use Exercise 4.12 to analyze the rank of certain matrices.

▶ **Example 4.13:** A convenient way to view the function LNE (Example 4.4) is by writing $\mathrm{LNE}_{\ell,k}(x, y) = \wedge_{j=1}^\ell \mathrm{NE}(x^j, y^j)$. With this view, it follows from Exercise 4.12 that $\mathrm{rank}(\mathrm{LNE}) = (\mathrm{rank}(\mathrm{NE}))^\ell$. Because M_{NE} has full rank, $\mathrm{rank}(\mathrm{LNE}) = (2^k)^\ell = 2^n$, which implies $D(\mathrm{LNE}) \geq n$. Now, consider the nondeterministic communication complexity of LNE. Clearly, $N^0(\mathrm{LNE}) = O(\log \ell + k)$, because Alice can "guess" the index j for which $x^j = y^j$ and send Bob the value j and x^j. Also, $N^1(\mathrm{LNE}) = O(\ell \log k)$, because Alice can "guess" for each j an index i such that $x_i^j \neq y_i^j$ and send Bob the list of indices and the values of the corresponding bits. In fact, by Example 4.5, $N^1(\mathrm{LNE}) \leq R^1(\mathrm{LNE}) = O(\ell + \log k)$. If, for example, $\ell = k = \sqrt{n}$, then $N^0(\mathrm{LNE}) = N^1(\mathrm{LNE}) = O(\sqrt{n})$, which, due to Theorem 2.11, are both optimal.

Exercise 4.14: Show that $D(\mathrm{EQ}^\ell) \geq \ell \cdot n$ (prove it once using a fooling set argument and again using Exercise 4.12).

The next application of Exercise 4.12 shows that the rank lower bound on $D(f)$ (Section 1.4) is always better (ignoring constants) than the fooling set lower bound (Section 1.3).

Lemma 4.15: *Let f be a Boolean function and let A be a fooling set for f. Then, $|A| \leq (\mathrm{rank}(f) + 1)^2$.*

PROOF: It is enough to prove that if A is a 1-fooling set, then $|A| \leq (\mathrm{rank}(f))^2$. The proof for 0-fooling sets can then be done by going through the function $not(f)$ whose matrix has a rank of at most $\mathrm{rank}(f) + 1$. Let $(x^{(1)}, y^{(1)}), \ldots, (x^{(r)}, y^{(r)})$ be the elements of A. Define a new function $g(x, y) = f(y, x)$. Obviously, $\mathrm{rank}(f) = \mathrm{rank}(g)$.

Consider the function $f \wedge g$. By Exercise 4.12,

$$\text{rank}(f \wedge g) = \text{rank}(f) \cdot \text{rank}(g) = (\text{rank}(f))^2.$$

Hence, it is enough to prove that $\text{rank}(f \wedge g) \geq |A|$. For this, it is enough to prove that $M_{f \wedge g}$ contains as a submatrix the identity matrix of order $r = |A|$. Consider the set S of the rows $(x^{(i)}, y^{(i)})$ $(1 \leq i \leq r)$ and the set T of the columns $(y^{(i)}, x^{(i)})$ $(1 \leq i \leq r)$. To see that the submatrix $S \times T$ is the identity matrix, note that the (i, j) entry in this submatrix is

$$(f \wedge g)\left[(x^{(i)}, y^{(i)}), (y^{(j)}, x^{(j)})\right] = f\left(x^{(i)}, y^{(j)}\right) \cdot g\left(y^{(i)}, x^{(j)}\right)$$
$$= f\left(x^{(i)}, y^{(j)}\right) \cdot f\left(x^{(j)}, y^{(i)}\right).$$

If $i = j$, then this value equals 1 because $f(x^{(i)}, y^{(i)}) = 1$ (because $(x^{(i)}, y^{(i)})$ is an element of A). On the other hand, if $i \neq j$, then this value equals 0 because at least one of $f(x^{(i)}, y^{(j)})$ and $f(x^{(j)}, y^{(i)})$ is 0 (because A is a fooling set). $\qquad \square$

Observe that both Lemma 4.15 and Exercise 4.12 hold in any field. This is used in the following example:

▶ **Example 4.16:** Consider the function IP. We proved that $\text{rank}(M_{IP}) = 2^n - 1$ (Example 1.29) and hence $D(\text{IP}) \geq n$. On the other hand, in Exercise 2.23 it is shown that over $GF(2)$ the rank is only $\text{rank}_{GF(2)}(M_{IP}) = n$. This implies, using the above lemma, that the size of a fooling set for the IP function is at most $(n + 1)^2$. Hence, in this case, the rank method gives an exponentially better lower bound than the bound given by the fooling set method.

4.2. Rounds

In the definition of communication complexity Alice and Bob alternate sending messages to each other. This is satisfactory as long as we are interested only in the number of bits exchanged. We may ask how much *interaction* is really necessary to obtain a low communication protocol. For example, maybe it always suffices for Alice to send one message (containing several bits) to Bob and then Bob can compute the answer by himself. We start by discussing one-round communication, where no interaction takes place; then, we consider protocols with limited interaction.

Definition 4.17: *A one-round protocol is a protocol where Alice sends a message to Bob, and then Bob sends the output. The one-round communication complexity of f, denoted $D^1(f)$, is the cost of the best one-round protocol for f. We use $D^{1, Bob}$ to denote the cost of one-round protocols in which Bob sends the first message. We use similar notation for randomized complexity ($R^1(f)$) and so forth.*

The one-round deterministic communication complexity of a function is quite easy to characterize.

Exercise 4.18: Prove that $D^1(f) = \log_2 t + 1$, where t is the number of different rows in the matrix M_f associated with f.

▶ **Example 4.19:** Let INDEX(x, i) denote the function where Bob gets an integer $1 \leq i \leq n$, and Alice gets a vector $x \in \{0, 1\}^n$, and the output is the bit x_i. The previous exercise implies that $D^1(f) = n + 1$, while $D^{1,Bob}(f) = \log_2 n + 1$.

Exercise 4.20: Prove that $R^1(\text{INDEX}) = \Theta(n)$ and that $R^{1,Bob}(\text{INDEX}) = \Theta(\log n)$.

We see that for both deterministic and randomized protocols, there may be an exponential gap between 1-round communication complexity and unrestricted communication complexity (or even between the 1-round complexities with different players starting). The next exercise claims that this is the largest gap possible for deterministic and randomized protocols. In contrast, for nondeterministic protocols there is no difference between 1-round and an arbitrary number of rounds (see Section 2.1).

Exercise 4.21: Show that $D(f) \geq \log_2 D^1(f)$ and also $R(f) \geq \log_2 R^1(f)$.

Exercise 4.22: We can consider an even more restricted type of protocols that are called *simultaneous* protocols. In this kind of protocol, Alice and Bob each send a single message (depending only on his own input) to a referee, who, based on these two messages, computes the value $f(x,y)$. Denote by $D^{||}(f)$ the deterministic communication complexity of computing the function f using simultaneous protocols and $R^{||}(f)$ the randomized communication complexity of computing the function f using simultaneous protocols. Let $f: \{0, 1\}^n \times \{0, 1\}^n \to \{0, 1\}$ be any function.

1. Prove that $D^{||}(f) = D^1(f) + D^{1,Bob}(f)$.
2. Prove that $R^{||}(f) = O(\sqrt{n} \cdot R^{||,pub}(f))$. Hint: Simulate the public coin protocol, for many different values of the coins. See also the proof of Theorem 3.14.
3. Prove that $D^{||}(f) = O(R^{||}(f)^2)$. Hint: First, reduce the probability of error by repeating the randomized protocol $O(R^{||}(f))$ times. Then, choose a specific random string for a deterministic simulation.
4. Determine $R^{||}(\text{EQ})$.

We now turn our attention to the case of limited interaction:

Definition 4.23: *A k-round protocol is a protocol where on every input there are at most k alternations between bits sent by Alice and bits sent by Bob. For example, a two-round protocol is a protocol where Alice sends a message to Bob; Bob sends a message to Alice; and then Alice sends the output.*
The k-round communication complexity of f, denoted $D^k(f)$, is the cost of the best k-round protocol for f, where Alice sends the first message. We use $D^{k,Bob}$ to denote the cost of k-round protocols where Bob sends the first message. We use similar notation for randomized complexity ($R^k(f)$), distributional complexity ($D_\varepsilon^{\mu,k}(f)$), and so forth.

It turns out that for any k, there are cases where restricting the number of rounds to k increases the communication complexity exponentially relative to even $k + 1$-round protocols. Proving such gaps for a certain function g consists of two parts: an upper bound on the $k+1$-round complexity of g, and a lower bound on its k-round complexity. The general technique used to prove such lower bounds proceeds by transforming any k-round protocol for g into a $k-1$-round protocol for some "restricted" case f of g, which by induction is known not to have efficient $k-1$-round protocols. The base case for this induction is one-round protocols, which, as we saw, are typically easier to handle. A transformation as described above can be done by arguing that the first message sent in the k-round protocol (for g) could not have conveyed too much information about f, and thus in the converted $k - 1$-round protocol, the parties will simply skip the first round of communication. A general scenario where this can be done is given in Theorem 4.26.

Definition 4.24: *Let $f(x, y)$ be a Boolean function on domain $X \times Y$. The two-party communication problem f^{*m} is as follows: Alice gets m strings $x_1, \ldots, x_m \in X$; Bob gets an integer $i \in \{1, \ldots, m\}$ and a string $y \in Y$. Their aim is to compute $f(x_i, y)$.*

Exercise 4.25: Recall the definition of f^m (Section 4.1). Prove that, for all k and m, $D^k(f) \leq D^k(f^{*m}) \leq D^k(f^m) \leq m \cdot D^k(f)$.

Consider a k-round protocol for computing f^{*m}. Intuitively, since Alice does not know i, she cannot know which x_i to speak about in her first message – and as long as she sends $o(m)$ bits in this message, she gives very little information on the right x_i. Thus, her first message can be skipped. This can be proven in the most clean and general way for public coin, randomized protocols. All randomized protocols in this section are in the public coin model, but for brevity we will simply use R^k instead of $R^{k,pub}$.

Theorem 4.26: *Let f be any function. Then,*

$$R^k(f^{*m}) \geq \min\left\{ \frac{m}{100 \log m}, \frac{R^{k-1,Bob}(f)}{10 \log m} \right\}.$$

In the proof of this theorem we will go back and forth between randomized and distributional complexities. We should observe that just like in the proof of Theorem 3.20, the k-round randomized complexity is exactly equal to the maximum over all distributions of the distributional k-round complexity (the same proof works).

We use the following notation: For a distribution D on a set X, denote by D^m the distribution on X^m obtained by choosing independently for each $1 \leq i \leq m$, an element $x_i \in X$ according to the distribution D. For a set S, denote the density of S according to the distribution D (that is $\Pr[x \in S]$ if x is chosen according to D) by $\Pr_D[S]$. If D is a joint distribution on $X_1 \times X_2$, we denote the conditional probability of event E given a fixed choice of x_1 by $\Pr_D[E|x_1]$.

Definition 4.27: *Let D be a distribution on X, let $S \subseteq X^m$ and let i $(1 \leq i \leq m)$ be an index. The index i is free in S (relative to D) if there exist $x_1, \ldots, x_{i-1} \in X$ and a set $G \subseteq X$ such that*

1. $\Pr_D[G] \geq 0.9$.

2. *For every $g \in G$ there exists $x_{i+1}, \ldots, x_m$ such that $\langle x_1, \ldots, x_{i-1}, g, x_{i+1}, \ldots, x_m \rangle \in S$.*

Intuitively, i is free in S if S has little information on x_i, even given $x_1, \ldots, x_{i-1}$. The following lemma states that if S is large, then it must have little information on one of the indices.

Lemma 4.28: *Let D be any distribution on X, and let $S \subseteq X^m$ such that for all $1 \leq i \leq m$, i is not free in S, then $\Pr_{D^m}[S] < 0.9^m$.*

PROOF: The proof is by induction on m. For $m = 1$, since 1 is not free in S, then $\Pr_D[S] < 0.9$ (otherwise, S itself can serve as the set G in the definition). Assume the lemma holds for $m - 1$, and prove it for m: Let A be the set of all $x_1 \in X$ that have an extension in S. Since 1 is not free in S, $\Pr_D[A] < 0.9$. For every $x \in A$ define $S_x = \{\langle x_2, \ldots, x_m \rangle | \langle x, x_2, \ldots, x_m \rangle \in S\}$. By the definition of D^m,

$$\Pr_{D^m}[S] = \sum_{x \in A} \Pr_D[x] \Pr_{D^{m-1}}[S_x].$$

By the fact that S has no free index, it follows that for all $x \in A$, the set S_x has no free index. By the induction hypothesis, $\Pr_{D^{m-1}}[S_x] < 0.9^{m-1}$. Thus

$$\Pr_{D^m}[S] < \Pr_D[A] \cdot 0.9^{m-1} < 0.9^m,$$

as needed. □

PROOF (OF THEOREM 4.26): Let $\mathcal{P}$ be a k-round randomized protocol for f^{*m} that achieves $R^k(f^{*m})$. We first reduce the probability of error of the protocol $\mathcal{P}$ for f^{*m} (by using Exercise 3.4) to $\frac{1}{40m}$. This results in a new protocol $\mathcal{P}'$ whose communication complexity is larger by at most a factor of $10 \log m$ than the communication complexity of $\mathcal{P}$. Hence, if $\mathcal{P}'$ has communication complexity of more than $m/10$, then the complexity of $\mathcal{P}$ is at least $m/(100 \log m)$ and we are done. Assume that this is not the case; that is, at most $m/10$ bits are exchanged by $\mathcal{P}'$.

For any distribution D on $X \times Y$ we will construct a deterministic $k - 1$-round protocol for f that errs on at most $\varepsilon = 0.15$ of the inputs weighted according to the distribution D. The number of bits exchanged by the protocol will be the same as the number of bits exchanged in $\mathcal{P}'$. Since we do this for all D, a randomized protocol for f follows as in Theorem 3.20, and the theorem follows.

Define a distribution D^* on $X^m \times Y \times \{1, \ldots, m\}$ of inputs for f^{*m} as follows: Choose (independently) m pairs (x_j, y_j) according to the distribution D, and an index i uniformly at random in $\{1, \ldots, m\}$. Set $y = y_i$ (and throw away all other y_js). Let $\mathcal{P}^*$ be a deterministic protocol for f^{*m} that errs on a fraction of at most $\frac{1}{40m}$ of the input weighted by the distribution D^* (such a protocol is obtained from $\mathcal{P}'$ using Theorem 3.20, and its communication complexity is the same).

Claim 4.29: *There exists a set $S \subseteq X^m$ such that*

1. *For all $\langle x_1, \ldots, x_m \rangle \in S$ Alice's first message in $\mathcal{P}^*$ is the same, call it α.*

2. $\Pr_{D^m}[S] > 0.9^m$.

3. *For all $\langle x_1, \ldots, x_m \rangle \in S : \Pr_{D^*}[\mathcal{P}^* \text{ errs} \mid \langle x_1, \ldots, x_m \rangle] \leq \frac{1}{20m}$.*

PROOF (OF CLAIM 4.29): Consider the set T of $\langle x_1, \ldots, x_m \rangle \in X^m$ that satisfy

$$\Pr_{D^*}[\mathcal{P}^* \text{ errs} \mid \langle x_1, \ldots, x_m \rangle] \leq \frac{1}{20m}.$$

Using the Markov inequality we see that $\Pr_{D^m}[T] \geq \frac{1}{2}$ (the distribution D^* induced on X^m is simply D^m). Since the first message contains at most $\frac{m}{10}$ bits it partitions T into at most $2^{\frac{m}{10}}$ sets. Let S be the subset of T that has maximum weight, its weight is at least $\Pr_{D^m}[S] \geq \frac{\Pr_{D^m}[T]}{2^{m/10}} > 0.9^m$. $\qquad\square$

We now proceed with the proof of the theorem. Let S be the set guaranteed by Claim 4.29, let i be a free index in S as guaranteed by Lemma 4.28, and let $x_1, \ldots, x_{i-1}$ and G be as guaranteed by the definition of i being free. Following is a $k - 1$-round protocol for f on input (x, y):

- Alice, given x, constructs an input for $\mathcal{P}^*$ as follows: If $x \in G$, then she picks a sequence $\langle x_1, \ldots, x_m \rangle \in S$ that starts with $x_1, \ldots, x_{i-1}, x$. Such a sequence exists by the definition of i being free. If $x \notin G$, then Alice picks an arbitrary sequence.

- Bob, given y, takes (y, i) as his input for $\mathcal{P}^*$, where i is the free index in S.

- The two players run the protocol $\mathcal{P}^*$, but skip the first round of communication, instead assuming that the first message sent is α.

The number of bits exchanged in the above protocol is exactly as in $\mathcal{P}^*$ (and $\mathcal{P}'$). That is, $10 \log m \cdot R^k(f^{*m})$. It remains to show that this protocol errs in computing f with probability at most 0.15 when (x, y) is chosen according to the distribution D. Let us call the distribution on $X^m \times Y \times \{1, \ldots, m\}$ induced by D, in the above construction, D'. The probability that our protocol errs when (x, y) is chosen according to D is given by

$$\Pr_{D'}[\mathcal{P}^* \text{ errs}] \leq \Pr_D[x \notin G] + \Pr_{D'}[\mathcal{P}^* \text{ errs} \mid x \in G].$$

The first term is bounded from above by $\frac{1}{10}$ (by the definition of G). To bound the second term we observe that for any $x \in G$, the sequence $x_1, \ldots, x_m$ is in S, and thus satisfies (by the definition of S):

$$\Pr_{D^*}[\mathcal{P}^* \text{ errs} \mid \langle x_1, \ldots, x_m \rangle] \leq \frac{1}{20m}$$

Now notice that the distribution D' conditioned on $x_1, \ldots, x_m$ is very similar to the distribution D^* under the same conditioning. The only difference is that in D^*, i is chosen at random, whereas in D' it is fixed deterministically (in both cases y is chosen such that (x_i, y) is distributed according to D). Thus,

$$\Pr_{D'}[\mathcal{P}^* \text{ errs } | \langle x_1, \ldots, x_m \rangle] = \Pr_{D^*}[\mathcal{P}^* \text{ errs } | \langle x_1, \ldots, x_m \rangle \text{ and } i]$$

$$\leq m \Pr_{D^*}[\mathcal{P}^* \text{ errs } | \langle x_1, \ldots, x_m \rangle]$$

$$\leq \frac{1}{20},$$

where the first inequality uses the fact that in D^* the index i is distributed uniformly. Thus the total probability of error is at most $\frac{1}{10} + \frac{1}{20} = 0.15$, which completes the proof of the theorem. $\qquad\square$

▶ **Example 4.30:** For any k define the tree problem, T_k, as follows: Consider the complete n-ary tree of depth k. A *labeling* of the tree assigns to each leaf a bit, and to each internal node a number in $\{1, \ldots, n\}$. An input to the tree problem is a particular labeling of the tree, where Bob gets as his input the labels of all nodes in odd levels (where the root is level 1), and Alice gets as her input all the labels of nodes in even levels. The labels of the internal nodes define in a natural way a path from the root to a leaf (the label of each internal node is viewed as a pointer to one of its children), and the output of T_k on this labeling is the label of the leaf reached by this path. Note that the input size N is $\Theta(n^k)$.

A k-round protocol for T_k, with Bob starting, proceeds by the parties simply following the path together, and each party sending the label of the node just reached. Thus $R^{k, Bob}(T_k) \leq D^{k, Bob}(T_k) \leq k \log n$. On the other hand, to get a lower bound for the k-round complexity where Alice speaks first, notice that T_k is, by definition, exactly $(T_{k-1})^{*n}$ (with the roles of Alice and Bob in T_{k-1} reversed). We get $R^1(T_1) = \Omega(n)$ from Exercise 4.20 and thus by induction, using Theorem 4.26, we get that $D^k(T_k) \geq R^k(T_k) = \Omega(n/\log^{k-1} n)$.

Exercise 4.31: For any k define the pointer jumping function, PJ_k, as follows: The input is a $2n$-vertex directed graph of out-degree 1. Bob holds the outgoing edges from vertices $1, \ldots, n$ of the graph, and Alice holds the outgoing edges from vertices $n+1, \ldots, 2n$ (that is $\Theta(n \log n)$ bits each). The value of PJ_k is the least significant bit of the k-th vertex reached by following the path starting at vertex 1. Use a reduction from T_k to show that $R^k(\text{PJ}_k) = \Omega(n^{1/k}/\log^{k-1} n)$. In contrast, note that $D^{k, Bob}(\text{PJ}_k) \leq k \log n$.

Exercise 4.32: Show that $R^k(\text{PJ}_k) \leq R^{k-1, Bob}(\text{PJ}_k) = O(\frac{n \log n}{k})$.

4.3. Asymmetric Communication

All our treatment of communication complexity so far has only counted the *total* number of bits exchanged during the execution of the protocol. We have not made a distinction between the number of bits sent by Alice and the number of bits sent by Bob. This distinction is important in certain applications and is particularly natural to consider in cases where one of the players has a much larger input size than the other.

Definition 4.33: *A* [k, ℓ]*-protocol is a protocol where on every input* (x, y) *Alice sends a total of at most k bits and Bob sends a total of at most ℓ bits.*

Exercise 4.34: Prove that each of the functions EQ, GT, IP, and DISJ has an $[\frac{n}{2} + 1, \frac{n}{2} + 1]$-protocol. In contrast, prove that for some constant c, most functions $f : \{0, 1\}^n \times \{0,1\}^n \rightarrow \{0,1\}$ do not have an $[n - c \log n, n - c \log n]$-protocol.

Consider the lower bound techniques we have seen so far. The reader can verify that both the rank method and the rectangle size method (and its special case – the fooling set method) are not sufficient to distinguish between bits sent by Bob and those sent by Alice. The round-by-round technique (Section 4.2) can naturally be applied while preserving this distinction but usually gives rather weak lower bounds. What we show here is that an extension of the rectangle size technique, which takes into account the lengths and widths of the rectangles (and not only their sizes), leads to better bounds.

Definition 4.35: *A function* f *is* (u, v)*-rich if at least* v *of the columns of the matrix* M_f *contain at least* u *1-entries each.*

In Figure 4.1, a $(6, 5)$-rich function is exhibited (the 5 "rich" columns are the 1st, 2nd, 4th, 7th, and 8th). Note that the definition of richness is asymmetric in the sense that rows and columns play different roles. This allows giving different costs to bits sent by Alice and bits sent by Bob. Definition 4.35 is formulated in a way that is appropriate in cases where Bob has a larger input than Alice. The next lemma shows how to use it.

Lemma 4.36: *Let* f *be* (u, v)*-rich. If* f *has an* $[a, b]$*-protocol, then* f *contains a* 1*-monochromatic rectangle of dimensions at least* $u/2^a \times v/2^{a+b}$.

PROOF: The proof is by induction on $a + b$. If $a + b = 0$, no communication takes place, hence f must be constant. Since f is (u, v)-rich, it follows that $f(x, y) = 1$ for all (x, y) and that its matrix $M_f = A \times B$ satisfies $|A| \geq u$ and $|B| \geq v$.

1	0	1	1	0	0	1	1
1	1	0	1	1	0	1	0
0	1	0	0	1	0	1	1
1	1	1	0	0	1	1	1
1	1	0	1	0	1	1	0
1	1	0	1	0	0	1	1
0	1	1	1	0	1	0	1
1	0	0	1	1	0	0	1

Figure 4.1: A $(6, 5)$-rich function

For the induction step, consider two cases depending on the player that sends the first bit in the protocol. Assume first that Bob sends the first bit. Let B_0 be the inputs for which he sends 0, and B_1 be the inputs for which he sends 1. Let f_0 be the restriction of f to $A \times B_0$ and let f_1 be the restriction of f to $A \times B_1$. Note that either f_0 or f_1 is $(u, v/2)$-rich (because each of the v columns guaranteed by f being (u, v)-rich belongs to either B_0 or B_1) and that both functions have an $[a, b-1]$-protocol. Therefore, either f_0 or f_1 contains, by the induction hypothesis, a 1-monochromatic rectangle of dimensions

$$\frac{u}{2^a} \times \frac{v/2}{2^{a+b-1}} = \frac{u}{2^a} \times \frac{v}{2^{a+b}},$$

as needed.

The second case is where Alice sends the first bit in the protocol. Let A_0, A_1, f_0, and f_1 be defined analogously. A simple averaging argument shows that either f_0 or f_1 is $(u/2, v/2)$-rich (because each of the v columns guaranteed by f being (u, v)-rich has at least $u/2$ of its 1-entries in either A_0 or A_1). Also, both f_0 and f_1 have an $[a - 1, b]$-protocol, so by the induction hypothesis, either f_0 or f_1 contains a 1-monochromatic rectangle of dimensions at least

$$\frac{u/2}{2^{a-1}} \times \frac{v/2}{2^{a-1+b}} = \frac{u}{2^a} \times \frac{v}{2^{a+b}},$$

as needed. $\square$

Exercise 4.37: Let f be a (u,v)-rich function. If f has an $[a, b]$-randomized protocol with one-sided error ε, then f contains a 1-monochromatic rectangle of dimensions at least $\frac{1-\varepsilon}{2} \frac{u}{2^a} \times \frac{1-\varepsilon}{2} \frac{v}{2^{a+b}}$. Hint: Fix the random coin tosses of the protocol in an appropriate way. Then, use Lemma 4.36.

▶ **Example 4.38:** For a vector x in Z_2^n and y a vector subspace of Z_2^n (that is, x is given by n bits and y by n^2 bits, for example, by specifying a basis of the subspace), let SPAN(x, y) be 1 iff x belongs to the subspace y. Clearly the problem can be solved by letting Alice send n bits (her input) to Bob. We show that any attempt to reduce the number of bits she sends essentially implies that Bob needs to send his input (which is much longer). More precisely, in every $[k, \ell]$-protocol for SPAN, either $k = \Omega(n)$ or $\ell = \Omega(n^2)$. For the proof, assume that y is of dimension exactly $n/2$ and is given by its basis. We show that

1. SPAN does not contain a $2^{n/3} \times 2^{n^2/6}$ 1-monochromatic rectangle, and
2. SPAN is $(2^{n/2}, 2^{n^2/4})$-rich.

By Lemma 4.36, the combination of (1) and (2) implies that there is no $[\frac{n}{6}, \frac{n^2}{12} - \frac{n}{6}]$-protocol for SPAN.

For (1), consider a 1-monochromatic rectangle R with at least $2^{n/3}$ rows. Note that any $2^{n/3}$ vectors span a subspace of Z_2^n of dimension at least $n/3$ and that this subspace, V, is contained in any subspace y that is a column of the rectangle R. The number of such ys (which are subspaces of dimension $n/2$) is bounded from above by the number of ways to choose an additional $n/6$ basis elements for V, which is at most $(2^n)^{n/6} = 2^{n^2/6}$, as needed.

For (2), notice that every subspace of Z_2^n of dimension exactly $n/2$ contains exactly $2^{n/2}$ vectors and that there are at least $2^{n^2/4}$ subspaces of dimension $n/2$. To see this, we count the number of ways to choose a basis for such a subspace (that is, to choose $n/2$ independent vectors). There are $2^n - 1$ possibilities to choose the first basis element (different from $\vec{0}$), $2^n - 2$ to choose the second, $2^n - 4$ to choose the third and so forth. Also note that each basis is chosen this way $\frac{n}{2}!$ times. Hence the number of bases is $(\prod_{i=0}^{n/2-1}(2^n - 2^i))/\frac{n}{2}!$. Each subspace has many bases. By a similar argument, the number of bases for a single subspace is $(\prod_{i=0}^{n/2-1}(2^{n/2} - 2^i))/\frac{n}{2}!$. Hence the total number of subspaces is:

$$\frac{\prod_{i=0}^{n/2-1}(2^n - 2^i)}{\prod_{i=0}^{n/2-1}(2^{n/2} - 2^i)} = \prod_{i=0}^{n/2-1}\frac{2^n - 2^i}{2^{n/2} - 2^i} \geq \prod_{i=0}^{n/2-1} 2^{n/2} = 2^{n^2/4},$$

as needed.

Exercise 4.39: Let $\mathrm{DISJ}_{k,\ell}$ be the disjointness function where Alice's set is of size k and Bob's set is of size ℓ (both sets are subsets of $\{1,\ldots,n\}$). Assume $k \leq \ell \leq n$. Prove that there exists a $[O(k\log\ell), O(k\log n)]$ protocol for $\mathrm{DISJ}_{k,\ell}$. Prove also that if there exists an $[a, b]$-protocol for $\mathrm{DISJ}_{k,\ell}$ where $a = o(k\log\ell)$, then $b = \ell^{1-o(1)}$.

4.4. Pseudorandomness

While discussing distributional communication complexity we assumed that inputs for the protocol are chosen according to some arbitrary probability distribution on $X \times Y$. It is sometimes beneficial to consider more restricted ways of generating inputs. A particular generation method we will be interested in is by using some (carefully chosen) function g, which on input z outputs pairs (x, y). Hence, any probability distribution on the zs induces a probability distribution on $X \times Y$.

Definition 4.40: *A function* $g : \{0, 1\}^m \rightarrow \{0, 1\}^n \times \{0, 1\}^n$ *is a pseudorandom generator for communication complexity* c *with parameter* ε *if for every two-party deterministic protocol* $\mathcal{P}$ *of at most* c *bits of communication*

$$|\Pr[\mathcal{P}(x, y) \text{ outputs } 1] - \Pr[\mathcal{P}(g(z)) \text{ outputs } 1]| \leq \varepsilon,$$

where x *and* y *are chosen uniformly and independently in* $\{0, 1\}^n$, *and* z *is chosen uniformly in* $\{0, 1\}^m$.

Intuitively, this says that there is no way to "distinguish" between truly random inputs and those that are generated by g, by using only c bits of communication. For $m = 2n$ (and any c and ε) it is trivial to get such a generator (the identity function).

Exercise 4.41: Prove that if g is a pseudorandom generator, then $m \geq n + c + \log(1 - \varepsilon)$.

A nearly optimal construction is presented below. For a graph $H = (V, E)$, let A_H be its incidence matrix (that is, an $n \times n$ matrix where the rows and columns correspond to the vertices of H, and the (u, v) entry of the matrix contains 1 if $(u, v) \in E$ and 0 otherwise). A parameter of interest is λ, the second largest eigenvalue of the matrix A_H (its interest comes from the close relation it has with the so-called "expansion" property of H). We will use a certain type of graphs, called Ramanujan graphs. These are D-regular graphs, for which it is known that $\lambda = \theta(\sqrt{D})$ [Lubotzky, Philips, and Sarnak 1986]. Finally, a standard inequality (see, for example, [Alon and Spencer 1992, page 122]) says that for every D-regular graph $H = (V, E)$, with second largest eigenvalue λ, and for every two subsets of vertices $S, T \subseteq V$

$$\left| \frac{|E(S, T)|}{|E|} - \frac{|S|\,|T|}{|V|\,|V|} \right| \leq \frac{\lambda}{D}, \qquad 4.1$$

where $E(S, T)$ denotes the number of edges with one vertex in S and the other in T. We are now ready to present the generator.

The Generator: Let $H = (V, E)$ be a D-regular $(D = 2^d)$ Ramanujan graph with $N = 2^n$ nodes. The input to the generator g is a name of a (directed) edge in E, and the two outputs are the two vertices of the edge. Thus g accepts an $m = n + d$ bit string (n bits to specify a vertex, and d bits to specify one of its neighbors) and produces two n bit strings.

Theorem 4.42: *The function g described above is a pseudorandom generator for communication complexity $c = (d - \log \lambda)/2$, with parameter $\varepsilon = 2^{-c}$.*

PROOF: Consider any protocol $\mathcal{P}$ that uses c bits of communication. Recall, that such a protocol partitions the inputs into at most 2^c monochromatic rectangles, say $S_i \times T_i$. Let I be the set of these rectangles on which $\mathcal{P}$ outputs 1. Consider a specific rectangle $S_i \times T_i$, for $i \in I$. The probability of getting a pair (x, y) in this rectangle in a truly random choice is exactly $\frac{|S_i|\,|T_i|}{|V|\,|V|}$. The probability of getting a pair in this rectangle as the output of the generator is the probability of having an edge whose first vertex is in S_i and the other is in T_i. That is, $\frac{|E(S_i, T_i)|}{|E|}$. Therefore, we get

$$|\Pr[\mathcal{P}(x, y) \text{ outputs } 1] - \Pr[\mathcal{P}(g(z)) \text{ outputs } 1]|$$

$$= \left| \sum_{i \in I} \frac{|S_i|\,|T_i|}{|V|\,|V|} - \sum_{i \in I} \frac{|E(S_i, T_i)|}{|E|} \right|$$

$$\leq \sum_{i \in I} \left| \frac{|S_i|\,|T_i|}{|V|\,|V|} - \frac{|E(S_i, T_i)|}{|E|} \right|$$

$$\leq 2^c \cdot \frac{\lambda}{D}$$

(by Equation (4.1)). This, by the choice of c, is at most 2^{-c}. $\qquad \square$

Note that although the definition requires that c-bit *deterministic* protocols will not be able to distinguish between truly random inputs and inputs generated by g, it actually says more. Consider c-bit *randomized* protocols in the public coin model (where now the probability of a protocol to output 1 is taken also on the random bits). Such protocols can be viewed as a collection of deterministic protocols, by fixing the random input to each

possible value (in fact this is the way Definition 3.12 is formalized). Because the generator is good for *any* deterministic protocol, we get that it is good against such randomized
protocols. Obviously, this implies that randomized protocols in the standard (private
coin) model cannot distinguish between random inputs and inputs generated by g.

4.5. Reductions and Complexity Classes

It is possible to categorize different communication problems into a "complexity hierarchy" similar to the one known in computational complexity. For this purpose, we
consider communication complexity of $polylog(n)$ as "efficient", and for each complexity measure we define a corresponding complexity class. In particular,

$$P^{cc} = \{f : D(f) = polylog(n)\},$$

$$NP^{cc} = \{f : N^1(f) = polylog(n)\},$$

$$coNP^{cc} = \{f : N^0(f) = polylog(n)\},$$

$$BPP^{cc} = \{f : R(f) = polylog(n)\},$$

and

$$RP^{cc} = \{f : R^1(f) = polylog(n)\}.$$

Formally, for these definitions to make sense, f is actually a sequence of functions on
different input lengths. That is, $f = \{f_n : \{0, 1\}^n x \{0, 1\}^n \rightarrow \{0, 1\}\}$. We emphasize
that the correspondence between the names of these complexity classes and the names
of computational complexity classes only reflects the view that $polylog(n)$ communication is "efficient." The implications that we get about these communication complexity
classes have nothing to do with the corresponding classes in computational complexity.
We have already seen various relationships among these classes. For example, Theorem 2.11 says in this terminology that $P^{cc} = NP^{cc} \cap coNP^{cc}$. Example 2.5 (the
function EQ) shows that $P^{cc} \neq coNP^{cc}$ and also $NP^{cc} \neq coNP^{cc}$. Example 3.5 (again,
the function EQ) shows that $P^{cc} \neq RP^{cc}$ and Example 3.22 (the function DISJ) shows
that $BPP^{cc} \setminus coNP^{cc} \neq \emptyset$. A natural thing to do is to define notions such as *reducibility*
and *completeness*:

Definition 4.43: *A function f is* reducible *to a function g (denote $f \leq g$) if there exist
$m = polylog(n)$ and a pair of functions $h_x : \{0, 1\}^n \rightarrow \{0, 1\}^{2^m}$ and $h_y : \{0, 1\}^n \rightarrow \{0, 1\}^{2^m}$ such that $f(x, y) = 1 \Leftrightarrow g(h_x(x), h_y(y)) = 1$. For a class C, the function g
is C-complete, if $g \in C$ and if every $f \in C$ is reducible to g.*

The notions of reducibility and completeness defined above have the same properties
that they have in other contexts. For example:

Exercise 4.44: (1) Prove that "$\leq$" is a transitive relation. That is, if $f_1 \leq f_2$ and $f_2 \leq f_3$,
then $f_1 \leq f_3$. (2) Prove that if $f \leq g$ and $g \in P^{cc}$, then also $f \in P^{cc}$.

▶ **Example 4.45:** We show that DISJ is $coNP^{cc}$-complete. Clearly, DISJ $\in coNP^{cc}$ because $N^0(\text{DISJ}) = O(\log n)$ (on input (x, y), Alice guesses an element of x that is in the intersection and sends it to Bob, who verifies that this element belongs to y). Now let f be any function in $coNP^{cc}$. This means that $N^0(f) = m = polylog(n)$ or, alternatively, that there is a cover of the 0s of f using 2^m rectangles. Therefore, we take $h_x(x)$ to be the set of 0-rectangles that x belongs to (represented by a 2^m-bit characteristic vector) and similarly $h_y(y)$ to be the set of 0-rectangles that y belongs to. Obviously, $f(x, y) = 0$ iff $h_x(x)$ and $h_y(y)$ intersect, or $f(x, y) = 1$ iff DISJ($h_x(x), h_y(y)) = 1$.

Exercise 4.46: Prove that, for every fixed k, the tree problem T_k (Example 4.30) is complete for the class $C = \{f : D^{k, \text{Bob}}(f) = polylog(n)\}$.

We can further extend the definitions of complexity classes and define the analogs of the polynomial hierarchy: Let Σ_0^{cc} be the set of all functions that are 1 on some rectangle R and 0 otherwise. $\Pi_0^{cc} = co \, \Sigma_0^{cc}$. Now, define

$$\Sigma_i^{cc} = \left\{ f \mid f = \bigvee_{j=1}^{2^{polylog(n)}} f_j, \ f_j \in \Pi_{i-1}^{cc} \right\}$$

and

$$\Pi_i^{cc} = \left\{ f \mid f = \bigwedge_{j=1}^{2^{polylog(n)}} f_j, \ f_j \in \Sigma_{i-1}^{cc} \right\}.$$

Exercise 4.47: (1) Prove that $\Sigma_1^{cc} = NP^{cc}$. (2) Prove that $\Sigma_1^{cc} \neq \Pi_1^{cc}$. (3) Prove that $BPP^{cc} \subseteq \Sigma_2^{cc} \cap \Pi_2^{cc}$. (4) Find complete problems for Σ_k^{cc} and Π_k^{cc}.

Open Problem 4.48: Is $\Sigma_2^{cc} = \Pi_2^{cc}$?

4.6. The Disjointness Function

In this section we study the *disjointness* function, DISJ. We prove a property of this function (Lemma 4.49) that is used (in Example 3.22) to show that the distributional communication complexity of DISJ, and hence its randomized communication complexity, is linear. These bounds are very strong and useful (see also, Example 2.19 and Section 5.2). Therefore we provide a detailed proof of this result.

Let $n = 4\ell - 1$ (for some integer ℓ). We define a probability distribution $\mu(x, y)$ by describing an algorithm $\mathcal{A}$ for producing pairs (x, y):

Choose a random partition $T = (T_1, T_2, \{i\})$ of $\{1, \ldots, n\}$ into three disjoint sets such that $|T_1| = |T_2| = 2\ell - 1$. Choose at random sets $x \subseteq T_1 \cup \{i\}$ and $y \subseteq T_2 \cup \{i\}$ such that $|x| = |y| = \ell$. Output (x, y).

Denote

$$A = \{(x, y) : \mu(x, y) > 0 \text{ and } x \cap y = \emptyset\}$$

and

$$B = \{(x, y) : \mu(x, y) > 0 \text{ and } x \cap y \neq \emptyset\}.$$

Note that if $(x, y) \in B$ then $x \cap y = \{i\}$ (in particular, $|x \cap y| = 1$). It is convenient to think of μ in the above manner although it can be noted, by a symmetry argument, that A is simply all pairs (x, y) such that $|x| = |y| = \ell$ and the intersection is empty (each such pair with the same probability) and similarly B is all pairs (x, y) such that $|x| = |y| = \ell$ and the intersection is of size 1 (again, each such pair with the same probability). We will prove the following lemma:

Lemma 4.49: *Let A, B and μ be as above. Let $R = C \times D$ be any rectangle. Then,* $\mu(B \cap R) \geq \alpha \cdot \mu(A \cap R) - 2^{-\delta n}$, *for some constants $\alpha, \delta > 0$.*

In other words, in any rectangle the weight of B-elements is at least some linear function of the weight of A-elements. Clearly, there are rectangles containing only A-elements and no B-elements, but the lemma says that these rectangles must be "small" (that is, of weight at most $2^{-\delta n}/\alpha$). For a given partition $T = (T_1, T_2, \{i\})$, we define

$$\begin{array}{ll}
\text{Row}(T) = \Pr[x \in C \mid T] & \text{Col}(T) = \Pr[y \in D \mid T] \\
\text{Row}_0(T) = \Pr[x \in C \mid T, i \notin x] & \text{Col}_0(T) = \Pr[y \in D \mid T, i \notin y] \\
\text{Row}_1(T) = \Pr[x \in C \mid T, i \in x] & \text{Col}_1(T) = \Pr[y \in D \mid T, i \in y]
\end{array}$$

where the probabilities are those induced by the algorithm $\mathcal{A}$. The following are basic observations:

1. $\Pr[i \in x \mid T] = \ell/2\ell = 1/2$. Therefore, for any partition T the probability of getting (x, y) that are not disjoint is simply $\Pr[i \in x \mid T] \cdot \Pr[i \in y \mid T] = 1/4$. Hence, $\mu(B) = \Pr[(x, y) \in B] = 1/4$.

2. Since $\Pr[i \in x \mid T] = 1/2$ we also get $\text{Row}(T) = (\text{Row}_0(T) + \text{Row}_1(T))/2$ and similarly $\text{Col}(T) = (\text{Col}_0(T) + \text{Col}_1(T))/2$.

3. Let $T = (T_1, T_2, \{i\})$ and $T' = (T_1', T_2', \{i'\})$ be two partitions such that $T_2 = T_2'$. Then, $\text{Col}_0(T) = \text{Col}_0(T')$ and $\text{Row}(T) = \text{Row}(T')$ (because in such a case $T_1 \cup \{i\} = T_1' \cup \{i'\}$). Similarly, if T and T' are such that $T_1 = T_1'$, then $\text{Row}_0(T) = \text{Row}_0(T')$ and $\text{Col}(T) = \text{Col}(T')$.

4. For all T_2, $E[\text{Row}_0(T) \mid T_2] = E[\text{Row}(T) \mid T_2]$ (where the expectation is taken uniformly over all partitions T with the given T_2). Note that for a specific T we may have $\text{Row}_0(T) \neq \text{Row}(T)$ but here we take the average over all partitions T with the same T_2. The reason for the above equality is that we get the same distribution of xs if we choose x at random in $\{1, \ldots, n\}\backslash T_2$ or if we first choose $i \notin T_2$ at random and then choose x at random in $\{1, \ldots, n\}\backslash(T_2 \cup \{i\})$. In particular, in both cases we have the same probability to get $x \in C$.

We need a few more definitions. We say that a partition T is *x-bad* if $\text{Row}_1(T) < \text{Row}_0(T)/3 - 2^{-\delta n}$ and is *y-bad* if $\text{Col}_1(T) < \text{Col}_0(T)/3 - 2^{-\delta n}$. We say that T is *bad* if it is either *x-bad* or *y-bad*. Let $\text{Bad}_x(T)$, $\text{Bad}_y(T)$, and $\text{Bad}(T)$ be random variables taking the value 1 if T is *x-bad*, *y-bad*, and bad (respectively) and 0 otherwise. The following technical claim gives a bound on the probability of bad partitions.

Claim 4.50: *For all* T_2, $\Pr[Bad_x(T) = 1 \mid T_2] < 1/5$. *(Symmetrically, for all* T_1, *we have* $\Pr[Bad_y(T) = 1 \mid T_1] < 1/5$.*)*

Suppose that the above claim is true. We show how to use it to prove Lemma 4.49 and only then we will provide the proof of the claim. The next claim says that the "contribution" of good partitions to the random variable $Row_0(T)Col_0(T)$ is significant.

Claim 4.51: $E[Row_0(T)Col_0(T)(1 - Bad(T))] > \frac{1}{5}E[Row_0(T)Col_0(T)]$.

PROOF: We need to prove $E[Row_0(T)Col_0(T)Bad(T)] \leq \frac{4}{5}E[Row_0(T)Col_0(T)]$. Because $Bad(T) \leq Bad_x(T) + Bad_y(T)$, it is enough to prove that

$$E[Row_0(T)Col_0(T)Bad_x(T)] \leq \frac{2}{5}E[Row_0(T)Col_0(T)].$$

A symmetric argument will show that this is also true with Bad_y instead of Bad_x. By Observation 3 above, if we look at all the partitions with some fixed T_2, then both $Row(T)$ and $Col_0(T)$ are fixed to some values r_{T_2} and c_{T_2} (respectively). Therefore it is sufficient to prove for each T_2 separately.

$$
\begin{aligned}
&E[Row_0(T)Col_0(T)Bad_x(T) \mid T_2] \\
&= c_{T_2}E[Row_0(T)Bad_x(T) \mid T_2] \\
&\leq c_{T_2}E[2Row(T)Bad_x(T) \mid T_2] && \text{by Observation 2} \\
&= 2c_{T_2}r_{T_2}E[Bad_x(T) \mid T_2] \\
&= 2c_{T_2}r_{T_2}\Pr[Bad_x(T) = 1 \mid T_2] \\
&< \frac{2}{5}c_{T_2}r_{T_2} && \text{by Claim 4.50} \\
&= \frac{2}{5}c_{T_2}E[Row(T) \mid T_2] \\
&= \frac{2}{5}c_{T_2}E[Row_0(T) \mid T_2] && \text{by Observation 4} \\
&= \frac{2}{5}E[Row_0(T)Col_0(T) \mid T_2],
\end{aligned}
$$

as desired. $\qquad\qquad\square$

To prove Lemma 4.49 we would like to express $\mu(A \cap R)$ and $\mu(B \cap R)$ in terms of the measures Row, Col, and so forth. We will show

Claim 4.52: $\mu(B \cap R) = \frac{1}{4}E[Row_1(T)Col_1(T)]$ *and* $\mu(A \cap R) = \frac{3}{4}E[Row_0(T) Col_0(T)]$.

PROOF: $\mu(B \cap R)$ can be written as $\mu(B) \cdot \mu(R \mid B)$. By Observation 1, $\mu(B) = 1/4$. To compute $\mu(R \mid B)$ we need to compute the probability that $(x, y) \in R$ given that x and y intersect. This occurs if and only if both $i \in x$ and $i \in y$. Therefore, we need to compute $\sum_T \Pr[T]\Pr[(x, y) \in R \mid T, i \in x, i \in y]$. Now, given T, the choice of x and the choice of y are independent, so this is the same as

$$\sum_T \Pr[T] \cdot \Pr[x \in C \mid T, i \in x, i \in y] \cdot \Pr[y \in D \mid T, i \in x, i \in y].$$

Also $i \in y$ is irrelevant to x (and $i \in x$ is irrelevant to y) so this is the same as

$$\sum_T \Pr[T] \cdot \Pr[x \in C \mid T, i \in x] \cdot \Pr[y \in D \mid T, i \in y].$$

However, this by definition is simply $\sum_T \Pr[T]\text{Row}_1(T)\text{Col}_1(T) = E[\text{Row}_1(T)\text{Col}_1(T)]$.

For the case of $\mu(A \cap R)$, we first note that the probability over pairs (x, y) obtained by conditioning on those pairs where x and y are disjoint (in which we can have $i \notin x, i \notin y$ or $i \in x, i \notin y$, or $i \notin x, i \in y$) is the same probability obtained by conditioning on $i \notin x \wedge i \notin y$ (in both cases, it is the uniform probability on disjoint x and y such that $|x| = |y| = \ell$). With this observation, the proof for this case becomes similar to the previous one. $\qquad\square$

PROOF (OF LEMMA 4.49): By Claim 4.52 we can write:

$$\mu(B \cap R) = \tfrac{1}{4}E[\text{Row}_1(T)\text{Col}_1(T)] \geq \tfrac{1}{4}E[\text{Row}_1(T)\text{Col}_1(T)(1 - \text{Bad}(T))].$$

Now, if $\text{Bad}(T) = 1$, then the partition T does not contribute anything to the expectation. On the other hand, when $\text{Bad}(T) = 0$ (that is, T is good), then by the definition of Bad this expectation is at least

$$\tfrac{1}{4}E\left[\left(\frac{\text{Row}_0(T)}{3} - 2^{-\delta n}\right)\left(\frac{\text{Col}_0(T)}{3} - 2^{-\delta n}\right)(1 - \text{Bad}(T))\right]$$

$$> \tfrac{1}{4}\tfrac{1}{9}E[\text{Row}_0(T)\text{Col}_0(T)(1 - \text{Bad}(T))] - 2^{-\delta n}$$

$$> \tfrac{1}{4}\tfrac{1}{9}\tfrac{1}{5}E[\text{Row}_0(T)\text{Col}_0(T)] - 2^{-\delta n} \qquad \text{by Claim 4.51}$$

$$= \tfrac{1}{4}\tfrac{1}{9}\tfrac{1}{5}\tfrac{4}{3}\mu(A \cap R) - 2^{-\delta n} \qquad \text{by Claim 4.52}$$

Set $\alpha = 1/135$ and the lemma follows. $\qquad\square$

PROOF (OF CLAIM 4.50): By Observation 3, all of the partitions with the same T_2 have the same value $\text{Row}(T)$. The easy case is where this value satisfies $\text{Row}(T) \leq 2^{-\delta n}$. In such a case, using Observation 2, $\text{Row}_0(T) \leq 2\text{Row}(T) \leq 2 \cdot 2^{-\delta n}$. Therefore,

$$\text{Row}_0(T)/3 - 2^{-\delta n} < 0 \leq \text{Row}_1(T).$$

Hence, in this case $\text{Bad}_x(T) = 0$ and $\Pr[\text{Bad}_x(T) = 1 \mid T_2] = 0$, and we are done. We now have to deal with the case where $\text{Row}(T) > 2^{-\delta n}$. Denote

$$S = \{x : x \in C, |x| = \ell, x \subseteq T_1 \cup \{i\}\}.$$

Then, $\text{Row}(T) = \Pr[x \in C \mid T] = |S|/\binom{2\ell}{\ell}$. Fix a partition $T = (T_1, T_2, \{i\})$ and denote $S' = \{x : x \in C, |x| = \ell, x \subseteq T_1\}$. Then,

$$\text{Row}_0(T) = \Pr[x \in C \mid T, i \notin x]$$

$$= \frac{|S'|}{\binom{2\ell-1}{\ell}} = \frac{|S'|}{|S|}\frac{|S|}{\binom{2\ell}{\ell}}\frac{\binom{2\ell}{\ell}}{\binom{2\ell-1}{\ell}} = \frac{|S'|}{|S|} \cdot \text{Row}(T) \cdot 2.$$

If we choose s uniformly in S, then $\Pr[i \notin s] = |S'|/|S|$ (because the condition $x \subseteq T_1$ is equivalent to $x \subseteq T_1 \cup \{i\} \wedge i \notin x$). Plugging this identity into the above equation we get $\text{Row}_0(T) = 2\text{Row}(T)\Pr[i \notin s]$. A similar argument shows $\text{Row}_1(T) = 2\text{Row}(T)\Pr[i \in s]$. Finally, note that if T is x-bad, then, in particular, $\text{Row}_1(T) < \text{Row}_0(T)/3$, hence by the last equalities $\Pr[i \in s] < \Pr[i \notin s]/3$, that is $\Pr[i \in s] < 1/4$.

Before we continue, let us denote the elements of $T_1 \cup \{i\}$ by $k_1, \ldots, k_{2\ell}$, and let $s_1, \ldots, s_{2\ell}$ be random variables such that $s_j = 1$ if $k_j \in s$ and 0 otherwise. Note that the random variable s is completely determined by the random variables $s_1, \ldots, s_{2\ell}$ and that these random variables are *not* independent (because exactly ℓ gets the value 1).

We are now ready to deal with the second case. Suppose toward a contradiction that $\Pr[\text{Bad}_x(T) \mid T_2] \geq 1/5$. Given T_2, the choice of i determines T. Hence for at least $1/5$ of the 2ℓ possible values of i $(k_1, \ldots, k_{2\ell})$ we get a T that is x-bad. For each such value k_j, we proved that $\Pr[k_j \in s] < 1/4$. Hence, the *entropy* of the corresponding random variable s_j satisfies $H(s_j) < H(1/4) < 0.82$. The other $4/5$ of the random variables s_j clearly satisfy $H(s_j) \leq H(1/2) = 1$. Also recall that for any two random variables s_1, s_2, $H(s_1, s_2) \leq H(s_1) + H(s_2)$. Then,

$$H(s) = H(s_1, \ldots, s_{2\ell}) \leq \sum_{j=1}^{2\ell} H(s_j) \leq \frac{2\ell}{5} H(1/4) + \frac{8\ell}{5} H(1/2)$$

$$< \frac{2\ell}{5} \cdot 0.82 + \frac{8\ell}{5} = 1.928\ell.$$

On the other hand, s is uniformly distributed in S. Recall that we proved that $|S| = \text{Row}(T)\binom{2\ell}{\ell}$ and that we are now handling the case where $\text{Row}(T) \geq 2^{-\delta n}$ (and that $n = 4\ell - 1$). We get,

$$H(s) = \log |S| \geq \log \left(\binom{2\ell}{\ell} 2^{-\delta n} \right)$$

which, using standard estimates of binomial coefficients, is larger (for some constant λ) than

$$\log \left(\frac{2^{2\ell}}{\lambda \sqrt{\ell}} 2^{-\delta n} \right) = 2\ell - \delta(4\ell - 1) - \log \lambda \sqrt{\ell} = \ell(2 - 4\delta - o(1)).$$

Combining all these together we get that

$$(2 - 4\delta - o(1))\ell \leq H(s) \leq 1.928\ell.$$

If we pick δ to be small enough this is a contradiction (to the assumption that the probability is greater than $1/5$) □

The analysis given here for the function DISJ was already used in Example 3.22 (to determine the distributional and randomized communication complexity of DISJ) and in Example 2.19 (to show a large gap between the rank lower bound and the communication complexity). Note that the distribution μ used in the proof is *not* a rectangular distribution (in the sense of Definition 3.24). Hence, this proof does not contradict Exercise 3.25.

4.7. Communication with Partial Information

The problems we have considered so far have all required Alice and Bob to compute the value $f(x, y)$ for *every* possible pair (x, y). In this section we consider the situation where not all pairs are possible. That is, where the players have some partial information on what the input pair might be. At this point even the problem of just sending the value of x from Alice to Bob is not trivial. *Information Theory* deals with this type of questions when communication is *noninteractive*. That is, the information should be delivered using a single message from Alice to Bob. However, modern communication systems allow *interaction* and hence may allow much more efficient communication.

This scenario is formalized as follows: There is some set of possible inputs $S \subseteq X \times Y$. Alice holds a value $x \in X$, Bob holds $y \in Y$, and these values are such that $(x, y) \in S$. The goal is for Bob to get the value of x. Note that there is a difference between this setting and the usual setting that we have discussed so far. Here the communication should enable Bob to learn what x is (using its knowledge of y) but an observer cannot necessarily determine what x is by just viewing the communication (nor it is necessary that Alice get any information about y). If we insist that x is determined by the communication, then clearly at least $\log_2 |X|$ bits must be communicated and no savings can be made.

▶ **Example 4.53:** The NBA problem is the following: Bob Holds $y = [z, w]$, where $z, w \in \{0, 1\}^n$ are two different strings (think about y and z as two NBA teams who played against each other last night). Alice holds a string $x \in \{0, 1\}^n$ that is known to be one of y and z (think about x as the winning team). She wants to send x to Bob. (Formally, define $S = \{(x, [z, w]) : z \neq w, x \in \{z, w\}\}$.) If Alice wants to send x to Bob using a one-round (that is, noninteractive), protocol, then she needs to send at least n bits. Otherwise, there are two strings x and x' on which Alice sends the same message. If Bob holds the input $[x, x']$ he will not be able to distinguish between them (because in both cases his input is the same and he gets the same message).

On the other hand, if we allow two rounds, then $\log n + 1$ bits are enough: Bob sends Alice an index i such that $z_i \neq w_i$ (such an index exists because $z \neq w$), and Alice answers with x_i. Because we are guaranteed that x is one of z, w, then this bit allows Bob to determine what x is. Hence, there may be an exponential gap between one-round and two-round protocols (see Section 4.2).

Let us denote by $D^k(S)$ the (deterministic) communication complexity of solving the problem associated with a set $S \subseteq X \times Y$, using a k-round protocol in which Bob is the last to get a message (by the nonsymmetric nature of the problem it makes no sense that Bob sends the last message). Similarly, $D(S)$ is the communication complexity when there is no restriction on the number of rounds.

Exercise 4.54: For every communication problem S, $D(S) \geq \log D^1(S)$.

This extends Exercise 4.21 in Section 4.2 It means that an exponential gap is the maximal possible, and hence the two-round protocol in Example 4.53 is optimal for that specific S.

Exercise 4.55: Let $0 \leq d \leq n/2$. Let S be the set of all pairs (x, y) such that $x, y \in \{0, 1\}^n$ and the Hamming distance between x and y (that is, the number of indices in which x and y differ) is at most d. Prove that $D(S)$ and $D^1(S)$ are both $\Theta(\log \binom{n}{d})$.

To analyze the rounds complexity associated with a problem S, define a *hypergraph* $G_S = (V, E)$ as follows: The vertices are the elements of X, and for every $y \in Y$ there is a hyperedge $e_y = \{x : (x, y) \in S\}$. A *coloring* of G_S with c colors is a function $\psi : V \to \{1, \ldots, c\}$ such that for every hyperedge $e \in E$ the vertices have different colors (that is, for all $v \in e$, the values $\psi(v)$ are distinct). The *chromatic number* of G_S, denoted $\chi(G_S)$, is the minimal value c for which a coloring exists. The *degree* of G_S, denoted $d(G_S)$, is the size (number of vertices) of the maximal hyperedge.

Exercise 4.56: For every communication problem S, $D^1(S) = \lceil \log \chi(G_S) \rceil$. (This extends Exercise 4.18.)

Exercise 4.57: For every communication problem S, $D(S) \geq \log(d(G_S))$.

For studying the two-round complexity, we need the following claim that guarantees the existence of a certain family of functions (sometime called "hash functions").

Claim 4.58: *Let m and t be any two integers. There exist constants c_1 and c_2, and a family of $k = c_2 t \ln m$ functions, $H_{m,t}$, such that (1) every function $h \in H_{m,t}$ goes from $\{1, \ldots, m\}$ to $\{1, \ldots, p\}$, where $p = c_1 t^2$, and (2) for every subset $A \subseteq \{1, \ldots, m\}$ of size at most t, at least half of the functions in $H_{m,t}$ are $1 - 1$ over A.*

PROOF: The proof is by a probabilistic argument. Choose k such functions at random (that is, the value of each h on each element of $\{1, \ldots, m\}$ is chosen at random in $\{1, \ldots, p\}$ independently of all other choices). For a fixed set A of size at most t, the probability that a random function h is $1 - 1$ is at least $1 \cdot \frac{p-1}{p} \cdots \frac{p-t+1}{p} \geq (1 - \frac{t}{p})^t = (1 - \frac{1}{c_1 t})^t$, which for an appropriate choice of c_1 is at least $3/4$. Now, if k random functions $h_1, \ldots, h_k$ are chosen, define random variables Z_i to be 1 if h_i is $1 - 1$ over A and 0 otherwise. By the above, $E[Z_i] \geq 3/4$. The probability that at least $1/2$ of them are $1 - 1$ over A is just the probability that $\sum_{i=1}^{k} Z_i \geq k/2$, which, using the Chernoff inequality, is at most $e^{-\theta(k)}$. Finally, the probability that there exists a set A for which less than half of the functions are $1 - 1$ is bounded by the number of such sets which is $m^{O(t)}$ times $e^{-O(k)}$. By an appropriate choice of c_2, this product is smaller than 1, which implies the existence of a family $H_{m,t}$ as required. □

We now use this claim to prove that two-round protocols are optimal (up to constants). This is in contrast to the regular scenario, of computing a function $f(x, y)$, where we proved that for every k, $k+1$-round protocols may be much more efficient than k-round protocols (Section 4.2).

Lemma 4.59: *For every communication problem S, $D^2(S) = O(D(S))$.*

PROOF: We present a two-round protocol for the communication problem S. This protocol uses the hypergraph G_S. Fix a coloring ψ of G_S with $\chi(G_S)$ colors, and fix a family of functions $H = H_{\chi(G_S),d(G_S)}$, as guaranteed by Claim 4.58. Bob considers the edge e_y, which determines all possible xs that Alice may hold. He chooses a function

———— 65 ————

$h \in H$ such that h is $1-1$ on the colors of the vertices in e_y and sends its name to Alice. Such an h exists by the properties of H and since the size of e_y is at most $d(G_S)$. Due to the size of H this requires $O(\log d(G_S) + \log \log \chi(G_S))$ bits. Alice sends the value $h(\psi(x))$, which is $O(\log d(G_S))$ bits long. Since h is $1-1$ on the colors of vertices in e_y, Bob can determine from $h(\psi(x))$ what $\psi(x)$ is and, by ψ being a legal coloring, what x is. The total number of bits transmitted is $O(\log d(G_S) + \log \log \chi(G_S))$. Finally note that, by Exercise 4.57 $D(S) \geq \log d(G_S)$ and, by combining Exercise 4.56 with Exercise 4.54, $D(S) \geq \log \log \chi(G_S)$. All together we get that $D^2(S) = O(D(S))$. $\square$

Now consider the direct-sum version of this problem (see Section 4.1): Alice is given $x^1, \ldots, x^\ell$, Bob is given $y^1, \ldots, y^\ell$ such that for all i, $(x^i, y^i) \in S$. The communication problem S^ℓ is for Bob to get from Alice the values $x^1, \ldots, x^\ell$. The naive approach for doing so is by solving the problem independently for each of the ℓ instances (x^i, y^i). The cost of this (using the above protocol) is $D^2(S^\ell) = O(\ell \cdot \log d(G_S) + \ell \cdot \log \log \chi(G_S))$. In what follows we show that sometimes a savings can be obtained.

Lemma 4.60: *For every communication problem S,*

$$D^2(S^\ell) = O(\ell \cdot \log d(G_S) + \log \ell \cdot \log \log \chi(G_S)).$$

PROOF: The idea is to use a protocol similar to the one presented in the proof of Lemma 4.59, but instead of using a different h for each instance the players "recycle" the hs. This uses the fact that not only does H contain a function that is $1-1$ on the colors of vertices in e_y but that at least half of the functions have this property.

Bob considers the colors of vertices in each of the edges $e_{y^1}, \ldots, e_{y^\ell}$. For each of them, half of the functions in H are $1-1$. Hence there exists a function $h_1 \in H$ that is $1-1$ for at least half of $e_{y^1}, \ldots, e_{y^\ell}$. Now Bob considers the remaining half of the hyperedges for which h_1 is not $1-1$ (there might be less than half but this can only help). He finds a function $h_2 \in H$ that is $1-1$ for at least half of those hyperedges and so forth. This way Bob finds $O(\log \ell)$ functions such that for every hyperedge e_{y^i} at least one of the functions, denoted $h_{j(i)}$, is $1-1$. Moreover, each h_j is "responsible" for $1/2^j$ of the hyperedges. Now Bob sends the names of these functions to Alice ($O(\log \ell (\log d(G_S) + \log \log \chi(G_S)))$ bits). In addition, for each i, Bob tells Alice which function in the list should be used on e_{y^i} (that is, $j(i)$). The obvious way for doing this is by sending $O(\ell \log \log \ell)$ bits. However, because h_1 is good for $\frac{1}{2}$ of the hyperedges, h_2 is good for $\frac{1}{4}$ of the hyperedges, and so forth, then, by using a better coding, $O(\ell)$ bits are enough (for example, if we encode h_i by a string of i 1s, then the total communication is of size $\sum_{i=1}^{O(\log \ell)} \frac{\ell}{2^i} \cdot i = O(\ell)$). Finally, in the second round, Alice sends for every i the value $h_{j(i)}(\psi(x^i))$, which as before enables Bob to determine what x^i is. This requires $O(\ell \log d(G_S))$ bits. All together the protocol has the desired complexity. $\square$

▶ **Example 4.61:** Consider the NBA communication problem S considered in Example 4.53. Let G_S be the corresponding hypergraph. Observe that $\chi(G_S) = 2^n$ (because every two vertices have a common edge) and that $d(G_S) = 2$. Hence $D(S^\ell)$ in this case is $O(\ell + \log \ell \log n)$, which is better than the $O(\ell \log n)$ bound that can be obtained just by repeating ℓ times the protocol for S.

4.8. Bibliographic Notes

The direct-sum question with respect to communication complexity was raised in the work of [Karchmer, Raz, and Wigderson 1991]. First results were obtained by [Feder et al. 1991] and then by [Karchmer et al. 1992a]. Related results were achieved by [Edmonds et al. 1991, Håstad and Wigderson 1993, Impagliazzo, Raz, and Wigderson 1994b, Ahlswede and Cai 1994] and by [Tamm 1995]. Example 4.13 is from [Mehlhorn and Schmidt 1982]. The direct-sum problem in the randomized case was handled in [Feder et al. 1991] (which, in fact, presents a somewhat better solution than the one given here) and in the nondeterministic case in [Feder et al. 1991, Karchmer et al. 1992a]. Lemma 4.15 and Example 4.16 are both due to [Dietzfelbinger, Hromkovic, and Schnitger 1994].

The issue of rounds versus communication complexity was first discussed in the work of [Papadimitriou and Sipser 1982]. Their results were later improved by [Ďuriš, Galil, and Schnitger 1984, McGeoch 1986] and [Nisan and Wigderson 1991]. Theorem 4.26, which is due to the work of [Miltersen et al. 1995], abstracts the technique used in most of these previous papers. The pointer jumping function PJ (Exercise 4.31) was the example used in most of the above work, and Example 4.30 is a special case of it. Randomized one-round communication complexity was discussed in [Ablayev 1993, Kremer, Nisan, and Ron 1995, Newman and Szegedy 1995]. The model of simultaneous protocols presented in Exercise 4.22 was considered in [Yao 1979, Kremer et al. 1995] and the randomized communication complexity of EQ was determined in [Newman and Szegedy 1996]. Part 3 of Exercise 4.22 is due to [Babal and Kimmel 1996].

The model of asymmetric communication complexity (Section 4.3) was considered in [Miltersen 1994, Miltersen et al. 1995]. Other lower bounds for asymmetric communication complexity were implicitly proved, using a round-by-round technique, in Ajtai 1988] and explicitly in [Miltersen 1994, Miltersen et al. 1995].

Pseudorandom generators for communication complexity were introduced (in a more general setting than what is presented here) in [Impagliazzo, Nisan, and Wigderson 1994a]. The construction of the generator presented here can use any other construction of regular expanders with $\lambda \ll D$.

Classes of communication complexity problems and the notions of reducibility and completeness were presented by [Babai et al. 1986]. In addition to the classes presented here, which are due to [Babai et al. 1986], analogues of various other complexity classes were discussed. In particular, the analogues of the complexity classes *FewP* and *UP* [Karchmer et al. 1992b], of the class *PP* [Paturi and Simon 1984, Alon et al. 1985], of the class $\oplus P$ [Krause and Waack 1991], counting classes [Damm et al. 1992], the class #*P* [Meinel and Waack 1994], Arthur–Merlin games [Lam and Ruzzo 1989], and the class *Quantum-P* [Yao 1993, Kremer 1995]. For a general treatment of the corresponding computational complexity classes see, for example, [Papadimitriou 1994].

The distributional (and randomized) communication complexity of the disjointness function (DISJ) was first handled by [Babai et al. 1986]. Their results were improved in the work of [Kalyanasundaram and Schnitger 1987]. A simplified proof was presented by [Razborov 1990a]. His proof is presented in this section.

Communication with partial information was extensively studied by [Orlitsky 1990, Orlitsky 1991a, Orlisky 1992, Orlitsky 1991b, Naor, Orlitsky, and Shor 1993, Zhang and Xia 1994] and [Alon and Orlitsky 1995] (in these papers the notion *Interactive communication* is used). An explicit construction of a family $H_{m,t}$, which has the properties required in Claim 4.58 (with slightly different parameters), appears in [Fredman 1984]. Lemma 4.60 is based on [Feder et al. 1991].

PART TWO

Other Models of Communication

CHAPTER 5

The Communication Complexity of Relations

In the first part of this book we were interested in computing *functions*. That is, for any input (x, y) there was a unique value $f(x, y)$ that Alice and Bob had to compute. More general types of problems are *relations*. In this case, on input (x, y) there might be several values that are valid outputs. Formally,

Definition 5.1: *A relation R is a subset $R \subseteq X \times Y \times Z$. The communication problem R is the following: Alice is given $x \in X$, Bob is given $y \in Y$, and their task is to find some $z \in Z$ that satisfies the relation. That is, $(x, y, z) \in R$.*

Note that functions are a special case of the above definition, where z is uniquely defined. Also note that it may be the case that for a certain input pair (x, y) there is no value z such that $(x, y, z) \in R$. We say that this input is *illegal* and we assume that it is never given as an input to Alice and Bob. Alternatively, we can assume that for every (x, y) there must exist a possible value z. For example, by extending the relation R and allowing every output z for the illegal pairs (that is, $(x, y, z) \in R$ for all $z \in Z$).

The definition of a *protocol* (Definition 1.1) remains unchanged. The complexity measures for relations are also simple extensions of the definitions given for functions:

Definition 5.2: *A protocol $\mathcal{P}$ computes a relation R if for every legal input $(x, y) \in X \times Y$, the protocol reaches a leaf marked by a value z such that $(x, y, z) \in R$. The deterministic communication complexity of a relation R, denoted $D(R)$, is the number of bits sent on the worst case input (legal or illegal) by the best protocol that computes R. Other complexity measures are defined in a similar manner.*

Note that the complexity of a protocol is the depth of its tree. An alternative definition of cost may restrict the tree to *legal* inputs only. It can be easily seen that the two possible definitions of cost are equivalent. Also note that measures such as $N^1(R)$ are not as interesting anymore, since the value "1" has no important role in this case. Yet, $N(R)$ is still defined and useful. Many of the basic properties of the complexity measures that were proved for functions hold for relations as well. However, we need

	000	001	010	011	100	101	110	111
000	∅	{3}	{2}	{2,3}	{1}	{1,3}	{1,2}	{1,2,3}
001	{3}	∅	{2,3}	{2}	{1,3}	{1}	{1,2,3}	{1,2}
010	{2}	{2,3}	∅	{3}	{1,2}	{1,2,3}	{1}	{1,3}
011	{2,3}	{2}	{3}	∅	{1,2,3}	{1,2}	{1,3}	{1}
100	{1}	{1,3}	{1,2}	{1,2,3}	∅	{3}	{2}	{2,3}
101	{1,3}	{1}	{1,2,3}	{1,2}	{3}	∅	{2,3}	{2}
110	{1,2}	{1,2,3}	{1}	{1,3}	{2}	{2,3}	∅	{3}
111	{1,2,3}	{1,2}	{1,3}	{1}	{2,3}	{2}	{3}	∅

Figure 5.1: Covering for a relation with monochromatic rectangles

to check carefully before applying any of these properties to relations. For example, we will see below that the gap between the deterministic communication complexity and nondeterministic communication complexity of relations may be exponential (as opposed to at most quadratic in the case of functions (Theorem 2.11)).

The notion of *monochromatic rectangles* is central to the study of relations as well. Formally,

Definition 5.3: $A \times B$ *is a* monochromatic rectangle (*with respect to relation R*) *if there exists a value z such that for every* $(x, y) \in A \times B$ *either* $(x, y, z) \in R$ *or* (x, y) *is illegal.*

For example, in Figure 5.1 a relation is considered for which $X = Y = \{0, 1\}^3$ and $Z = \{1, 2, 3\}$. A triple (x, y, z) satisfies the relation if the z-th bit of x is different than the z-th bit of y. The figure shows a partition of $X \times Y$ into monochromatic rectangles (each row in the figure represents $x \in X$, each column represents $y \in Y$, and the entry (x, y) contains the set of all z such that $(x, y, z) \in R$). Note, for example, that the upper-right rectangle is monochromatic, because the value 1 is common to all entries. Also note that the upper-left rectangle is monochromatic, because the value 3 is common for all legal inputs (the pair (000,000) for example is illegal). This partition corresponds to the protocol in which Alice sends her first bit. Bob outputs 1 if his first bit is different or "continue" if not. Then Alice sends her second bit and Bob outputs 2 if his second bit is different or otherwise he outputs 3.

As in the case of functions, the following is true:

Proposition 5.4: *Any t-bit protocol $\mathcal{P}$ that computes the relation R induces a partition of $X \times Y$ into at most 2^t monochromatic rectangles.*

As before, the main issue is how to prove lower bounds. The following example shows that the fooling set method and the rectangle size method (Section 1.3), appropriately modified for the case of relations, may still be useful.

▶ **Example 5.5:** We saw that given sets $x, y \subseteq \{1, \ldots, n\}$, it is difficult for Alice and Bob to decide whether these sets are disjoint or not. That is, we proved that the communication complexity of the function DISJ is $\Omega(n)$ both in the deterministic case (Example 1.23) and in the randomized case (Example 3.22). Certainly, computing the size of the intersection can only be more difficult. Consider the *approximation* variant of this problem. That is, the relation

$$R = \left\{ (x, y, m) \mid |x \cap y| - \frac{n}{12} \le m \le |x \cap y| + \frac{n}{12} \right\}.$$

We will show that $D(R) = \Omega(n)$ by exhibiting the existence of a large "fooling set." To do so, we pick t random subsets $S_1, \ldots, S_t$ of $\{1, \ldots, n\}$ and consider the pairs of inputs $(S_1, \bar{S}_1), \ldots, (S_t, \bar{S}_t)$. In each such pair the two sets are disjoint. Hence, Alice and Bob need to output some value m that is at most $n/12$. We claim that in a "successful" choice of the sets no two of these pairs can be in the same monochromatic rectangle. For this, it is enough to prove that $|S_i \cap \bar{S}_j| > n/6$ (for all $i \ne j$), because this implies that any output that is at most $n/12$ is invalid for $(S_i, \bar{S}_j)$. Therefore, we now compute the probability that two random subsets S_i and $\bar{S}_j$ of $\{1, \ldots, n\}$ have intersection of size at most $n/6$ (if S_j is a random subset then so is $\bar{S}_j$). Let Z_k be a random variable, which gets the value 1 if k belongs to both S_i and $\bar{S}_j$. Hence, $E[Z_k] = 1/4$. By the Chernoff inequality,

$$\Pr\left[\sum_{k=1}^{n} Z_k \le n/6 \right] \le \Pr\left[\left| \frac{\sum_{k=1}^{n} Z_k}{n} - \frac{1}{4} \right| \ge \frac{1}{12} \right] \le 2e^{-\frac{(1/12)^2}{2 \cdot 1/4 \cdot 3/4} n} < \frac{1}{2^{cn}},$$

for some constant c. Hence, the probability that $|S_i \cap \bar{S}_j| \le n/6$ for some $S_i, \bar{S}_j$, is smaller than $t^2 2^{-cn}$. For $t = 2^{cn/2}$ this probability is smaller than 1. In other words, there exist $t = 2^{\Omega(n)}$ sets S_i such that the pairs $(S_1, \bar{S}_1), \ldots, (S_t, \bar{S}_t)$ must all belong to distinct monochromatic rectangles. That is, $D(R) = \Omega(n)$.

On the other hand, the randomized communication complexity of R is low; $O(1)$ in the public coin model, and $O(\log n)$ in the private coin model. To see this, let Alice and Bob pick at random (using the public coin, with no communication) $\ell = 200$ points in $\{1, \ldots, n\}$. For each of these points Alice sends a bit indicating whether $i \in x$. Bob computes $Z_i = 1$ if i belongs to both x and y and outputs $m = n \cdot \sum_{j=1}^{\ell} Z_j / \ell$ (rounded to the closest integer). The probability that the output is wrong, that is, m is too far from $|x \cap y|$ is, by Hoeffding inequality,

$$\Pr\left[\left| \frac{\sum_{j=1}^{\ell} Z_j}{\ell} - \frac{|x \cap y|}{n} \right| \ge \frac{1}{12} \right] \le 2e^{-2\ell(1/12)^2} < \frac{1}{4},$$

as desired.

Exercise 5.6: For $x, y \in \{0, 1\}^n$, denote by $d(x, y)$ the Hamming distance between x and y (that is, the number of indices in that x and y differ). Let R be a relation consisting of all triples (x, y, m) such that $|m - d(x, y)| \le n/3$. In other words, computing R is the problem of approximating the Hamming distance between x and y. Prove that $D(R) = \Omega(n)$. (Observe that computing the Hamming distance *exactly* is as hard as computing the equality function, EQ.)

Many of the relations we will analyze are of the following nature: Alice holds an input $x \in X$, Bob holds an input $y \in Y$, and they are looking for an index i such that the

i-th bit of x is different from the i-th bit of y. The motivation for studying these relations (as well as explanations for the choice of names for them) will become clear only in Chapter 10 when we discuss the applications of the results for lower bounds on circuit depth. One property that we will prove for this type of relation is that the gap between the deterministic communication complexity and the nondeterministic communication complexity may be huge. Hence, the fooling set method and the rectangle size method, that actually give lower bounds for the nondeterministic communication complexity, cannot yield strong lower bounds. In addition, it is not clear how to generalize the rank lower bound method (Section 1.4) so as to make it applicable to relations. Hence, we need to develop new lower bound techniques.

5.1. Basic Examples

We start by giving some upper and lower bounds for simple relations.

▶ **Example 5.7:** The *universal relation* $U \subseteq \{0, 1\}^n \times \{0, 1\}^n \times \{1, \ldots, n\}$ consists of all triples (x, y, i) such that $x_i \neq y_i$ (pairs (x, y) such that $x = y$ are illegal). The case $n = 3$ is exactly the relation shown in Figure 5.1. An obvious upper bound for this relation is $D(U) \leq n + \log n$ (Alice sends x and Bob finds an index i as needed). On the other hand, we prove $D(U) \geq D(\text{NE}) - 2 = n - 2$ (where NE is the nonequality function, as in Example 1.21). To see this, assume a protocol $\mathcal{P}_U$ for U is given and construct a protocol for NE as follows: Alice and Bob use $\mathcal{P}_U$ on (x, y). If the communication does not correspond to any output $i \in \{1, \ldots, n\}$, then the output is 0 (that is, $x = y$). Otherwise, if they get an output i, then Alice sends x_i to Bob, who outputs 1 if indeed $x_i \neq y_i$ and 0 otherwise. If $x \neq y$, then $\mathcal{P}_U$ is guaranteed to output i such that $x_i \neq y_i$ so the output will be 1. If $x = y$, then although $\mathcal{P}_U$ was not designed to take care of such inputs, still its communication on (x, y) may correspond to some output i (if it does not then the protocol outputs 0). However, no matter what the output i of $\mathcal{P}_U$ may be, the result in this case will always be 0.

Note that $N(U) = O(\log n)$. Alice "guesses" i and sends i together with x_i to Bob, who can verify this guess (recall that inputs with $x = y$ are illegal). This implies that, when relations are considered, the gap between deterministic and nondeterministic communication complexity may be exponential.

The universal relation allows the input x to be *any* n-bit string, and similarly y could be any n-bit string. We will be interested in the communication complexity of relations for which X and Y are restricted.

▶ **Example 5.8:** Let $X \subseteq \{0, 1\}^n$ be the set of all strings whose parity is 1 (that is, x such that $\sum_{i=1}^n x_i \mod 2 = 1$) and $Y \subseteq \{0, 1\}^n$ be the set of all strings whose parity is 0. Let the parity relation, $R_\oplus$, be the set of all triples (x, y, i) such that $x \in X, y \in Y$, and $x_i \neq y_i$ ($X \cap Y = \emptyset$, hence $x \neq y$ and so such index i always exists). We show that $D(R_\oplus) \leq 2 \log n$. Alice and Bob will do a binary search for a bit i such that $x_i \neq y_i$. At each stage they will have a set $\{j, \ldots, k\}$ such that the parity of $x_j, \ldots, x_k$ is different than the parity of $y_j, \ldots, y_k$. They start with the set $\{1, \ldots, n\}$. At each stage they compute

$\ell = \lfloor (j + k)/2 \rfloor$. Alice sends the parity of $x_j, \ldots, x_\ell$ (one bit) and Bob sends the parity of $y_j, \ldots, y_\ell$ (one bit). If these parities are different, then they set $k = \ell$ and continue. If the parities are equal, they conclude that the parity of $x_{\ell+1}, \ldots, x_k$ and the parity of $y_{\ell+1}, \ldots, y_k$ are different, so they set $j = \ell + 1$ and continue. In each case the size of the set $\{j, \ldots, k\}$ is divided by two. All together there are $\log n$ stages, at each stage 2 bits are exchanged, and when the set is of size 1, then the index $j = k$ is the desired bit.

The next lemma shows that this is the best possible protocol for $R_\oplus$. In fact, the lemma is much more general.

Lemma 5.9: *Let X and Y be* disjoint *subsets of $\{0, 1\}^n$. Let*

$$C = \{(x, y) : x \in X, y \in Y, d(x, y) = 1\},$$

where $d(x, y)$ denotes the Hamming distance between x and y (that is, the number of indices in which x and y differ). Let R be the relation defined by all triples (x, y, i) such that $x \in X, y \in Y$, and $x_i \neq y_i$. Then the partition number of R satisfies $C^D(R) \geq \frac{|C|^2}{|X||Y|}$.

PROOF: Let $R_1, \ldots, R_t$ be the monochromatic rectangles (with respect to the relation R) in the optimal partition of $X \times Y$. Denote by m_i the number of C-elements in R_i and by $|R_i|$ the number of elements in the rectangle. By definition,

$$|C| = \sum_{i=1}^{t} m_i. \qquad 5.1$$

Also, since we start from a partition,

$$\sum_{i=1}^{t} |R_i| = |X||Y|. \qquad 5.2$$

On the other hand, let j be the output corresponding to the rectangle R_i. In every row x of R_i there is at most one C-element; this is because all ys in the rectangle differ from x in the j-th bit and for (x, y) to be in C the string y must differ from x in *exactly* one bit. Similarly, in every column of R_i there is at most one C-element. Hence, both the number of rows and the number of columns in R_i are greater than m_i and so

$$|R_i| \geq m_i^2. \qquad 5.3$$

We get

$$|C|^2 = \left(\sum_{i=1}^{t} m_i \right)^2 \qquad \text{By Equation 5.1}$$

$$\leq t \sum_{i=1}^{t} m_i^2 \qquad \text{By Cauchy–Schwartz inequality}$$

$$\leq t \sum_{i=1}^{t} |R_i| \qquad \text{By Equation 5.3}$$

$$= t|X||Y| \qquad \text{By Equation 5.2}$$

Altogether we get $t \geq \frac{|C|^2}{|X||Y|}$. $\qquad \qquad \square$

To use Lemma 5.9 for the relation $R_\oplus$, we take X to be the set of all strings whose parity is 1 and Y to be the set of all strings whose parity is 0. In this case, the relation R defined in Lemma 5.9 is exactly $R_\oplus$. In addition, note that $|X| = |Y| = 2^{n-1}$, whereas $|C| = n2^{n-1}$ (because for every $x \in X$ each of the n strings in Hamming distance 1 from x is in Y). Hence, $C^D(R_\oplus) \geq n^2$, which implies $D(R_\oplus) \geq 2\log n$.

Exercise 5.10*: Let $X \subseteq \{0, 1\}^n$ be the set of all strings in that the number of 1s is larger than the number of 0s, and $Y \subseteq \{0, 1\}^n$ be the set of all strings in that the number of 1s is at most as large as the number of 0s. Let the majority relation, R_{MAJ}, be the set of all triples (x, y, i) such that $x \in X$, $y \in Y$, and $x_i \neq y_i$. Prove that $D(R_{\text{MAJ}}) = \Theta(\log n)$. Hint: For the upper bound, prove first that $D(R_{\text{MAJ}}) = O(\log^2 n)$ and then improve this bound.

Exercise 5.11: Prove that $C^D(R) \geq n^2$ is the best lower that can be proven by using Lemma 5.9.

▶ **Example 5.12:** We now return to the universal relation and show that its randomized complexity, $R(U)$, is $O(\log n)$. In fact, for convenience, we will prove $R^{\text{pub}}(U) = O(\log n)$. However, the transformation of public coin protocols to private coin protocols, presented in Section 3.3, works for relations as well.

Alice and Bob repeat the following t times: They choose (using the public coin) a random string $r \in \{0, 1\}^n$. Alice sends Bob the inner product $\langle x, r\rangle$ (one bit) and similarly Bob sends $\langle y, r\rangle$. If these two bits are different, then Alice and Bob restrict x and y (respectively) to the bits where $r_i = 1$. On these bits the parity of x is different than the parity of y, and so they can use a (deterministic!) binary search, as in Example 5.8, to find a bit i such that $x_i \neq y_i$ (and the protocol terminates with i as its output). The cost of the binary search is $O(\log n)$ bits. If they fail in all t attempts to find a string r such that $\langle x, r\rangle \neq \langle y, r\rangle$ they output an arbitrary i. The number of bits exchanged is $2t + O(\log n)$. The error probability is 2^{-t} because for $x \neq y$ the probability that $\langle x, r\rangle \neq \langle y, r\rangle$, for a random r, is exactly $1/2$. For $t = \log n$ we get $O(\log n)$ communication and error probability of $1/n$.

Note that this can be extended to show that the *zero error* complexity, $R_0(U)$ is also $O(\log n)$. This is done by letting Alice, in case that in all t stages no r was found, send her input x to Bob. Because the probability of this event happening is only $1/n$, then the expected number of bits exchanged remains logarithmic and error never occurs.

▶ **Example 5.13:** A similar relation is the universal *monotone* relation $U_m \subseteq \{0, 1\}^n \times \{0, 1\}^n \times \{1, \ldots, n\}$ that consists of all triples (x, y, i) such that $x_i = 1$ and $y_i = 0$ (pairs (x, y) for that no such i exists are illegal). As for U, here we also have $D(U_m) \leq n + \log n$. Also, $D(U_m) \geq D(\text{DISJ}) - 2 = n - 2$ (see Example 1.23). To see this, assume we are given a protocol $\mathcal{P}_{U_m}$ for U_m and construct a protocol for DISJ as follows: Given an inputs (x, y), Alice and Bob, use $\mathcal{P}_{U_m}$ on (x, y'), where y' is obtained from y by flipping all the bits. Note that x and y intersect if and only if there exists some i such that $x_i = y_i = 1$, which occurs if and only if there exists some i such that $x_i = 1$ and $y'_i = 0$. When they get an output i, then Alice sends x_i to Bob, who outputs 0 if indeed $x_i = 1$ and $y'_i = 0$

and 1 otherwise. If indeed x intersects y, then $\mathcal{P}_{U_m}$ is guaranteed to output i such that $x_i = 1$ and $y'_i = 0$ so the output will be 0. If x and y are disjoint, then no matter what the output i of $\mathcal{P}_{U_m}$ is, the result in this case will always be 1.

The same proof shows that $R(U_m) \geq R(\text{DISJ}) - 2 = \Omega(n)$ (see Example 3.22), which exhibits a significant difference between U and U_m.

5.2. The Pair–Disjointness Relation

Examples 5.7 and 5.13 show that sometimes lower bounds on the communication complexity of relations can be proven by reducing the problem of computing these relations to that of computing certain functions and then using results (and machinery) developed for the case of computing functions. The following example goes in the same direction but is much less obvious.

Let $n = 3m$. Let X consist of all ordered sets P of m *pairs* of elements out of $\{1, \ldots, n\}$, where the $2m$ elements in P are all distinct. Let Y consist of all sets S of $m-1$ elements out of $\{1, \ldots, n\}$. The pair–disjointness relation $M \subseteq X \times Y \times \{1, \ldots, m\}$ consists of all triples (P, S, i) where P and S are as above and i is such that the i-th pair of P contains no element of S. Note that due to the cardinalities of S and P such an index i always exists. For example, let $m = 5$, $P = \{(4, 7), (2, 13), (1, 3), (15, 10), (8, 11)\}$, and $S = \{3, 4, 10, 15\}$, then (P, S, i) satisfies M for $i = 2$ and $i = 5$. We will prove that $D(M) = \Omega(m)$.

First, note that the problem only becomes easier if the input is restricted to (P, S) such that any pair in P contains at most one element of S (that is, all other input pairs are illegal). Call this new relation M'. We have $D(M') \leq D(M)$. Now consider the following relation f (in fact, f is what we call a *partial* function): Bob gets as an input a set S, this time of size m. Alice gets P as before, where again (P, S) is such that no pair in P contains two elements of S. If there is a pair in P that does not contain any element of S, then $f(P, S) = 0$ and if each pair contains an element of S (S is of size m, so this is possible), then $f(P, S) = 1$.

Lemma 5.14: $R^{pub}_{1/4}(f) \leq 2(D(M') + \log n)$.

PROOF: Given a deterministic protocol $\mathcal{P}_{M'}$ for M', we construct a randomized protocol (in the public coin model), $\mathcal{P}_f$, that computes f with about the same communication complexity and makes an error, with probability at most $1/2$, only when the output is 0 (by repeating this twice, we reduce the error probability to $1/4$). The protocol $\mathcal{P}_f$ works as follows: On input (P, S) for f, Bob erases the smallest element x from S to get a set S^* of size $m - 1$. Now Alice and Bob choose, using their public coin, a random permutation π of $\{1, \ldots, n\}$. Bob applies π to S^* to get a set S'. Alice applies the same permutation π to the elements of P. In addition, she permutes the order of the m pairs using another random permutation τ. Denote by P' the resulting list of pairs (so far there was no communication). Alice and Bob run the protocol $\mathcal{P}_{M'}$ on (P', S') and get some output i. Finally, Bob sends the element removed, x, to Alice ($\log n$ bits), who outputs 1 if $\pi(x)$ belongs to the i-th pair of P' and 0 otherwise. For the analysis, consider two cases:

If $f(P, S) = 1$, this means that each pair of P contains exactly one element of S. Therefore, when x is omitted from S, there is exactly one pair in P that does not contain an element of S. After applying π and τ to P, there is still exactly one pair p_i' of P' that contains no element of S' (and $\pi(x) \in p_i'$). Therefore, the output of the protocol $\mathcal{P}_{M'}$ must be this i, which implies that in this case Bob *always* outputs the correct answer (that is, 1). (Note that in this case permuting the elements neither helps nor hurts.)

If $f(P, S) = 0$, this means that there is at least one pair in P, say p_k, that does not contain an element of S. Also, in this case some of the elements of S are not among the $2m$ elements of P. If x is such an element, then obviously $\pi(x)$ is not in the i-th pair found by the protocol $\mathcal{P}_{M'}$ and so $\mathcal{P}_f$ always computes the correct answer (that is, 0). The difficult case is when x is an element of some pair p_ℓ. In such a case there are at least two pairs in P' – the images of p_k and p_ℓ – that contain no element of S'. We use this fact to prove that with probability at least $1/2$ the protocol for M' outputs a pair that does not contain $\pi(x)$. For this, we associate, in a $1 - 1$ manner, with each pair of permutations π, σ another pair π', σ' under that we get the same (P', S') but $\pi(x)$ and $\pi'(x)$ are in different pairs of P'. Hence, because the permutations are chosen at random, no matter what the output i on (P', S') is, with probability at least $1/2$ the element $\pi(x)$ is not in the i-th pair. For this, let $p_\ell' = (a', b')$ be the image of $p_\ell = (a, b)$ under π, σ and, similarly, $p_k' = (c', d')$ is the image of $p_k = (c, d)$. Let π' be identical to π except that $\pi'(a) = c'$, $\pi'(b) = d'$, $\pi'(c) = a'$ and $\pi'(d) = b'$, and τ' be identical to τ except that $\tau'(\ell) = k'$ and $\tau'(k) = \ell'$ (see Figure 5.2). Under π and τ we get $\pi(x) \in p_\ell'$, whereas under π' and τ' we get $\pi'(x) \in p_k'$, as desired. $\qquad\square$

Finally, we show,

Lemma 5.15: $R_{1/4}^{pub}(\text{DISJ}) \leq R_{1/4}^{pub}(f)$, *where* DISJ *is the disjointness function for inputs in* $\{0, 1\}^m \times \{0, 1\}^m$.

PROOF: We show how to use a protocol $\mathcal{P}_f$ for f to compute the function DISJ with the same communication complexity and the same error probability. Alice on input $x \in \{0, 1\}^m$ constructs a set P of m pairs as follows: for every i $(1 \leq i \leq m)$ the set P includes the pair $p_i = (3i - x_i - 1, 3i)$. Bob on input $y \in \{0, 1\}^m$ constructs a set S of size m as follows: for every i $(1 \leq i \leq m)$ the set S includes the element $s_i = 3i - y_i$ (that is, both p_i and s_i are chosen from $\{3i - 2, 3i - 1, 3i\}$). Alice and Bob execute $\mathcal{P}_f$ on (P, S).

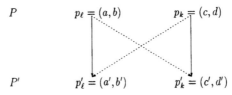

Figure 5.2: The permutations π and τ (solid lines) have the same image as the permutations π' and τ' (dashed lines)

If $\text{DISJ}(x, y) = 0$ (that is, the sets x and y are not disjoint), then there exists i such that $x_i = y_i = 1$. For such i, the list P includes the pair $p_i = (3i - 2, 3i)$, whereas S includes the element $s_i = 3i - 1$ (clearly, for $j \neq i$, s_j is not an element of p_i). Therefore, p_i contains no element of S and the value of f in this case is 0. On the other hand, if $\text{DISJ}(x, y) = 1$, then the sets x and y are not intersecting. Hence, for all i either $y_i = 0$ or $y_i = 1$ and $x_i = 0$. Therefore, after the transformation, for all i either $s_i = 3i$, in which case obviously the pair p_i contains an element from S, or S contains the element $s_i = 3i - 1$ and so does p_i. Therefore, all pairs in P contain elements of S so the value of f is 1. Hence, the success probability of the protocol for DISJ equals the success probability of $\mathcal{P}_f$, as desired. $\qquad\qquad\square$

By Example 3.22, the randomized communication complexity of the function DISJ is $\Omega(m)$ and because the difference between the public coin complexity and the private coin complexity is at most $O(\log m)$, then also $R_{1/4}^{pub}(\text{DISJ}) = \Omega(m)$. All together we get,

$$D(M) \geq D(M') = \Omega\big(R_{1/4}^{pub}(f) - \log m\big) = \Omega\big(R_{1/4}^{pub}(\text{DISJ}) - \log m\big) = \Omega(m).$$

5.3. The FORK Relation

The following lower bound does not reduce relations to functions but rather gives a direct proof using the properties of the specific relation.

Let Σ be an alphabet consisting of w letters, say $\{1, \ldots, w\}$. Let FORK be the relation consisting of all triples (x, y, i) such that $x, y \in \Sigma^\ell$ and i is such that $x_i = y_i$ and $x_{i+1} \neq y_{i+1}$. To simplify things, we think of x and y as having also a 0-coordinate in that $x_0 = y_0 = 1$ and an $\ell + 1$ coordinate in which $x_{\ell+1} = w$ and $y_{\ell+1} = w - 1$. This in particular implies that for all x and y there exists an index i such that $(x, y, i) \in$ FORK. For example, let $w = 3$, $x = 231213$, and $y = 321223$, then FORK(x, y, i) is satisfied for $i = 0, 4, 6$.

Exercise 5.16: Prove that $D(\text{FORK}) = O(\log \ell \log w)$.

Our goal is to show that this upper bound is tight. For $0 \leq \alpha \leq 1$, we say that a protocol is an (α, ℓ) protocol if there exists a set $S \subseteq \Sigma^\ell$ of size $|S| \geq \alpha \cdot w^\ell$ such that the protocol succeeds in solving FORK whenever $x, y \in S$. That is, there is a fraction α of the strings of size ℓ for that the protocol works correctly. With this terminology, a deterministic protocol for FORK is just a $(1, \ell)$ protocol. The proof of the lower bound is by a series of transformations. The first kind of transformations actually holds for any relation.

Lemma 5.17: *If there exists a c-bit (α, ℓ) protocol for the relation* FORK, *then there is also a $c - 1$-bit $(\alpha/2, \ell)$ protocol for* FORK.

PROOF: Assume without loss of generality that Alice sends the first bit in the (α, ℓ) protocol $\mathcal{P}$. Let S be the set guaranteed by the (α, ℓ) property, let $S_0 \subseteq S$ be those strings in S for that Alice sends 0 as the first bit, and similarly let $S_1 \subseteq S$ be those strings in S for that Alice sends 1 as the first bit. Let S_σ be the larger of the two sets, that is $|S_\sigma| \geq |S|/2$. Let $\mathcal{P}'$ work like $\mathcal{P}$ but without sending the first bit, and the players assuming that this value is σ. Then, $\mathcal{P}'$ is a $c-1$ -bit $(\alpha/2, \ell)$ protocol for FORK. □

The main tool will be the following "amplification" lemma, that allows us, using an (α, ℓ) protocol, to construct another protocol that works for shorter strings (of length $\ell/2$) but with a larger fraction of successful pairs. More precisely:

Lemma 5.18: *Let* $\alpha \geq \lambda/w$ *(for a large enough constant* λ*). If there exists a c-bit* (α, ℓ) *protocol for* FORK, *then there is also a c-bit* $(\sqrt{\alpha}/2, \ell/2)$ *protocol for it.*

The proof uses the following technical claim:

Claim 5.19: *Consider an* $n \times n$ $0-1$ *matrix. Let m be the number of* 1s *in it, and* m_i *be the number of* 1s *in the i-th row. Denote by* $\alpha = m/n^2$ *the fraction of 1-entries in the matrix and by* $\alpha_i = m_i/n$ *the fraction of the 1-entries in the i-th row. Then, either (a) there is some row i with* $\alpha_i \geq \sqrt{\alpha/2}$ *or (b) the number of rows for that* $\alpha_i \geq \alpha/2$ *is at least* $\sqrt{\alpha/2} \cdot n$.

PROOF (OF CLAIM): Intuitively, the claim says that either one of the rows is "very dense" or there are a lot of rows that are "pretty dense." Consider $\sum_{i=1}^{n} \alpha_i$. On one hand, $\sum_{i=1}^{n} \alpha_i = \sum_{i=1}^{n} m_i/n = m/n = \alpha \cdot n$. On the other hand, suppose both (a) and (b) do not hold. This means that for all rows $\alpha_i < \sqrt{\alpha/2}$ and that for less than $\sqrt{\alpha/2} \cdot n$ rows $\alpha_i \geq \alpha/2$. Therefore,

$$\sum_{i=1}^{n} \alpha_i < (\sqrt{\alpha/2} \cdot n) \cdot \sqrt{\alpha/2} + n \cdot \alpha/2 = \alpha n.$$

A contradiction. □

PROOF (OF LEMMA 5.18): Let S be the set corresponding to the (α, ℓ) protocol. Consider a matrix whose rows and columns correspond to strings in $\Sigma^{\ell/2}$ and whose (u, v) entry contains 1 if the string $u \circ v$ is in S and 0 otherwise. Note that by the assumptions on S the density of 1s in the matrix is at least α. Applying the claim to this matrix, we get that it satisfies either (a) or (b). For each of the two cases we construct the desired c-bit $(\sqrt{\alpha}/2, \ell/2)$ protocol. In case (a) there exists a row, corresponding to some string u, whose density is at least $\sqrt{\alpha/2}$. The new protocol works as follows: on input $x, y \in \Sigma^{\ell/2}$ Alice and Bob use the original c-bit protocol on the length-ℓ strings $u \circ x$ and $u \circ y$ (and subtract $\ell/2$ from the output). Because the same string u is concatenated to both x and y, then the output of the protocol is guaranteed to be in the second half of the string. The protocol succeeds whenever the entries corresponding to x and y (in row u) contain 1. The fraction of strings with this property is at least $\sqrt{\alpha/2} > \sqrt{\alpha}/2$, as needed.

In case (b) we need to do something else: Let S' be the set of all rows with density at least $\alpha/2$. We will find two function $f, g : \Sigma^{\ell/2} \to \Sigma^{\ell/2}$ and a set $S'' \subseteq S'$ such that the following properties hold:

1. for all $x \in S''$, $x \circ f(x) \in S$,

2. for all $y \in S''$, $y \circ g(y) \in S$,

3. for all $x, y \in S''$, the strings $f(x)$ and $g(y)$ are different in all coordinates, and

4. S'' contains $\sqrt{\alpha}/2$ of the strings in $\Sigma^{\ell/2}$.

Assuming that such functions exist, the new protocol works as follows: on input $x, y \in \Sigma^{\ell/2}$ Alice and Bob use the original c-bit protocol on the length-ℓ strings $x \circ f(x)$ and $y \circ g(y)$ (each player can modify its own input). By property (3), for all x and y in S'' the output of the protocol is guaranteed to be in the first half of the string, and therefore the protocol succeeds. By property (4) (combined with (1) and (2)), this is a $(\sqrt{\alpha}/2, \ell/2)$ protocol.

It remains to prove the existence of such f, g, and S''. Consider $\ell/2$ subsets A_i of Σ where each A_i is of size $w/2$. If we guarantee that $f(x)$ is a string in $A = A_1 \times \cdots \times A_{\ell/2}$ and $g(y)$ is a string in $B = \bar{A}_1 \times \cdots \times \bar{A}_{\ell/2}$, then property (3) immediately holds. So it remains to show that there exist such sets for that the other properties also hold. The idea is to choose each of the A_is at random and to show that this happens with non-zero probability. To simplify the analysis we choose the A_is as follows: We first choose at random $w/2$ strings $v^1, \ldots, v^{w/2}$ each of length $\ell/2$. Then we define A_i to include the i-th letter in each of these $w/2$ strings and extend it into a set of size $w/2$ randomly. (Note that this indeed gives random and independent A_is.) Now, fix $x \in S'$. We wish to compute the probability that it has an extension $f(x) \in A$ such that $x \circ f(x) \in S$. It is enough to show that with high probability one of the vectors v_j is such an extension. This is because the probability that none of the vectors is good is smaller than $(1 - \alpha/2)^{w/2} < e^{-\alpha w/4}$. Therefore, the probability that either A or the corresponding B (that also consists of $\ell/2$ sets each of size $w/2$) are not good is at most $2e^{-\alpha w/4}$. In other words, for every $x \in S'$ a fraction of $1 - 2e^{-\alpha w/4}$ of the partitions (A, B) is good. Hence, there is a partition that is good for $1 - 2e^{-\alpha w/4}$ of the elements of S'. Let S'' be this set of elements. The fraction of elements in S'' is $(1 - 2e^{-\alpha w/4}) \cdot \sqrt{\alpha}/2$, which is at least $\sqrt{\alpha}/2$, as long as $\alpha \geq \lambda/w$ (for some constant λ). $\quad\square$

We get:

Corollary 5.20: $D(\text{FORK}) = \Omega(\log \ell \log w)$.

PROOF: Denote by $c(\alpha, \ell)$ the number of bits required by an (α, ℓ) protocol for FORK. Clearly, $c(1, \ell) \geq c(1/w^{1/3}, \ell)$ so it is enough to prove that $c(1/w^{1/3}, \ell) = \Omega(\log \ell \log w)$. By applying Lemma 5.17 $\Theta(\log w)$ times, $c(1/w^{1/3}, \ell) \geq \Omega(\log w) + c(1/w^{2/3}, \ell)$. By Lemma 5.18, $c(1/w^{2/3}, \ell) \geq c(1/w^{1/3}, \ell/2)$, hence $c(1/w^{1/3}, \ell) \geq \Omega(\log w) + c(1/w^{1/3}, \ell/2)$. Using this inductively $\Theta(\log \ell)$ times, we get $c(1/w^{1/3}, \ell) \geq \Omega(\log \ell \log w)$. $\quad\square$

Exercise 5.21: Let FORK' be the relation consisting of all triples (x, y, i) such that $x, y \in \Sigma^\ell$ and i is such that $x_i = y_i$ and either $x_{i+1} \neq y_{i+1}$ or $x_{i-1} \neq y_{i-1}$. Prove that $D(\text{FORK}') = \Omega(\log \ell \log w)$.

5.4. Bibliographic Notes

The generalization of communication complexity to the case of relations was initiated by [Karchmer and Wigderson 1988]. Their motivation was the connection between the communication complexity of a certain type of relations and the complexity of Boolean circuits. We will discuss this application of communication complexity in Chapter 10. For an excellent text on this topic see [Karchmer 1989]. In particular, Karchmer and Wigderson proved the bounds for the universal relation U and the relation $R_\oplus$. The pair–disjointness relation (Section 5.2) was analyzed by [Raz and Wigderson 1990]. The relation FORK was analyzed by [Gringi and Sipser 1991]. Again, the motivation for these papers was also proving lower bounds on the depth of (monotone) Boolean circuits. The direct-sum problem with respect to relations was discussed in [Karchmer et al. 1991]. The problem of computing the Hamming distance exactly, mentioned in Exercise 5.6, was considered in [Pang and El-Gamal 1986].

CHAPTER 6

Multiparty Communication Complexity

It is very natural to generalize the two-party model of communication complexity to more than two parties. The obvious generalization that we may imagine is to let k players evaluate a k-argument function $f(x_1, \ldots, x_k)$, where the i-th player only knows the i-th argument, x_i. The exact form of communication between the k players should be specified somehow. For example, we can assume that every message by any one of the players is seen by all the others (that is, a broadcast).

This model is in a sense weaker than the two-party model, because the input is distributed among more players and hence evaluating functions may be more difficult. Therefore, it should not be surprising that the techniques we already have from the two-party model are strong enough to prove good lower bounds in this model.

Exercise 6.1: Let $x_1, \ldots, x_k$ each be an n-bit string. Define the generalized equality function $\mathrm{EQ}_n^k(x_1, \ldots, x_k)$ to be 1 iff all k strings are equal, and the generalized nonequality function $\mathrm{NE}_n^k(x_1, \ldots, x_k)$ to be 1 iff all k strings are distinct (EQ_n^k and NE_n^k are complements only for $k = 2$). Use reductions from the two-party model to show that if player i knows only x_i, then the communication complexity of EQ_n^k is $\Theta(n)$ and the communication complexity of NE_n^k is $\Theta(kn)$.

In what follows we will be interested in a different model, which is stronger than the above model. The main new ingredient that this model captures is the *overlap of information*. Each part of the input will be known by many of the players. Because this model is stronger than the two-party model, we will require stronger tools to prove lower bounds. On the other hand, these lower bounds will teach us new things on the nature of communication and will have more applications.

6.1. The "Number on the Forehead" Model

Let $f(x_1, \ldots, x_k)$ be a Boolean function whose input is k arguments each n-bit long. There are k parties, denoted $P_1, \ldots, P_k$, each having unlimited computational power, who wish to collaboratively evaluate f. The twist in this model is the large overlap of information: The i-th party knows *all* the input arguments *except* x_i. In other words, x_i is known to all parties but P_i. It is convenient to imagine the i-th party having x_i written on his forehead – observed by all players but himself.

The communication between the parties is by "writing on a blackboard" (broadcast): any bit sent by any party is seen by all others. They exchange messages according to a fixed protocol. The protocol must specify the following information for each possible sequence of bits that is written on the board so far:

- Whether the run is over. If the run is over then the protocol should also specify the value computed by the protocol. This should be completely determined by the information written on the board.

- If the run is not over then the protocol should specify which party writes the next bit; this as well should be completely determined by the information written on the board so far.

- What that party writes: this should be a function of the information written on the board so far and of the parts of the input that the party knows.

Definition 6.2: *The cost of a protocol is the number of bits written on the board for the worst case input. The multiparty (deterministic) communication complexity of f, $D(f)$, is the minimal cost of a protocol that computes f.*

As in the two-party case, the definition of multiparty protocols is clearly equivalent to protocol trees, where the internal nodes may query functions depending on at most $k-1$ of the x_is, and the leaves hold the value computed. The cost of the protocol is the depth of the protocol tree. Obviously, for every function f, $D(f) \leq n+1$ (say, P_1 writes on the board x_2, and P_2, which now knows all the k parts of the input, computes $f(x_1, \ldots, x_k)$). The following examples show that the overlap of information may be very useful.

▶ **Example 6.3:** Consider the function EQ_n^k from Exercise 6.1. We show that for $k \geq 3$, $D(\text{EQ}_n^k) = 2$. In contrast, for $k = 2$, $D(\text{EQ}_n^2) = D(\text{EQ}) = n+1$ (Example 1.21). Player P_1 sends a single bit indicating whether $x_2 = x_3 = \cdots = x_k$ and Player P_2 sends a single bit indicating whether $x_1 = x_3$. Both tests succeed if and only if all x_is are equal to each other.

▶ **Example 6.4:** For bits a, b, c denote by $\text{MAJ}(a, b, c)$ their majority. Consider the 3-argument function MIP defined on $(\{0, 1\}^n)^3$ as follows:

$$\text{MIP}(x_1, x_2, x_3) = \sum_{i=1}^{n} \text{MAJ}(x_{1,i}, x_{2,i}, x_{3,i})(mod\ 2).$$

This may seem like a generalization of the inner product function IP (Example 1.25) to three vectors (and three parties), where we take the bitwise majority. However, while IP has high communication complexity, we get $D(\text{MIP}) = 3$. To see this, note that

$$\text{MAJ}(a, b, c) = ab + ac + bc\ (mod\ 2),$$

thus

$$\text{MIP}(x_1, x_2, x_3) = \sum_{i=1}^{n} x_{1,i} x_{2,i} + \sum_{i=1}^{n} x_{1,i} x_{3,i} + \sum_{i=1}^{n} x_{2,i} x_{3,i}\ (mod\ 2).$$

The value of each of these three terms can be computed by one of the three parties alone and communicated to the rest using one bit of communication.

In this chapter we present the known lower bounds on multiparty communication complexity of explicit functions. It is quite interesting that in most of these examples there are also surprising upper bounds that we also present. Note that lower bounds for nonexplicit functions can be easily proven:

Exercise 6.5: Prove that for most Boolean functions $f : (\{0,1\}^n)^k \to \{0,1\}$, $D(f) = \Omega(n)$. Hint: Count the number of protocols of a given cost.

6.2. Cylinder Intersections

In two-party communication complexity the main objects of study are rectangles—these are the pieces into which a protocol partitions the space of inputs. These objects are obtained by the fact that each message sent by a player depends on his input only. The analogous objects for multiparty complexity are "cylinder intersections," which are obtained by the fact that each message sent by a player depends on $k - 1$ of the inputs.

Definition 6.6: Let X_i be the set of possible values for x_i. A subset $S \subseteq X_1 \times \cdots \times X_k$ is called a cylinder in the i-th dimension, if membership in S does not depend on the i-th coordinate. That is, for all $x_1, \ldots, x_{i-1}, x_i, x_{i+1}, \ldots, x_k$ and x_i',

$$(x_1, \ldots, x_{i-1}, x_i, x_{i+1}, \ldots, x_k) \in S \Leftrightarrow (x_1, \ldots, x_{i-1}, x_i', x_{i+1}, \ldots, x_k) \in S.$$

A subset S is called a cylinder intersection if it can be represented as an intersection of k cylinders, that is $S = \bigcap_{i=1}^k S_i$, where S_i is a cylinder in the i-th dimension.

Figure 6.1 shows a cylinder (for $k = 3$). As is shown below, cylinder intersections play a central role in the analysis of multiparty protocols. The following definition gives us a different way to look at cylinder intersections.

Definition 6.7: A star in $X_1 \times \cdots \times X_k$ is a set of k points of the form:

$$(x_1', x_2, \ldots, x_k), (x_1, x_2', \ldots, x_k), \ldots, (x_1, x_2, \ldots, x_k'),$$

where for each i, $x_i \neq x_i'$ and $x_i, x_i' \in X_i$. The point $(x_1, x_2, \ldots, x_k)$ is called the center of the star (the center does not belong to the star).

An example of a star (for $k = 3$) is shown in Figure 6.2. The star consists of the 3 points (x_1', x_2, x_3), (x_1, x_2', x_3) and (x_1, x_2, x_3'). Its center, (x_1, x_2, x_3), is not part of the star. The following lemma connects the notion of star to the notion of cylinder intersection.

Lemma 6.8: A set S is a cylinder intersection iff for every star that it contains it also contains its center.

85

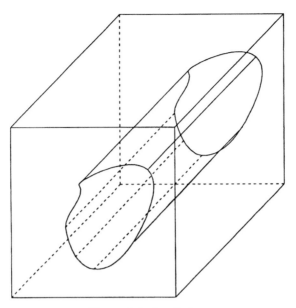

Figure 6.1: A cylinder

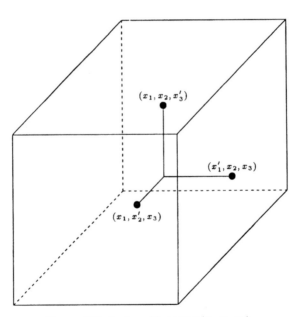

Figure 6.2: A star with center (x_1, x_2, x_3)

PROOF: (Only if): Let S be a cylinder intersection. That is, $S = \bigcap_i S_i$, and S_i a cylinder in the i-th dimension. Assume that S contains a star

$$(x_1', x_2, \ldots, x_k), (x_1, x_2', \ldots, x_k), \ldots, (x_1, x_2, \ldots, x_k').$$

Thus, for each i, $(x_1, \ldots, x_i', \ldots, x_k) \in S \subseteq S_i$. Since membership in S_i does not depend on the i-th coordinate, also $(x_1, \ldots, x_i, \ldots, x_k) \in S_i$. Thus, the center of the star $(x_1, \ldots, x_i, \ldots, x_k)$ belongs to $\bigcap_i S_i = S$.

(If): Define the set

$$S_i = \{(x_1, \ldots, x_i, \ldots, x_k) | \exists \, x_i' \in X_i(x_1, \ldots, x_i', \ldots, x_k) \in S\}.$$

By its definition, S_i is a cylinder in the i-th dimension. We will show that if S contains the center of every star it contains then $S = \bigcap_i S_i$. One direction, that $S \subseteq \bigcap_i S_i$ is immediate from the definition (it is true for any S and not only S with the "star property"). For the other direction, consider a point $(x_1, \ldots, x_i, \ldots, x_k) \in \bigcap_i S_i$. Then, for each i, by the definition of S_i, there exists x_i' such that $(x_1, \ldots, x_i', \ldots, x_k) \in S$. But this set of k points is a star contained in S, and thus its center, $(x_1, \ldots, x_i, \ldots, x_k)$ is also in S. $\square$

Lemma 6.9: *Fix a k-party protocol $\mathcal{P}$ and consider a leaf ℓ of the protocol tree. Then, the set R_ℓ, of inputs that reach this leaf, is a cylinder intersection.*

PROOF: As in the two-party case (Proposition 1.14), we can prove by induction, using the first definition, that the set of inputs reaching a node of the protocol tree is indeed a cylinder intersection. Again, it is perhaps more instructive to consider a proof that uses the second definition.

Fix a star in R_ℓ. That is, k points such that for every i, $(x_1, \ldots, x_i', \ldots, x_k) \in R_\ell$. We will show that its center, $(x_1, \ldots, x_i, \ldots, x_k)$ is also in R_ℓ. That is, we need to show that on input $(x_1, \ldots, x_i, \ldots, x_k)$ the protocol still reaches the same leaf ℓ. At each step, the party that needs to send the next message, say P_i, cannot distinguish between the input $(x_1, \ldots, x_i, \ldots, x_k)$ and the input $(x_1, \ldots, x_i', \ldots, x_k)$, because he does not see the i-th part of the input. Thus, P_i will send the same message in both cases. Hence the whole communication on the center is the same as on all elements of the star, as needed. $\square$

We can now summarize this section by:

Lemma 6.10: *Any c-bit multiparty protocol for f partitions $X_1 \times \cdots \times X_k$ into at most 2^c f-monochromatic cylinder intersections.*

6.3. Bounds Using Ramsey Theory

In this section we present a lower bound technique for multiparty communication complexity that is based on Ramsey theory.

▶ **Example 6.11:** For an n-bit integer N let the exactly-N function, $E_N^k(x_1, \ldots, x_k)$, be 1 iff $\sum_{i=1}^k x_i = N$, where the inputs, $x_1, \ldots, x_k$, are each an n-bit integer in $\{1, \ldots, N\}$. To analyze the communication complexity of the function E_N^k, we use the Ramsey number, $\xi_k(N)$, defined next: $\xi_k(N)$ is the smallest number of colors needed to color $\{1, \ldots, N\}^{k-1}$ such that for all vectors $(x_1, \ldots, x_{k-1})$ and for all integers $\lambda \neq 0$, if the k vectors

$$(x_1, \ldots, x_{k-1}),$$
$$(x_1 + \lambda, x_2, \ldots, x_{k-1}),$$
$$(x_1, x_2 + \lambda, \ldots, x_{k-1}),$$
$$\vdots$$
$$(x_1, x_2, \ldots, x_{k-1} + \lambda)$$

are all in $\{1, \ldots, N\}^{k-1}$, then not all of them are colored with the same color (see, for example, [Graham et al. 1990, Section 2.3]).

For an upper bound, we present a protocol with communication complexity of $O(k + \log \xi_k(N))$. Fix a proper coloring of $\{1, \ldots, N\}^{k-1}$ with $\xi_k(N)$ many colors. Now, for $1 \leq i \leq k - 1$, player P_i first computes $x_i' = N - \sum_{j \neq i} x_j$ (that is, x_i' is the number that together with the $k - 1$ parts of the input that P_i sees would make the sum exactly N). If $x_i' \leq 0$, then P_i already knows that the sum is larger than N. In this case he can already output 0. Otherwise, P_i computes the color with which the vector $(x_1, \ldots, x_i', \ldots, x_{k-1})$ is colored. Player P_k computes the color of the vector $(x_1, \ldots, x_{k-1})$. The players now compare the k colors they computed and output 1 iff they are all the same. For doing this, only the first player actually needs to send his color ($\log \xi_k(N)$ bits) and each of the other players only needs to send a single bit indicating whether or not he has the same color. It remains to prove the correctness of the protocol. If $\sum_i x_i = N$, then each of the first $k - 1$ players computes $x_i' = x_i$ and hence all players compute the color of the same vector (that is, $(x_1, \ldots, x_{k-1})$). Therefore, in this case, the output is 1. On the other hand, if $\sum_i x_i = N - \lambda \neq N$, then the colors they computed belong to the vectors $(x_1, \ldots, x_{k-1})$ (player P_k), $(x_1 + \lambda, \ldots, x_{k-1})$ (player P_1), up to $(x_1, \ldots, x_{k-1} + \lambda)$ (player P_{k-1}). All these vectors are in $\{1, \ldots, N\}^{k-1}$ therefore, by the legality of the coloring, the colors of these k vectors are not all the same and so the output in this case is 0.

For a lower bound, we show that $D(E_N^k) \geq \log \xi_k(\lfloor \frac{N-1}{k-1} \rfloor)$. For this, we present a legal coloring of $\{1, \ldots, \lfloor \frac{N-1}{k-1} \rfloor\}^{k-1}$ with at most L colors, where $L \leq 2^{D(E_N^k)}$ is the number of leaves of the optimal protocol for E_N^k. The point $(x_1, \ldots, x_{k-1})$ is colored by the name of the leaf reached by the input $(x_1, \ldots, x_{k-1}, N - \sum_{i=1}^{k-1} x_i)$ (for every $1 \leq i \leq k - 1$, we have $1 \leq x_i \leq \lfloor \frac{N-1}{k-1} \rfloor$ and therefore the k-th component of the input is a number in $\{1, \ldots, N\}$ as needed). This coloring is legal, because if there are k vectors in $\{1, \ldots, \lfloor \frac{N-1}{k-1} \rfloor\}^{k-1}$ of the form

$$
\begin{aligned}
&(x_1, \ldots, x_{k-1}), \\
&(x_1 + \lambda, x_2, \ldots, x_{k-1}), \\
&(x_1, x_2 + \lambda, \ldots, x_{k-1}), \\
&\qquad\vdots \\
&(x_1, x_2, \ldots, x_{k-1} + \lambda)
\end{aligned}
$$

which are colored with the same color, then there exist k inputs (in $\{1, \ldots, N\}^k$)

$$
\left(x_1, \ldots, x_{k-1}, N - \sum_{i=1}^{k-1} x_i\right),
$$

$$
\left(x_1 + \lambda, \ldots, x_{k-1}, N - \sum_{i=1}^{k-1} x_i - \lambda\right),
$$

$$
\left(x_1, x_2 + \lambda, \ldots, x_{k-1}, N - \sum_{i=1}^{k-1} x_i - \lambda\right),
$$

$$
\vdots
$$

$$
\left(x_1, \ldots, x_{k-1} + \lambda, N - \sum_{i=1}^{k-1} x_i - \lambda\right)
$$

which are all in the same 1-monochromatic cylinder intersection. However, such points form a star whose center is $(x_1, \ldots, x_{k-1}, N - \sum_{i=1}^{k-1} x_i - \lambda)$, hence by the results of Section 6.2 the center also belongs to the same cylinder intersection. But this center has a sum of $N - \lambda$ and hence it cannot be in the same cylinder intersection. Therefore, the coloring must be legal.

The reader can verify that $\xi_k(N) \leq k \cdot \xi_k(N/k)$. Hence, for any fixed k, we get $D(E_N^k) = \Theta(\log \xi_k(N))$. Although this gives an exact characterization of $D(E_N^k)$, it is not clear at all what this value is, that is what is the value of $\xi_k(N)$. The best lower bound known states that for any fixed k, $\xi_k(N) = \omega(1)$ (see [Graham et al. 1990]), which implies that E_N^k cannot be computed with a constant number of bits. On the other hand, a surprising upper bound for $k = 3$ is known: $\xi_3(N) \leq exp(\sqrt{\log N} \log \log N)$ [Chandra, Furst, and Lipton 1983]. This implies that $D(E_N^3) = O(\sqrt{n} \log n)$. Also note that $D(E_N^2) = D(\text{EQ}) = n + 1$.

Exercise 6.12: As in the two-party case, we can define the nondeterministic communication complexity of a function as the number of bits that the players need to exchange in order to be convinced that $f(x_1, \ldots, x_k) = 1$. Similarly, the co-nondeterministic communication complexity of a function is the number of bits that the players need to exchange in order to be convinced that $f(x_1, \ldots, x_k) = 0$. Prove that the nondeterministic communication complexity of E_N^k, for every fixed k, is $\theta(\log \xi_k(N))$, whereas the co-nondeterministic complexity is $\theta(\log \log \xi_k(N))$.

Exercise 6.13: Prove that the randomized communication complexity of E_N^k, for every fixed k, is $\theta(\log \log \xi_k(N))$ in the private coin model and $\theta(1)$ in the public coin model.

6.4. Discrepancy Lower Bound

The basic lower bound techniques we use for the two-party model cannot be used for $k \geq 3$ parties. The only technique from two-party communication complexity that generalizes to the multiparty case is the discrepancy method (Section 3.5).

Definition 6.14: *Let $f : X_1 \times \cdots \times X_k \to \{0, 1\}$ be a function. Let μ be a probability distribution on $X_1 \times \cdots \times X_k$. The discrepancy of f according to μ, $Disc_\mu(f)$, is*

$$\max_S \left| \Pr_\mu[f(x_1, \ldots, x_k) = 0 \wedge (x_1, \ldots, x_k) \in S] \right.$$
$$\left. - \Pr_\mu[f(x_1, \ldots, x_k) = 1 \wedge (x_1, \ldots, x_k) \in S] \right|,$$

where the maximum is taken over all cylinder intersections S.

As in the two-party case, upper bounds on the discrepancy give lower bounds on the multiparty communication complexity. In fact they even give lower bounds on the randomized complexity.

Exercise 6.15: Let f be a function. For every distribution μ,

1. $D^{\mu}_{\frac{1}{2}-\epsilon}(f) \geq log(2\epsilon/Disc_{\mu}(f))$; and

2. $R_{\frac{1}{2}-\epsilon}(f) \geq log(2\epsilon/Disc_{\mu}(f))$.
   (Obviously this implies $D(f) = \Omega(log(1/Disc_{\mu}(f)))$.)

Hint: The first part is the analogue of Proposition 3.28, and the second part is obtained from the first part together with the analogue of Theorem 3.20.

In the next subsection we use this exercise to prove a lower bound for a natural generalization of the inner product function, IP. We start with the upper bound for it.

▶ **Example 6.16:** The k-wise *generalized inner product* function on k n-bit strings is defined by $GIP^k_n(x_1, \ldots, x_k) = 1$ if the number of locations in which all of the x_is have 1 is odd, and 0 otherwise. We show in the next subsection that $D(GIP^k_n) = \Omega(n/4^k)$. This lower bound deteriorates exponentially with k. The following protocol for GIP^k_n shows that at least for this function this is unavoidable.

It is convenient to view the input for GIP^k_n as a $k \times n$ matrix whose rows are $x_1, \ldots, x_k$. With this view, the task is only to count (modulo 2) the number of $(1, \ldots, 1)$ columns. The protocol goes as follows: the players divide the columns into blocks, each block contains (at most) $2^{k-1} - 1$ columns. The first observation is that if we compute the GIP^k_n with respect to each block, then by summing the results (modulo 2) we get the desired value of GIP^k_n with respect to the whole matrix. Consider a specific block. Player P_1 announces a k-bit vector α that is not a column in this block. Although P_1 does not know the first row (x_1), this is still possible because there are only $2^{k-1} - 1$ columns that the sees without their first bit, and for each of them he can eliminate both ways to extend them (with 0 or 1). Still, this eliminates at most $2^k - 2$ of the 2^k combinations.

Now all players know a vector α that is not a column in the block and they use it to compute the GIP^k_n in this block. If $\alpha = (1, \ldots, 1)$ we are done because this implies that $GIP^k_n = 0$ (without any communication). Otherwise, α contains at least one 0. Assume, without loss of generality, that α is of the form $(0, \ldots, 0, 1, \ldots, 1)$, that is it starts with ℓ 0s and then $k - \ell$ 1s (if this is not the case we can permute the indices and the players accordingly). Let y_i be the number of vectors (in the block) of the form $(0, \ldots, 0, 1, \ldots, 1)$, that is, those that start with i 0s and the rest are 1s. Let z_i be the number of vectors of the form $(0, \ldots, 0, *, 1, \ldots, 1)$, that is, those that start with $i - 1$ 0s then an arbitrary bit in the i-th position and the rest are 1s. Each player P_i ($1 \leq i \leq \ell$) announces the value of z_i. Note that P_i has the information needed to do so. Also note that $z_i = y_{i-1} + y_i$ and that $y_\ell = 0$ by the assumption that α does not appear as a column. Hence the players can use the z_is to compute the values of all the y_is and in particular of y_0, which is the number of $(1, \ldots, 1)$ columns, and hence GIP^k_n can be computed for this block.

During this stage the players communicate k numbers and hence need $k \log n$ bits. A more careful observation shows that nothing is changed if all calculations are done mod 2, hence k bits are enough. All together, there are $O(\frac{n}{2^k})$ blocks, in each of them k bits are used to communicate α and k to compute the GIP^k_n, in total $O(k \cdot \frac{n}{2^k})$ bits.

6.4.a. The Discrepancy of GIP

In this subsection we prove a lower bound for GIP by using the discrepancy method. Specifically, we show that $Disc_{uniform}(\text{GIP}_n^k) \leq exp(-n/4^k)$.

We first introduce a slightly modified notation to facilitate easier algebraic handling. Define a function f as follows: $f(x_1, \ldots, x_k)$ is 1 if $\text{GIP}_n^k(x_1, \ldots, x_k) = 0$ and -1 if $\text{GIP}_n^k(x_1, \ldots, x_k) = 1$. In this case, instead of working directly with the discrepancy we will use:

$$\Delta_k(n) = \max_{\phi_1, \ldots, \phi_k} |E_{x_1, \ldots, x_k}[f(x_1, \ldots, x_k) \cdot \phi_1(x_1, \ldots, x_k) \cdots \phi_k(x_1, \ldots, x_k)]|,$$

where the maximum is taken over all functions $\phi_i : (\{0, 1\}^n)^k \to \{0, 1\}$ such that ϕ_i does not depend on x_i, and the expectation is over all 2^{nk} possible choices of $x_1, \ldots, x_k$.

First, it should be clear that $Disc_{uniform}(\text{GIP}_n^k) = \Delta_k(n)$. This is because the product $\phi_1(x_1, \ldots, x_k) \cdots \phi_k(x_1, \ldots, x_k)$ gives 1 on a collection of points that forms a cylinder intersection, and, conversely, any cylinder intersection can be written as such a product. In addition, because we changed to the $\{-1, +1\}$ notation, the expectation plays the same role as the difference in probabilities previously did.

We define constants β_k recursively: $\beta_1 = 0$, and $\beta_k = \sqrt{\frac{1+\beta_{k-1}}{2}}$. It follows by induction that $\beta_k \leq 1 - 4^{1-k} < e^{-4^{1-k}}$. We will prove the following upper bound on $\Delta_k(n)$.

Lemma 6.17: $\Delta_k(n) \leq (\beta_k)^n$, for all $k \geq 1, n \geq 0$.

PROOF: Observe that $\Delta_1(n) = 0$, because in this case ϕ_1 must be constant and $E_{x_1}[f(x_1)] = 0$ (in the case that $n = 0$, we get $\Delta_1(0) = 1$. To overcome this, we define $0^0 = 1$ for this proof). We proceed by induction on k. Let $k \geq 2$, and fix $\phi_1, \ldots, \phi_k$ that achieve the value of $\Delta_k(n)$. Because ϕ_k does not depend on x_k, and is bounded in absolute value by 1,

$$\Delta_k(n) \leq E_{x_1, \ldots, x_{k-1}}[|E_{x_k} f(x_1, \ldots, x_k) \cdot \phi_1(x_1, \ldots, x_k) \cdots \phi_{k-1}(x_1, \ldots, x_k)|].$$

In order to estimate the right-hand side, we will use a special case of the Cauchy–Schwartz inequality stating that for any random variable z: $(E[z])^2 \leq E[z^2]$. Thus our estimate is:

$$\Delta_k(n) \leq (E_{x_1, \ldots, x_{k-1}}[E_{x_k}[f(x_1, \ldots, x_k) \cdot \phi_1(x_1, \ldots, x_k) \cdots \phi_{k-1}(x_1, \ldots, x_k)]]^2)^{1/2}$$
$$= (E_{u,v,x_1, \ldots, x_{k-1}}[f(x_1, \ldots, x_{k-1}, u) \cdot f(x_1, \ldots, x_{k-1}, v)$$
$$\cdot \phi_1^u \cdot \phi_1^v \cdots \phi_{k-1}^u \cdot \phi_{k-1}^v])^{1/2}$$

where ϕ_i^u stands for $\phi_i(x_1, \ldots, x_{k-1}, u)$, and ϕ_i^v for $\phi_i(x_1, \ldots, x_{k-1}, v)$.

Now observe that for every particular choice of u and v, we can express the product $f(x_1, \ldots, x_{k-1}, u) f(x_1, \ldots, x_{k-1}, v)$ in terms of the function f on $k - 1$ strings of possibly shorter length. Inspection reveals that the value of $f(x_1, \ldots, x_{k-1}, u) f(x_1, \ldots, x_{k-1}, v)$ is simply $f(z_1, \ldots, z_{k-1})$, where z_i is the restriction of x_i to the coordinates j such that $u_j \neq v_j$ (here is where the particular properties of f are used). We will now view each x_i as composed of two parts: z_i and y_i, where z_i is the part of x_i where $u_j \neq v_j$, and y_i the part of x_i where $u_j = v_j$ (this is done separately for every u, v).

For every particular choice of u, v and consequently $y_1, \ldots, y_{k-1}$, we define functions of the "z-parts":

$$\xi_i^{u,v,y_1,\ldots,y_{k-1}}(z_1, \ldots, z_{k-1}) = \phi_i(x_1, \ldots, x_{k-1}, u)\phi_i(x_1, \ldots, x_{k-1}, v),$$

where the x_is are obtained by the concatenation of the corresponding y_i and z_i. We can now rewrite the previous estimate as

$$\Delta_k(n) \le (E_{u,v}[E_{y_1,\ldots,y_{k-1}}[S^{u,v,y_1,\ldots,y_{k-1}}]])^{1/2},$$

where $S^{u,v,y_1,\ldots,y_{k-1}}$ is defined as

$$E_{z_1,\ldots,z_{k-1}}\left[f(z_1, \ldots, z_{k-1}) \cdot \xi_1^{u,v,y_1,\ldots,y_{k-1}}(z_1, \ldots, z_{k-1})\right.$$
$$\left. \cdots \xi_{k-1}^{u,v,y_1,\ldots,y_{k-1}}(z_1, \ldots, z_{k-1})\right].$$

Now $S^{u,v,y_1,\ldots,y_{k-1}}$ can be estimated via the induction hypothesis, because f and the ξ_is are all functions of $k-1$ strings. Moreover, note that $\xi_i^{u,v,y_1,\ldots,y_{k-1}}$ does not depend on z_i. Thus the previous estimate of $\Delta_k(n)$ is bounded by

$$\Delta_k(n) \le (E_{u,v,y_1,\ldots,y_{k-1}}[\Delta_{k-1}(m_{u,v})])^{1/2} \le \left(E_{u,v,y_1,\ldots,y_{k-1}}[\beta_{k-1}^{m_{u,v}}]\right)^{1/2},$$

where $m_{u,v}$ is the length of the strings z_i, which is equal to the number of locations j such that $u_j \ne v_j$.

Because u and v are distributed uniformly in $\{0, 1\}^n$, $m_{u,v}$ is distributed according to the binomial distribution. For any constant m, the probability that $m_{u,v} = m$ is exactly $\binom{n}{m}2^{-n}$. Thus the previous estimate gives:

$$\Delta_k(n) \le \left[\sum_{m=0}^n \binom{n}{m}2^{-n}\beta_{k-1}^m\right]^{1/2} = [2^{-n}(1 + \beta_{k-1})^n]^{1/2} = \beta_k^n,$$

which completes the proof of the lemma. $\qquad\square$

To conclude, this shows that $Disc_{uniform}(\text{GIP}_n^k) \le 1/e^{\frac{n}{4^{k-1}}}$, which implies that the deterministic (and even randomized) communication complexity of GIP_n^k is $\Omega(n/4^k)$. In fact, by Exercise 6.15, we also get a bound for $D_{\frac{1}{2}-\varepsilon}^{uniform}(f)$ and $R_{\frac{1}{2}-\varepsilon}(f)$ of $\Omega(\log \varepsilon + n/4^k)$.

6.5. Simultaneous Protocols

The protocols presented in Examples 6.3 and 6.4 are of a very restricted form: the communication sent by each party does not depend at all on the previous communication sent by other parties. We can imagine all parties speaking "simultaneously" and each writing, on a common blackboard, a function of the $k-1$ parts of the input it can see. After all parties have spoken, the answer should be determined by what is written on the blackboard. We call such protocols simultaneous.

Definition 6.18: *The* simultaneous communication complexity of f, $D^{\|}(f)$, *is the cost of the best simultaneous protocol that computes f.*

Exercise 6.19: Show that $D^{\|}(E_N^k) = O(k \cdot log\,\xi_k(N))$, where E_N^k is the exactly-N function of Example 6.11.

It turns out that simultaneous protocols, although very simple, have surprising power as is shown by the following generalization of Example 6.4.

Lemma 6.20: *Fix a ring R. Let $R[x_{i,j}]$ ($1 \le i \le k$, $1 \le j \le n$) be the set of all poly-nomials over the ring R with variables $x_{i,j}$. For every polynomial p in $R[x_{i,j}]$ of degree at most $k - 1$, associate a k-party communication problem where $x_i = (x_{i,1}, \ldots, x_{i,n})$ (each $x_{i,j}$ is an element of R, that is $\log |R|$-bit long) and the goal is to evaluate p. Then $D^{\|}(p) \le k \log |R|$.*

PROOF: Because p is of degree at most $k - 1$, each monomial of p contains at most $k - 1$ variables. Thus, some party can compute the value of this monomial by itself. The protocol will first fix a partition of the monomials of p into k sets, with set i only containing monomials that can be computed by P_i. Each party will compute all the monomials assigned to it, add them up (in R), and write the answer (an element in R that takes $\log |R|$ bits) on the blackboard. Clearly, the value of p can be determined by what is on the blackboard, because this value is just the sum of values written by the k parties. □

The power of this lemma will be best appreciated when we consider the complexity class ACC^0 in Section 11.4 This also motivates the following open problem:

Problems 6.21: For some explicit function $f : (\{0,1\}^n)^k \to \{0,1\}$, prove a super-logarithmic lower bound on $D^{\|}(f)$ with $k \ge log\,n$ parties.

Recall that in two-party communication complexity proving strong lower bounds for 1-round communication was rather easy (Exercise 4.18). For multiparty communication we can obtain easily only rather weak bounds even for the simultaneous case.

▶ **Example 6.22:** Let A be a $k - 1$ dimensional array of bits, where each dimension has n entries. For every j ($1 \le j \le k - 1$), let i_j be an integer $1 \le i_j \le n$. Thus A is repre-sented by $N = n^{k-1}$ bits and each i_j by $\log n$ bits. The function INDEX($i_1, i_2, \ldots, i_{k-1}, A$) is defined to be the $(i_1, \ldots, i_{k-1})$-th entry of A, that is $A[i_1, \ldots, i_{k-1}]$.

We will show that $D^{\|}(\text{INDEX}) = \Omega(n/k) = \Omega(N^{1/(k-1)}/k)$ using a reduction to 1-round two-party communication complexity. Let us consider the two-party variant where Alice gets A and Bob gets all the indices $i_1, \ldots, i_{k-1}$. This problem is completely equivalent to the one considered in Example 4.19 (on N bits) and its 1-round (Alice speaks, then Bob can tell the answer) complexity is $N = n^{k-1}$. Now, assume that the k-party version can be solved with cost c. We will build a 1-round protocol for the two-party case where Alice only sends kcn^{k-2} bits. Thus, $ckn^{k-2} \ge n^{k-1}$ and the lower bound on c follows.

Alice will simulate all the parties except the k-th party (the one not seeing A), that is simulated by Bob. The difficulty is that party j in the multiparty case has access to all indices but i_j, whereas Alice does not. Alice will thus simulate the j-th party for all possible values of these $k - 2$ indices. The number of these values is n^{k-2}. Each possibility requires c bits of communication, and this should be done for all $1 \le j \le k - 1$. All together Alice sends $O(ckn^{k-2})$ bits. Bob knows $i_1, \ldots, i_{k-1}$, which is all the information required to simulate the k-th party (he will do so without actually sending the message). In addition, using his information, Bob can also figure out what the real message sent by the simulated j-th party is. Therefore, he can determine the answer.

Exercise 6.23: Prove that $D(\text{INDEX}) = \theta(\log n)$. That is, k parties without the restriction to simultaneous protocols can do better. Hint: For the lower bound generalize Exercise 4.21.

Problems 6.24: How big can the gap between $D(f)$ and $D^{||}(f)$ be when $k \ge \log n$?

Exercise 6.25: Let A be an n-bit string, and $1 \le j, i \le n$. Define the 3-argument function SUM-INDEX$(A, j, i) = A[j \oplus i]$, where $\oplus$ denotes bitwise xor. Prove that $D^{||}$ (SUM-INDEX) $= \Omega(\sqrt{n})$. Hint: Reduction from INDEX.

▶ **Example 6.26:** Surprisingly, the function SUM-INDEX can be computed with less communication than the obvious $O(n)$ upper bound. Below is an $O(n^{0.92})$ protocol for this function.

The first idea is that A can be thought of as a Boolean function $A : \{1, \ldots, n\} \to \{0, 1\}$, instead of a string, by letting $A(k)$ be the k-th bit of A. The second idea is that such a function A can be written as a multilinear polynomial over $GF(2)$ in the Boolean variables $x_1, \ldots, x_t$, where $t = \log n$. Let $k_1, \ldots, k_t$ be the binary representation of k, then to get $A(k)$ we evaluate the polynomial on the assignment $x_1 = k_1, \ldots, x_t = k_t$. To see how to get this polynomial, note that for every k there is a multilinear polynomial p_k that gets 1 only for the value k. For example, if $k = 1010$, then the polynomial p_k is obtained by simplifying the expression $x_1 \cdot (1 - x_2) \cdot x_3 \cdot (1 - x_4)$. The multilinear polynomial corresponding to A is obtained as $A(x) = \sum_{k:A(k)=1} p_k(x)$. So we can write, $A(x) = \sum_{S \subseteq \{1,\ldots,t\}} a_S \prod_{\ell \in S} x_\ell$, where each a_S is a 0-1 coefficient of the corresponding monomial. In this terminology, the players are required to evaluate

$$A(j \oplus i) = \sum_S a_S \prod_{\ell \in S} (j_\ell + i_\ell) = \sum_{S:|S| \le 2t/3} a_S \prod_{\ell \in S} (j_\ell + i_\ell) + \sum_{S:|S| > 2t/3} a_S \prod_{\ell \in S} (j_\ell + i_\ell),$$

where the motivation for decomposing the sum into two terms will soon become clear. The protocol for SUM-INDEX will work as follows: The player holding both j and i writes on the board these two values (this is only $O(\log n)$ bits). Now note that each player who sees A knows all the values a_S. Therefore, if one of these two players broadcasts, all the values a_S, for S such that $|S| > 2t/3$, then from this communication (and the values of j and i, which are already on the board) the second term in the above summation can be computed. This requires $\sum_{m > \frac{2t}{3}}^{t} \binom{t}{m}$ bits. The question is how the first term can be computed. Note that if the players write all these coefficients as well, then the communication will exceed $2^t = n$ bits, which is not useful. To overcome this difficulty, we manipulate the first term:

$$\sum_{S:|S|\leq 2t/3} a_S \prod_{\ell\in S}(j_\ell + i_\ell) = \sum_{S:|S|\leq 2t/3} a_S \sum_{T_1,T_2\,:\,T_1\cup T_2=S,T_1\cap T_2=\emptyset} \prod_{\ell\in T_1} j_\ell \prod_{\ell\in T_2} i_\ell$$

$$= \sum_{|T_1|+|T_2|\leq 2t/3,T_1\cap T_2=\emptyset} a_{T_1\cup T_2} \prod_{\ell\in T_1} j_\ell \prod_{\ell\in T_2} i_\ell$$

$$= \sum_{T_1:|T_1|\leq t/3} \left(\sum_{T_2:|T_2|\leq 2t/3-|T_1|,T_1\cap T_2=\emptyset} a_{T_1\cup T_2} \prod_{\ell\in T_2} i_\ell \right) \prod_{\ell\in T_1} j_\ell$$

$$+ \sum_{T_2:|T_2|\leq t/3} \left(\sum_{T_1:t/3<|T_1|\leq 2t/3-|T_2|,T_1\cap T_2=\emptyset} a_{T_1\cup T_2} \prod_{\ell\in T_1} j_\ell \right) \prod_{\ell\in T_2} i_\ell.$$

Therefore, we get a sum of two terms. The first term can be considered as a polynomial in j, whose coefficients are known to the player holding A and i, whereas the second term is a polynomial in i, whose coefficients are known to the player holding A and j. Each of these two players writes on the board all the coefficients of the corresponding polynomial ($\sum_{m=0}^{t/3} \binom{t}{m}$ bits). Hence, we get a *simultaneous* protocol, such that the value of $A(j \oplus i)$ can be computed from its communication. The communication complexity of this protocol is

$$2t + \sum_{m>\frac{2t}{3}}^{t} \binom{t}{m} + 2\sum_{m=0}^{t/3} \binom{t}{m} < 2t + 3\sum_{m=0}^{t/3} \binom{t}{m}$$

$$= 2t + O\left(\frac{2^{tH(1/3)}}{\sqrt{t}} \right)$$

$$= 2\log n + O\left(\frac{n^{H(1/3)}}{\sqrt{\log n}} \right),$$

where H denotes the entropy function. Since $H(1/3) = 0.918, \ldots$, this is $O(n^{0.92})$.

Problems 6.27: Does there exist a protocol for SUM-INDEX where two parties are allowed to send *poly− log(n)* bits each, and the third $o(n)$? See Section 11.3 for motivation.

6.6. Bibliographic Notes

Several models for multiparty communication were introduced in the literature. See for example [Dolev and Feder 1989]. The "Number on the Forehead" model was presented by [Chandra, Furst, and Lipton 1983]. The notion of cylinder intersection was defined in the work of [Babai, Nisan, and Szegedy 1989]. The notion of star is from [Chandra et al.1983]. The Ramsey technique for proving lower bounds in due to [Chandra et al.1983] (for an excellent introduction to Ramsey theory see [Graham et al. 1983]. The lower bound for GIP is due to [Babai et al. 1989]. It was later improved by [Chung and

Tetali 1993], who proved a lower bound of $\Omega(n/2^k)$ for the GIP function; this matches the upper bound, that is due to [Grolmusz 1994].

Simultaneous protocols were defined in [Babai, Kimmel, and Lokam 1995]. Lemma 6.20 is from the work of [Håstad and Goldmann]. Examples 6.22 and 6.26 are by [Babai et al. 1995]. Similar results for different functions appear in [Pudlák and Rödl 1993].

CHAPTER 7

Variable Partition Models

In the standard two-party model the input (x, y) is partitioned in a fixed way. That is, Alice always gets x and Bob always gets y. In this chapter we discuss models in which the partition of the input among the players is not fixed. The main motivation for these models is that in many cases we wish to use communication complexity lower bounds to obtain lower bounds in other models of computation. This would typically require finding a communication complexity problem "hidden" somewhere in the computation that the model under consideration must perform. Because in such a model the input usually is not partitioned into two distinct sets $x_1, \ldots, x_n$ and $y_1, \ldots, y_n$, such a partition must be given by the reduction. In some cases the partition can be figured out and *fixed*. In some other cases we must use arguments regarding *any* partition (of a certain kind). That is, we require a model where the partition is not fixed beforehand but the protocol determines the partition (independently of the particular input). Several such "variable partition models" are discussed in this chapter.

Throughout this chapter the input will be m Boolean variables $x_1, \ldots, x_m$, and we consider functions $f : \{0, 1\}^m \to \{0, 1\}$. We will talk about the communication complexity of f between two disjoint sets of variables S and T. That is, one player gets all bits in S and the other all bits in T

7.1. Worst-Case Partition

The simplest variable partition model we may consider is the "worst-case" partition: split the input into two sets in the way that maximizes the communication complexity.

Definition 7.1: *Let* $f : \{0, 1\}^m \to \{0, 1\}$ *be a function. Let S and T be a partition of the variables $x_1, \ldots, x_m$ into two disjoint sets. The* (deterministic) *communication complexity of f between S and T, denoted $D^{S:T}(f)$, is the complexity of computing f where Alice sees all bits in S, and Bob sees all bits in T. The* worst-case communication complexity *of f, denoted $D^{worst}(f)$, is the maximum of $D^{S:T}(f)$ over all such partitions.*

Note that for all f, $D^{worst}(f) \leq \frac{m}{2} + 1$ (because for any partition $S : T$, the player with the least number of bits can send them to the other player). Proving lower bounds for the worst-case communication complexity is quite simple because it suffices to find a single hard partition and then rely on techniques (and results) for the regular two-party model.

▶ **Example 7.2:** Let the function $\text{PAL}_m(x_1, \ldots, x_m)$ be 1 iff the string $x_1 \cdots x_m$ is a palindrome (that is, the string $x_1 \cdots x_m$ equals the string $x_m \cdots x_1$). Then $D^{worst}(\text{PAL}_m) = \frac{m}{2} + 1$. The hard partition is the first $m/2$ bits versus the last $m/2$ bits. Computing PAL_m, according to this partition, is equivalent to computing the function EQ on two $m/2$-bit strings (that is, check whether $x_1 \cdots x_{m/2} = x_m \cdots x_{m/2+1}$). By the lower bound of Example 1.21, the result follows.

Exercise 7.3: Let the function $f_m(x_1, \ldots, x_m)$ be 1 iff the m-bit string $x_1 \cdots x_m$ contains two consecutive 1s. Prove that $D^{worst}(f_m) = \Theta(m)$.

▶ **Example 7.4:** Let MAJ_m be the majority function on m-bit strings. We show that $D^{worst}(\text{MAJ}_m) = \log m$. For the upper bound, let the player whose set in the partition is smaller send the number of 1s in its input ($\log \frac{m}{2}$ bits) and the other player can compute the output. For the lower bound, we need to show a hard partition. Consider *any* partition $S : T$ of the bits into two sets of size $m/2$ (all such partitions are equivalent because the function is symmetric). Let n_1 be the number of 1s in S and n_2 be the number of 1s in T. Intuitively, the parties must simply check whether $n_1 + n_2 > m/2$, or equivalently whether $n_1 > m/2 - n_2$. This is simply the GT problem on $(\log m - 1)$-bit strings (formally, given $\log \frac{m}{2}$-bit inputs (i_1, i_2) to the GT function, Alice can produce a string with exactly i_1 1s and Bob can produce a string with exactly $m/2 - i_2$ 1s. The output of MAJ_m on this string is exactly the output of $\text{GT}(i_1, i_2)$). The required bounds for this function are given in Exercise 1.22.

A similar argument shows that $D^{worst}(\text{TH}_m^k) = \log \min(k, m - k) + 1$, where for an integer k (the "threshold"), TH_m^k is a function that gives 1 iff at least k of the m input bits are 1s.

We can also talk about variable partitions for multiparty communication complexity (where "multiparty" refers to the "number on the forehead" model discussed in Chapter 6.

Definition 7.5: *The k-party worst-case communication complexity of f, $D^{worst\,k-party}(f)$, is the worst-case multiparty communication complexity over all partitions of the variables of f into k disjoint subsets (where each player sees the variables in $k - 1$ of these subsets).*

▶ **Example 7.6:** Recall Lemma 6.20. In our terms it states the following: Fix a ring R, and let $p : R^m \to R$ be a polynomial in $R[x_1, \ldots, x_m]$ of degree d. Then, $D^{worst(d+1)-party}(p) \leq d \log |R|$. (Here the input is m elements of R. These m elements are partitioned among the players and not the $m \log |R|$ bits representing them.)

Below we prove lower bounds for stronger variable partition models. All these lower bounds also apply to the worst-case partition complexity.

7.2. Best-Case Partition

In many cases we are faced with models that may choose the locations in that input variables are accessed (in some specific sense depending on the model) according to the function that must be computed. In some cases lower bounds in the model would only follow if all partitions (of a certain kind) yield hard communication complexity problems. The simplest way to capture this is the following model:

Definition 7.7: *Let* $f(x_1, \ldots, x_m)$ *be a function. The* best-case communication complexity *of* f, $D^{best}(f)$, *is the minimum* $D^{S:T}(f)$ *over all partitions of* $x_1, \ldots, x_m$ *into two sets* S, T *of equal size.*

Note that here we insist that S and T are of equal size (as opposed to the "worst partition" case where they could be of any size) because otherwise the partition of all the variables versus none of them clearly has 0 complexity. Lower bounds for the best-case complexity do not follow directly from the two-party model because we must argue somehow that *all* partitions are hard. Indeed, in some cases in the best partition the problem is much easier than in the worst partition:

▶ **Example 7.8:** $D^{best}(\text{PAL}_m) = 2$ (in contrast, Example 7.2 shows that $D^{worst}(\text{PAL}_m) = \frac{m}{2} + 1$). An easy partition is the second and third quarters of the bits versus the first and last quarters. Alice simply verifies that the second quarter is the reverse of the third quarter, and Bob verifies that the first quarter is the reverse of the last quarter. They output 1 iff both tests succeed, which requires one bit of communication from each.

For some functions there is no big difference between the various partitions. For example, consider the function MAJ_m (Example 7.4). By the symmetry of the function all the partitions of bits into two equal size sets are equivalent. Example 7.4 therefore shows that $D^{best}(\text{MAJ}_m) = \log m$. Next we show a more interesting example, and a technique that is often very useful.

▶ **Example 7.9:** For $x, y \in \{0, 1\}^n$ and $0 \le i \le n - 1$, define the "shifted equality" function $\text{SEQ}(x, y, i)$ to be 1 iff the string $x = x_0 x_1 \cdots x_{n-1}$ equals to the string y shifted circularly by i-bits to the right, that is to $y_i y_{i+1} \cdots y_{n-1} y_0 \cdots y_{i-1}$. In other words, $\text{SEQ}(x, y, i) = 1$ iff for all $0 \le j < n$, $x_j = y_{i+j \bmod n}$. Then $D^{best}(\text{SEQ}) = \Omega(m)$, where $m = 2n + \log n$ is the size of the input.

As is the case in Example 7.8, for certain partitions checking equality may be easy. The idea will be to show that for some values of i the bits are partitioned between the players in a way that makes the equality-test "hard." First, observe that each of the two players holds a "significant" number of bits from a different string. To see this, note that each player gets $\frac{m}{2} = n + \frac{1}{2} \log n$ bits, out of them at least $n - \frac{1}{2} \log n$ are bits of either x or y. Without loss of generality, Alice holds $\frac{n}{2}$ bits of x, and hence Bob holds at least $k = \frac{n}{2} - \frac{1}{2}\log n$ bits of y. Let $A \subseteq \{0, 1, \ldots, n-1\}$ be k bits of $x_0, \ldots, x_{n-1}$ held by Alice, and $B \subseteq \{0, 1, \ldots, n-1\}$ be k bits of $y_0, \ldots, y_{n-1}$ held by Bob (each player possibly holds other bits as well from x, y, and i).

Consider the special case where all bits of x and y not in A and B (respectively) are 0s (as we are proving a lower bound, we are allowed to restrict the input). We are now going to fix the value of i in a way that yields high communication complexity between Alice and Bob. For this, let us see what is the communication complexity for some *fixed* value of i. Denote $B_i = \{j|(i + j \bmod n) \in B\}$. We claim that for any fixed i, the communication complexity between A and B is at least $|A \cap B_i|$. To see this, we further restrict the input by letting $x_j = 0$ and $y_{i+j\bmod n} = 0$, for all $j \notin A \cap B_i$. Now observe that the induced function is 1 iff for all $j \in A \cap B_i$, $x_j = y_{i+j\bmod n}$. Because $j \in A$ the bit x_j is held by Alice, and because $j \in B_i$, we have $(i + j \bmod n) \in B$, that is, the bit $y_{i+j\bmod n}$ is held by Bob (and none of these bits is already fixed). By the lower bound for EQ (Example 1.21) applied to strings of length $|A \cap B_i|$, the claim follows (in the sense that a better protocol for this problem implies a protocol for EQ whose communication complexity is better than the lower bound). Finally, it remains to show that for some i, $|A \cap B_i| = \Omega(m)$. For this, we write

$$\sum_i |A \cap B_i| = \sum_{j \in A} |\{i | j \in B_i\}|$$

(to see this, think of a matrix whose rows are $j \in A$ and columns are the sets B_i; The entry (j, B_i) is 1 if $j \in B_i$ and 0 otherwise. With this view, the right-hand term of the equality counts the 1s of this matrix row-by-row, whereas the left-hand term counts the 1s column-by-column). Now,

$$\sum_{j \in A} |\{i | j \in B_i\}| = |A| \cdot |B| = k^2.$$

Hence, for some i we have $|A \cap B_i| \geq k^2/k = k = \Omega(m)$, as needed.

Exercise 7.10: Let MATCH be the function that accepts a $3m$-bit string x and an m-bit string y and returns 1 iff y is a substring of x. Prove that D^{best}(MATCH)$= \Omega(m)$.

Exercise 7.11: Let SUM(a,b,i) be the function that takes two n-bit integers a,b and a $\log n$-bit integer i and returns the i-th bit of the binary representation of the sum $a + b$ (the length of the input is $m = 2n + \log n$). Similarly, let PROD(a,b,i) be the function that takes the same inputs and returns the i-th bit of the product $a \cdot b$. Prove

1. D^{best}(SUM) $= O(\log m)$; but
2. D^{best}(PROD) $= \Omega(m/\log(m))$.

We may think of several generalizations of D^{best}. Perhaps the most natural one is to allow partitions into two sets that are not exactly of equal size, but only approximately so. Say, each set must hold at least a third of the input bits. Lower bounds for such a generalization may be proved in similar ways as for D^{best} but may be used more easily in proving lower bounds in some models. A generalization that is significantly stronger is considered in the next section. Thus, the lower bounds proven below directly imply lower bounds on D^{best}.

7.3. Best Partition with Information Overlap

Let S and T be two disjoint subsets of $x_1, \ldots, x_m$, which do not necessarily cover all the variables. The definition of $D^{S:T}(f)$ (Definition 7.1) can be extended to be the complexity of computing f where Alice sees all bits in S, Bob sees all bits in T, and all bits not in $S \cup T$ are seen by *both* Alice and Bob. This is equivalent to the maximum over all possible values for the bits not in $S \cup T$ of the communication complexity of the induced function on the variables of $S \cup T$.

Definition 7.12: *Let* $f : \{0, 1\}^m \to \{0, 1\}$ *be a function. The n-best communication complexity of* f, $D^{n-best}(f)$, *is the minimum of* $D^{S:T}(f)$ *over all disjoint sets* S, T *of size n each.*

By the definitions, $D^{best}(f) = D^{m/2-best}(f)$. In some cases, the overlap of information may be very useful. For example, the function SEQ (Example 7.9) can be computed with $O(1)$ bits as long as each player holds at most $n/2$ bits (and the rest are common). This is because partitions in which the two players get, say, only bits of x (and y and i are common) are easy; each player checks for every bit x_j that he holds whether $x_j = y_{i+j \bmod n}$.

▶ **Example 7.13:** Consider the function MAJ_m defined in Example 7.4. We show that $D^{n-best}(\text{MAJ}_m) = \log n$. For the upper bound, notice that for any setting of the bits not in $S \cup T$ (which are known by both parties) a protocol for MAJ_m can start by Alice sending to Bob the number of 1s in her part of the input ($\log n$ bits), and Bob can then compute the value of the function. Because the function is symmetric, the choice of S and T does not matter. To prove the lower bound, it suffices to exhibit some setting for variables not in $S \cup T$ that gives complexity $\log n$. For example, set exactly half of these variables to 0 and half to 1. This returns us to the case of majority on n variables, and because the function is symmetric this is the same as in Example 7.4.

▶ **Example 7.14:** Let ED be the element distinctness function: its input is k integers in the range $0, 1, \ldots, 4k - 1$ (thus, each integer is given by $\log(4k)$ bits). It returns 1 iff all k integers are distinct. We show that, for all n, $D^{n-best}(\text{ED}) = \Omega(n/\log m)$, where $m = k(\log k + 2)$ is the size of the input (in particular, $D^{best}(\text{ED}) = \Omega(m/\log m)$).

Let S and T be two disjoint sets of n bits each. Each of these bits is the j-th coordinate (for some $0 \le j < \log(4k)$) of one of the k numbers. Let j_S be the coordinate most often used in S and j_T be the coordinate most often used in T. Let A be the subset of the k input numbers for which S contains the j_S-th coordinate. Similarly, let B be the subset of the k input numbers for which T contains the j_T-th coordinate. Then, $|A| \ge n/\log(4k)$ and $|B| \ge n/\log(4k)$. Without loss of generality, we assume that the sizes are actually equal (otherwise, we simply reduce the larger of A and B). We also assume that A and

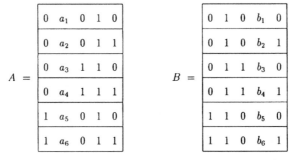

$$A = \begin{array}{|ccccc|}
\hline
0 & a_1 & 0 & 0 & 0 \\
\hline
0 & a_2 & 0 & 0 & 1 \\
\hline
0 & a_3 & 0 & 1 & 0 \\
\hline
0 & a_4 & 0 & 1 & 1 \\
\hline
0 & a_5 & 1 & 0 & 0 \\
\hline
0 & a_6 & 1 & 0 & 1 \\
\hline
\end{array}
\qquad
B = \begin{array}{|ccccc|}
\hline
0 & b_1 & 0 & 0 & 0 \\
\hline
0 & b_2 & 0 & 0 & 1 \\
\hline
0 & b_3 & 0 & 1 & 0 \\
\hline
0 & b_4 & 0 & 1 & 1 \\
\hline
0 & b_5 & 1 & 0 & 0 \\
\hline
0 & b_6 & 1 & 0 & 1 \\
\hline
\end{array}$$

Figure 7.1: Case 1 ($j = j_S = j_T = 2$); Reducing EQ to ED

$$A = \begin{array}{|ccccc|}
\hline
0 & a_1 & 0 & 1 & 0 \\
\hline
0 & a_2 & 0 & 1 & 1 \\
\hline
0 & a_3 & 1 & 1 & 0 \\
\hline
0 & a_4 & 1 & 1 & 1 \\
\hline
1 & a_5 & 0 & 1 & 0 \\
\hline
1 & a_6 & 0 & 1 & 1 \\
\hline
\end{array}
\qquad
B = \begin{array}{|ccccc|}
\hline
0 & 1 & 0 & b_1 & 0 \\
\hline
0 & 1 & 0 & b_2 & 1 \\
\hline
0 & 1 & 1 & b_3 & 0 \\
\hline
0 & 1 & 1 & b_4 & 1 \\
\hline
1 & 1 & 0 & b_5 & 0 \\
\hline
1 & 1 & 0 & b_6 & 1 \\
\hline
\end{array}$$

Figure 7.2: Case 2 ($j_S = 2, j_T = 4$); Reducing DISJ to ED

B are disjoint. Otherwise, we split common elements equally between the two sets (this may reduce the size of A and B by a factor of at most two).

We now fix all input bits, except for the j_S-th and j_T-th coordinates of the numbers in $A \cup B$, as follows: For all $0 \le i < |A|$, the i-th number in A and the i-th number in B get the binary representation of i (padded with 0s) written in the coordinates excluding j_S and j_T (see Figures 7.1 and 7.2). All numbers not in $A \cup B$ get unique binary representations of numbers larger than $|A| - 1$ written in these coordinates. This is possible since there are (at least) $\log k$ "free" coordinates and only k numbers. For numbers not in $A \cup B$ we also fix the j_S-th and j_T-th coordinate to 0. Notice that these restrictions already ensure that the only equalities between input numbers that may occur are between the i-th number in A and the i-th number in B, for some i. For all other pairs, inequality is ensured. We distinguish two cases, whether $j_S = j_T$ or not.

Case 1: $j_S = j_T = j$ (see Figure 7.1). In this case ED is 1 if and only if for all $0 \le i < |A|$, the j-th bit in the i-th number in A is equal to the complement of the j-th bit in the i-th number in B. This problem is equivalent to the equality function (EQ) on $|A|$-bit strings, for which we have the required lower bound of $|A|$ (Example 1.21).

Case 2: $j_S \ne j_T$ (see Figure 7.2). We further restrict the input by fixing the j_S-th coordinate of all numbers in B to 1, and the j_T-th coordinate of all numbers in A to 1. Now ED is 0 if and only if for some $0 \le i < |A|$, the j_S-th bit in the i-th number in A (held by Alice) is 1 and also the j_T-th bit in the i-th number in B (held by Bob) is 1. This is equivalent to the disjointness function (DISJ) on subsets of $1, \ldots, |A|$, for which again we have the required lower bound of $|A|$ (Example 1.23).

Exercise 7.15*: The undirected $s - t$-connectivity problem, USTCON, accepts as input a graph on ℓ vertices (that is, $m = \binom{\ell}{2}$ input bits representing the edges), and outputs 1 if and only if there exists a path between vertices s and t in the input graph ($s \neq t$). Prove that for all n, $D^{n-best}(\text{USTCON}) = \Omega(n/\ell)$. Conclude that $D^{best}(\text{USTCON}) = \Omega(\sqrt{m})$.

7.4. Bibliographic Notes

The *Best-Case Partition* model was introduced by [Papadimitriou and Sipser 1982], and in fact many results in communication complexity were first introduced in this model. It was heavily used for proving lower bounds for VLSI [Lengauer 1990, Chu and Schnitger 1991] (also see references in [Lengauer 1990], as well as Section 8.3 below). In particular, the technique used in Example 7.9 was developed in this context.

In [Lam and Ruzzo 1989] a general transformation is given from a fixed partition to the *best* partition. The *n–best* complexity is implicit in [Alon and Maass 1986]. Exercise 7.15 is implicit in [Meinel and Waack 1994]. The graph connectivity problem in the best partition case was considered in [Hajnal, Maass, and Turan 1988]. Other graph theoretic problems were considered, for example, in [Ďuriš and Pudlák 1989].

The definitions given in this chapter can be extended in various ways. In particular, there is no special reason to discuss only the deterministic case and we may define in a similar way measures like $R^{worst}(f)$ (the randomized communication complexity of f with respect to the worst partition), and so forth.

PART THREE

Applications

CHAPTER 8

Networks, Communication, and VLSI

Results about communication complexity have all kinds of applications. The most obvious ones are applications to communication problems. For example, for the management of a distributed system it is often required to check whether two copies of a file that reside in two different sites are the same. Clearly, this is just solving the "equality" problem EQ, whose communication complexity was extensively studied in the first part of this book. It is also very useful to compare a whole directory. Namely, to get for each file in the directory a bit indicating whether the copies of this particular file are the same or not. This is the same as solving the direct-sum version of EQ (see Section 4.1).

Most of the results in Part III of this book are devoted to applications in which communication does not appear explicitly in the statement of the problem. These applications show that in fact communication is an essential part of more problems than it may seem at first glance. We start (in Sections 8.1 and 8.2) with several applications in which the relation to communication complexity is obvious. Then, we show (in Section 8.3) how to apply communication complexity results to the study of VLSI chips.

8.1. Bisection Width of Networks

A network of k processors can be viewed as a graph G, where nodes correspond to the processors in the network and edges represent the connection of two processors by a communication channel. We will be proving lower bounds and we will do so regardless of the implementation of "processors" and "channels." We will only rely on the assumption that in each time step a single bit can be sent on each of the channels.

The network consists of k processors $P_1, \ldots, P_k$. Each processor P_i of the network gets as an input some value x_i and together they wish to compute the value of $f(x_1, \ldots, x_k)$. Let $T_G(f)$ be the time required to compute this value on the network G by the best protocol. There are essentially two general lower bound techniques for such networks. The first is the "network diameter" lower bound. It claims that (for nontrivial functions) information must travel from one end of the graph to the other

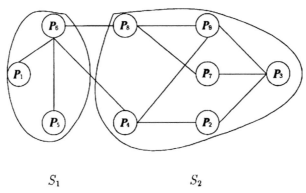

$$S_1 \qquad\qquad\qquad\qquad S_2$$

Figure 8.1: A network partitioned into two sets $S_1 : S_2$

end, and thus the computation requires Ω (diameter (G)) time. The other method for proving lower bounds is based on identifying communication bottlenecks in the network. This method, which is presented here, makes use of communication complexity lower bounds.

For any partition of the nodes in the graph into two sets S_1, S_2 denote by $B(S_1 : S_2)$ the number of edges connecting S_1 and S_2. For example, in Figure 8.1 a network of 9 nodes is presented, whose nodes are partitioned into two sets: S_1 of size 3 and S_2 of size 6. For this partition, $B(S_1 : S_2) = 2$. The next lemma relates the time complexity of computing f on the network G (that is, $T_G(f)$) to the communication complexity of computing f by two players, Alice and Bob, with respect to a certain partition of the input bits. For this, recall the definition of $D^{S:T}(f)$ (Definition 7.1). In this section, we denote by $D^{S_1 : S_2}(f)$ the communication complexity with respect to the partition in which Alice sees all input bits seen by processors in S_1 and Bob sees all input bits seen by processors in S_2 (note that here S_1 and S_2 are sets of processors and not sets of bits; the input of each processor may consist of several bits).

Lemma 8.1: *Let G and f be as above. Let $S_1 : S_2$ be any partition of G. Then*

$$T_G(f) \geq \frac{D^{S_1:S_2}(f)}{B(S_1 : S_2)}.$$

PROOF: Consider the best protocol for computing f on the network G. We construct a two-party protocol for f (with respect to the partition $S_1 : S_2$) as follows. Alice will simulate all processors in S_1 (her input is exactly the input to these processors) and Bob will simulate all processors in S_2 (his input is exactly the input to these processors). The only communication needed at any time step is the bits going between the processors of S_1 and the processors of S_2. The number of these bits is at most $B(S_1 : S_2)$ and hence $D^{S_1:S_2}(f) \leq T_G(f) \cdot B(S_1 : S_2)$. $\qquad\square$

▶ **Example 8.2:** Consider a ring of $k = 2\ell$ processors. That is, a network consisting of k edges $(P_1, P_2), \dots, (P_{k-1}, P_k), (P_k, P_1)$. Each processor holds an n-bit string x_i and the goal is to determine whether every two opposing processors hold the same string. That is, for each i ($1 \leq i \leq \ell$) $x_i = x_{i+\ell}$. By partitioning the network into two equal parts (that is, $S_1 = \{P_1, \ldots, P_\ell\}$ and $S_2 = \{P_{\ell+1}, \ldots, P_k\}$, we get $B(S_1 : S_2) = 2$. The induced two-argument function is simply the function EQ on strings of length ℓn. Hence, by Lemma 8.1, a lower bound of $\Omega(\ell n)$ on the time required to complete this computation follows.

In general, the *bisection width* of a network G, denoted $B(G)$, is the minimum of $B(S_1 : S_2)$ over all S_1, S_2 that form a partition of V. Usually, the bisection width is defined with respect to sets S_1, S_2 of equal size (assume for simplicity that $|V|$ is even so $|S_1| = |S_2| = \frac{k}{2}$). The above lemma says that for our purposes it is not necessary to consider only balanced partitions as long as good bounds on $D^{S_1:S_2}(f)$ can be proven. In fact, as can be seen by Example 8.3, it is sometimes better that S_1 and S_2 be only almost balanced sets (for example, each is of size at least $k/3$).

▶ **Example 8.3:** Consider the following problem ED′, which is a variant of the element distinctness function, ED, of Example 7.14. The input for each of the k processors is a number in the range $1, \ldots, k^2$ ($O(\log k)$ bits each). The goal of the processors is to check whether these k numbers are distinct. We first show that for any partition $S_1 : S_2$ of the processors in which each of the two sets is of size $\Omega(k)$ the communication complexity is $D^{S_1:S_2}(\text{ED}') = \Omega(k \log k)$. Observe that a protocol for ED′ under a partition $S_1 : S_2$ gives a protocol for the disjointness function, DISJ, on inputs of size $n = k^2$, where Alice gets as an input a set of size $|S_1|$ and Bob gets as an input a set of size $|S_2|$. In fact, this problem is no easier from the function $\text{DISJ}_{k'}$ of Example 2.12, where $k' = \min(|S_1|, |S_2|) = \Omega(k)$. (Here the sizes of the sets are not necessarily equal, but we do not change the problem by much if we increase the domain to $k^2 + k$. Then, we only restrict the input if we insist that for the larger set only k' elements are in the range $1, \ldots, k^2$ and the rest are in the range $k^2 + 1, \ldots, k^2 + k$.) It follows from Example 2.12, that $D^{S_1:S_2}(\text{ED}') = \Omega(k \log k)$.

Now, we consider computing ED′ on several networks. In each case we partition the network into two sets S_1 and S_2 each of $\Omega(k)$ processors and hence, by using Lemma 8.1, we can use the communication complexity lower bound $D^{S_1:S_2}(\text{ED}') = \Omega(k \log k)$ to get lower bounds on the time required to compute ED′ on the corresponding network.

- Suppose that the network is a linear array (that is, a line graph). Then the network can be partitioned into two sets S_1 and S_2 in the middle (that is, each set contains about $k/2$ processors). In this case $B(S_1 : S_2) = 1$, hence $T_{ARRAY}(\text{ED}') = \Omega(k \log k)$.
- Suppose that the network is a two-dimensional array (that is, a $\sqrt{k} \times \sqrt{k}$ grid, also known as a *mesh*). Again, we can partition the network in the middle into two sets S_1 and S_2 of $\sqrt{k} \times (\sqrt{k}/2) = k/2$ processors. In this case $B(S_1 : S_2) = \sqrt{k}$ and hence $T_{MESH}(\text{ED}') = \Omega(\sqrt{k} \log k)$.
- Suppose that the network is a binary tree. Then there is always a single edge that cuts the tree into two parts, each of at least $1/3$ of the nodes (see for example, the proof of Lemma 2.8). Hence $T_{TREE}(\text{ED}') = \Omega(k \log k)$.
- Suppose that the network is planar. It is known that such a network can be partitioned into two sets S_1, S_2, each of size at least $k/3$ such that $B(S_1 : S_2) = O(\sqrt{k})$. Hence, $T_{PLANAR}(\text{ED}') = \Omega(\sqrt{k} \log k)$.

Note that in all these cases we get bounds that are better than the bounds that are obtained by considering only the diameter of the network.

▶ **Example 8.4:** Suppose we are given a network, and an order of its processors so that adjacent processors in this order are also neighbors in the network. For example, such an order on the *MESH* network will be to take the rows in the natural order, inside even rows to take the processors from left to right, and inside odd rows to take the processors from right to left. In the SORT problem, each of the k processors of the network is given an input number in the range $1, \ldots, k^2$ ($O(\log k)$ bits); at the end the input numbers are permuted so that if we look at the processors according to the specified order, we get a nondecreasing sequence of numbers. We claim that lower bounds proved for ED can be transformed into lower bounds for SORT as well. To see this, note that $T_G(\text{ED}) \le T_G(\text{SORT}) + O(\log k)$. This is because to compute ED (that is, to check whether all k numbers are distinct) the processors can simply compute SORT, and then adjacent processors check in $O(\log k)$ time (because they are neighbors) whether their numbers are equal. Hence, for example $T_{MESH}(\text{SORT}) = \Omega(\sqrt{k} \log k)$. A matching upper bound for SORT exists.

Similar types of lower bounds can be applied to other multiprocessor computing devices:

Exercise 8.5: Consider a parallel machine where the k processors communicate via a shared memory whose total size is b bits. Each time unit a processor can read an arbitrary number of bits from the shared memory and write an arbitrary number of bits into the shared memory (the values written in time unit t will be read only in time unit $t + 1$). If more than one processor tries to write into the same bit, then conflicts are resolved by assuming that the value written by the lower numbered processor is the value that is actually written into this bit. Denote by $T_b(f)$ the time needed to compute the function f in this model and recall the definition of the measure D^{worst} (Definition 7.1). Prove that $T_b(f) \ge D^{worst}(f)/b$.

8.2. Total Communication

Consider a network that has to compute some function f. In the previous section we considered the *time* that it takes to compute the function f on the network, ignoring the number of bits transmitted in each time step. It is interesting to ask what is the *total* number of bits exchanged between the processors of the network. Of a particular interest is the *line network*, consisting of $k + 1$ processors $P_0, P_1, \ldots, P_k$ with edges only between P_i and P_{i+1}, for $0 \le i \le k - 1$ (see Figure 8.2). The processors wish to compute a function $f(x, y)$ where x is stored in P_0 and y is stored in P_k. The complexity of a protocol is the *total* number of bits exchanged on all edges. Let $D_k(f)$ be the complexity of the best protocol for f. Obviously, $D_k(f) \le k \cdot D(f)$. This is because the processors can simulate the best two-party protocol for f (P_0 simulates Alice, P_k simulates Bob, and the intermediate processors behave as a relay; that is, they

Figure 8.2: A line network (for $k = 7$)

just propagate the messages they receive). The main question here is whether we can do better.

Open Problem 8.6: Is it true that for every function f, $D_k(f) = \Omega(k \cdot D(f))$?

Many of the techniques that were used to prove lower bounds for the two-party (deterministic) communication complexity, $D(f)$, can be extended for $D_k(f)$.

Exercise 8.7: Let $f : \{0,1\}^n \times \{0,1\}^n \to \{0,1\}$ be a function.

1. Let $D_k^1(f)$ be the complexity of computing f in such a line network when communication is one-way. That is, message are allowed only from P_i to P_{i+1}. Assume that t is the number of distinct rows in the matrix M_f, associated with f (see Section 1.4). Then, $D_k^1(f) = \Theta(k \log t)$. (This extends Exercise 4.18.)

2. If f has a fooling set S (see Section 1.3) of size t, then $D_k(f) \geq k \log_2 t$. (This extends Lemma 1.20.)

The best general lower bound that we know for $D_k(f)$ is the following.

Lemma 8.8: *For every function* $f : \{0, 1\}^n \times \{0, 1\}^n \to \{0, 1\}$, $D_k(f) \geq k \cdot R_0^{pub}(f)$.

PROOF: Given a protocol for the line network that uses a total of $D_k(f)$ bits, we construct a public coin, randomized, zero error, two-party protocol for f. Alice and Bob choose together (using their public coin, with no communication), uniformly at random, one of the k edges (P_i, P_{i+1}). They simulate the line protocol, where Alice simulates $P_0, \ldots, P_i$ and Bob simulates $P_{i+1}, \ldots, P_k$. Note that the only bits that they actually need to exchange are those going through the chosen edge. The expected number of bits used by the simulation is therefore at most $D_k(f)/k$. Hence, $R_0^{pub}(f) \leq D_k(f)/k$. $\square$

Corollary 8.9: *For every function* $f : \{0, 1\}^n \times \{0, 1\}^n \to \{0, 1\}$,

$$D_k(f) = \Omega(k \cdot (\sqrt{D(f)} - \log n)).$$

PROOF: By Exercise 3.15, $R_0(f) = O(R_0^{pub}(f) + \log n)$. By Section 3.2, $R_0(f) = \Omega(\sqrt{D(f)})$. Combining these two facts with Lemma 8.8 the corollary follows. $\square$

Exercise 8.10: Show that for every function f, $D_k(f) \geq k \cdot (R_0(f) - \log k)$. Conclude that $D_k(f) = \Omega(k \cdot (\sqrt{D(f)} - \log k))$.

8.3. AT^2 Lower Bounds for VLSI

Without getting into any details concerning the technology involved in VLSI chips, we can abstractly view a chip as follows (in practice chips are more restricted but because we are mainly interested in proving lower bounds, this only makes the results stronger): A chip is a planar rectangle, whose size is measured in terms of Δ, which is essentially the minimal width of a wire (Δ is of course, technology-dependent). On this rectangle (of size $a \times b$, where the size is measured in units of Δ), there are gates (processors) and there are wires connecting them. A chip has m input ports and 1 output port (connected at any point on the chip) and its goal is to compute some function $f: \{0, 1\}^m \to \{0, 1\}$. Figure 8.3 shows a chip with 10 input ports (denoted $x_1, \ldots, x_{10}$) and one output port.

A chip works in cycles; in each cycle a (single) signal can "cross" a wire connecting two gates and all gates can complete their computation. The work *time*, T, of the chip is the (worst case) number of cycles from the time the inputs were fed into the input ports until the result appears at the output port. The *area* A of the chip is simply $a \cdot b$. One of the main advantages that a designer of such a chip has is the ability to choose where to locate the ports and which input bit to feed into which input port as to make the chip layout efficient (in area and time). The following lemma gives a way to prove lower bounds on the quantity AT^2, using the measure D^{best} introduced in Section 7.2.

Lemma 8.11: *Suppose that there is a VLSI chip as above (with area A and time T) that computes a function f. Then $D^{best}(f) \le \sqrt{AT}$.*

PROOF: Assume that the chip is an $a \times b$ rectangle with $a \le b$. We can find a cut in the chip of length at most $a + 1 \le \sqrt{A} + 1$ that separates the input ports into two sets of size $m/2$. This is because we can "sweep" an imaginary line in parallel to the length a axis of the rectangle until reaching the maximal location where the number of input ports to the left of the imaginary line is at most $m/2$. Then, if this number is not exactly $m/2$ we may need to add a "shoulder" to our line, in order to get a cut as required (see Figure 8.3 for such a cut with a "shoulder").

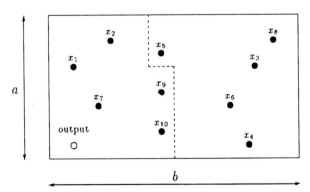

Figure 8.3: A chip partitioned into two parts.

With this cut in mind, we choose a partition of the m input bits between Alice and Bob exactly as the partition of input bits between the two sides of the cut. Alice and Bob simulate the chip, cycle by cycle, where each player is responsible for the simulation of one side of the chip. At each cycle the only information needed for continuing the simulation is the information that "crosses" the cut. By definition, the number of wires (and hence number of bits) that cross the cut is at most $|C|$, the size of the cut. Hence, in each of the T cycles this many bits could be sent, which gives $T \cdot |C| = O(T\sqrt{A})$ in total.

$\square$

▶ **Example 8.12:** Consider the "shifted equality" function (SEQ) for which we proved (Example 7.9) that $D^{best}(\text{SEQ}) = \Omega(m)$. By the above lemma, any VLSI chip for this function satisfies $AT^2 = \Omega(m^2)$.

Many other models for VLSI chips are discussed in the literature. The same type of bounds apply for most of them.

Exercise 8.13: Consider a model similar to the one defined above but in which many input bits can appear at the same input port at different, predefined, time units (still any particular input bit appears in a single input port). Prove that computing the function SEQ in this model still requires $AT^2 = \Omega(m^2)$.

8.4. Bibliographic Notes

For a discussion on the notion of bisection width and its applications for proving lower bounds in various architectures, see [Leighton 1991]. In Example 8.3, we use the fact that the nodes of any planar graph can be partitioned into two sets, each with at least $|V|/3$ nodes and with $O(\sqrt{|V|})$ edges connecting the two parts. This fact was proved in [Lipton and Tarjan 1980].

The question of total communications, discussed in Section 8.2, is due to [Tiwari 1984]. It is interesting to note that, in addition to the methods mentioned in Exercise 8.7, he proved that $D_k(f) \geq k \cdot \log rank(f)$. Hence, whenever the rank lower bound (Section 1.4) is tight, then $D_k = \Omega(k \cdot D(f))$. The largest known gap between $D_k(f)$ and $k \cdot D(f)$ is given by [Kushilevitz et al. 1995].

For an extensive survey on VLSI and especially of applications of communication complexity for VLSI, see [Lengauer 1990].

CHAPTER 9

Decision Trees and Data Structures

9.1. Decision Trees

One of the simplest models of computation is the decision tree model. In this model we are concerned with computing a function $f: \{0, 1\}^m \rightarrow \{0, 1\}$ by using queries. Each query is given by specifying a function q on $\{0, 1\}^m$ taken from some fixed family Q of allowed queries (the queries need not be Boolean). The answer given for the query is simply the value of $q(x_1, \ldots, x_m)$. The algorithm is completely adaptive, that is the i-th query asked may depend in an arbitrary manner on the answers received for the first $i - 1$ queries. The only way to gain information about the input x is through these queries. The algorithm can therefore be described as a labeled *tree*, whose nodes are labeled by queries $q \in Q$, the outgoing edges of each node are labeled by the possible values of $q(x_1, \ldots, x_m)$, and the leaves are labeled by output values. Each sequence of answers describes a path in the tree to a node that is either the next query or the value of the output. In Figure 9.1 a decision tree is shown that computes (on inputs $x_1, \ldots, x_4$) whether at least three of the input bits are 1s. It uses a family of queries Q consisting of all disjunctions of input variables and conjunctions of input variables.

The cost measure we are interested in is the number of queries performed on the worst case input; that is, the depth of the tree.

Definition 9.1: *The decision tree complexity of a function f using the family of queries Q, denoted $T_Q(f)$, is the minimum cost decision tree algorithm over Q for f.*

Recall the definition of the measure D^{worst} (Definition 7.1).

Lemma 9.2: *Denote $c_Q = max_{q \in Q} D^{worst}(q)$. Then, for all f, $T_Q(f) \geq D^{worst}(f)/c_Q$.*

PROOF: Fix an arbitrary partition of the input bits into two disjoint sets. Here is a possible communication protocol for f with this partition: Alice and Bob simulate the decision tree for f; each time they encounter a query q they compute $q(x_1, \ldots, x_m)$ using the best protocol for computing q with respect to that partition. This requires at

———— 114 ————

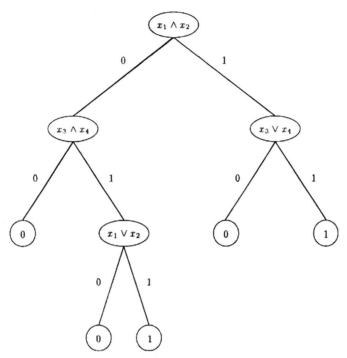

Figure 9.1: A decision tree

most c_Q bits, for all queries q and for all possible partitions. Because the tree has depth $T_Q(f)$, the whole simulation uses $c_Q \cdot T_Q(f)$ bits. Therefore, $D^{worst}(f) \leq c_Q \cdot T_Q(f)$.

$\square$

Decision trees are often used with queries that are just single variables (that is, of the type $q(x_1, \ldots, x_m) = x_i$). In this case, obviously $c_Q = 1$ so by Lemma 9.2, for all f, $T_Q(f) \geq D^{worst}(f)$. We now show that we can get good lower bounds on the decision tree complexity even when considering stronger families of queries.

▶ **Example 9.3:** Consider a decision tree whose queries are "unweighted threshold queries" (UT); that is queries of the form "$\sum_{i \in S} x_i > \theta$?" for some subset S of the input bits and integer θ. Then, $T_{UT}(\text{IP}) = \Omega(m/\log m)$, where $\text{IP}(x_1, \ldots, x_{\frac{m}{2}}; x_{\frac{m}{2}+1}, \ldots, x_m)$ is the inner product function defined in Example 1.25. The proof is immediate from the above lemma together with the communication complexity lower bound $D^{worst}(\text{IP}) = \Omega(m)$ (Example 1.25), and the upper bound $D^{worst}(\text{TH}_m^\theta) = O(\log m)$ (Example 7.4).

Exercise 9.4: Let a weighted threshold query (in WT) be of the form "$\sum_i w_i x_i > \theta$?" where w_i and θ are arbitrary reals. Show that $T_{WT}(\text{IP}) = \Omega(m/polylog(m))$. Hint: Use (1) the fact that without loss of generality, each w_i and θ are $O(m \log m)$-bit integers, and, (2) randomized communication complexity.

Exercise 9.5: Let $P(d, R)$ be the set of all degree d polynomials over the ring R (see Lemma 6.20). Prove that $T_{P(d, R)}(\text{GIP}_n^{d+1}) = \Omega(n/(4^d d \log |R|))$, where GIP is the generalized inner product function defined in Example 6.16. Hint: Use multiparty communication complexity and Example 7.6.

9.2. Data Structures and the Cell Probe Model

Suppose we want to implement a data structure that allows storing a "database" D in a way that queries in a certain family Q of queries can be answered. For example, we may want to store a k-element subset S of $\{1, \ldots, N\}$ such that we can answer *membership queries* of the form "$i \in S$?" for each i. A very abstract model for studying time/space tradeoffs in this setting is the cell probe model described below.

An implementation for the family Q in the cell probe model consists of a way of mapping a "database" D into s cells (numbered $1, \ldots, s$), where each cell consists of b bits of information (that is, D determines the values of all cells; however, this is not necessarily done by distributing the bits of D among the s cells). Each query q, in this model, is defined by a decision tree, where each node of the tree probes (that is, reads the value of) a single cell, and branches according to the 2^b different values that may appear in that cell. Each leaf is labeled by an answer to the query. The *time* used, t, is the maximum number of probes to the database needed; that is, the depth of the worst decision tree (over all possible queries $q \in Q$). Considering for example the case of membership queries, a simple solution, which requires a single step, is to use $s = N$ cells with the i-th cell indicating whether $i \in D$. However, we want to minimize the time while at the same time keeping the *space*, s, as small as possible.

Lemma 9.6: *Consider the function $f(q, D)$ defined as the answer to the query q on database D. Assume that there is an implementation that allows storing D using s cells of b bits each so that any query q can be solved using at most t probes. Then f can be computed by a t-round communication protocol where at each round Alice (who holds q) sends $\log s$ bits and Bob (who holds D) sends b bits.*

PROOF: Alice simulates the decision tree corresponding to the query q, starting from the root. Each probe is implemented by Alice sending the cell index to Bob ($\log s$ bits), Bob replying with the cell's content (b bits), and Alice updating her current node accordingly. Since there are at most t such probes, the lemma follows. $\qquad\square$

▶ **Example 9.7:** Suppose we want to store U, a vector subspace of Z_2^n, in such a way that for every vector $q \in \{0, 1\}^n$ we can answer the query "$q \in U$?". Consider the case where the cell size, b, is exactly n bits. One possible way to store the subspace U is by keeping a set of $n - dim(U)$ linear equations defining U. This requires a cell for each equation (since an equation in Z_2^n is described by n bits). On a query q, we need to access all cells and check whether q satisfies each of them. This requires in the worst case $s = n$ cells and the query time is $t = n$. Suppose we want to answer queries faster; that is, in $t = o(n)$ time. How many cells are needed?

To obtain a lower bound using communication complexity note that here $f(q, U)$ is exactly the SPAN problem discussed in Example 4.38, where it is shown that either Alice sends $\Omega(n)$ bits or Bob sends $\Omega(n^2)$ bits. By Lemma 9.6, an s cell solution would imply a protocol where Alice sends $t \log s$ bits and Bob sends tn bits. Since we wish to have $t = o(n)$, this implies that Bob sends $o(n^2)$ bits, and hence Alice must send $\Omega(n)$ bits. Thus $s \geq 2^{\Omega(n/t)}$.

Exercise 9.8: Show that for every value of $1 \leq t \leq n$, there exists a solution that uses only $s = t \cdot 2^{O(n/t)}$ cells.

9.3. Dynamic Data Structures

In the dynamic data-structure problem, we need to maintain a database D under various update operations, as to allow a set of queries Q. The model employed is again the cell probe model, described above, where, in addition, update operations may also change the values of cells. Thus each node in the decision tree for an (update or query) operation may also be a "store" node in which some value is written into a cell.

For any k we can associate with the dynamic problem a function $f_k(q, \vec{u})$, where $\vec{u} = u_1, \ldots, u_k$ is a sequence of k updates and q is a query. The value of f is the answer to that query after all updates in $\vec{u}$ have been performed on the initial content of the database. Clearly, maintaining a data structure that allows *dynamic* changes (and is not static, as is the case considered in the previous section) is only more difficult. The following lemma allows getting *time* lower bounds for dynamic data structures (in opposition to time–space tradeoffs we had in the static case).

Lemma 9.9: *If every update operation and every query operation can be performed in at most t probes, in the cell probe model with cell size b, then f_k has a communication protocol where Alice sends $O(t \log(kt))$ bits and Bob sends $O(t(b+\log|Q|)+\log(kt))$ bits.*

PROOF: Bob first simulates (with no communication) the sequence of updates $u_1, \ldots, u_k$ and fixes W to be the set of cells whose values were changed during these updates. Because during each update at most t cells may be written, we have $|W| \leq kt$. Bob then finds a prime p, $p \leq |W|^3$ such that for all $w, w' \in W$, $w \neq w' \mod p$, and sends p ($O(\log(kt))$ bits) to Alice (a random prime in the range $1, \ldots, |W|^3$ will have this property). Alice now simulates the decision tree corresponding to query q as follows.

Every probe into cell m is handled as follows. Alice sends $m \mod p$ to Bob. Bob finds the unique $w \in W$ such that $w = m \mod p$, if such w exists, and sends to Alice a "description of w" as well as the value stored in the cell w. Alice first checks whether $w = m$, and, if so, Bob has sent her the contents of cell m. Otherwise, if $w \neq m$, Alice knows that none of the update operations changed the value of cell m and thus its value is still the initial value that is known and fixed. In both cases she now has the value stored in cell m. For each of the t probes, Alice sends $m \mod p$, which is an $O(\log(kt))$ bit number, and Bob replies with b bits, and the amount of information needed to specify the name of the cell w. This can be done by simply sending the address of the cell ($\log s$ bits). Therefore, we get that Alice sends $O(t \log(kt))$ bits and Bob sends $O(t(b + \log s) + \log(kt))$ bits.

This complexity is small if we know that the number of cells, s, is small enough. However, it may be the case that the number of cells, s, is much larger than the number of queries $|Q|$ (because the database not only needs to keep the answers to all queries but it should also be possible to answer all queries after future updates to the database). In other words, the communication complexity of Bob that involves both t and s may be useful for getting time–space tradeoffs but is not useful if we wish to get time lower bounds. To get the complexity as in the statement of the lemma, Bob uses the following encoding of w with $\log |Q|$ bits. For this, Bob considers all the queries that are consistent with the communication so far. For each of these queries, there is the cell that is supposed to be probed next (according to the corresponding decision tree). Bob sends Alice the name of an arbitrary query q' on which the next probe is w (or says that no such q' exists). Notice that if $m = w$, then such a query exists ($q' = q$) and so Alice gets the value w. If $m \neq w$, either Bob says that he does not find an appropriate query, or Alice will know that $m \neq w$ by determining the cell w that is probed by q'.   □

▶ **Example 9.10:** Suppose we want to maintain a vector subspace $U \subseteq Z_2^n$ under an update operation: $add(u)$ which replaces U by $span(U \cup \{u\})$, so as to allow the single query $dim(U)$ which returns the dimension of U. Assume again that the cell size, b, is n. First, observe that any solution to this problem also allows answering queries of the form "$q \in U$?" for any given vector $q \in Z_2^n$, because such a query can be simulated by asking the query $dim(U)$ before and after adding q to U. Therefore, it is sufficient to prove a lower bound for the later problem.

The function $f_n(q, \vec{u})$ for queries of the type "$q \in U$?" is equivalent to the SPAN problem (Example 4.38), where here the subspace is not necessarily given by a basis but by any set of vectors. Thus, any protocol for it requires $\Omega(n^2)$ bits from Bob or $\Omega(n)$ bits from Alice. In both cases, by Lemma 9.9 (with $|Q| = 2^n$), the number of probes needed is $t = \Omega(n/\log n)$.

9.4. Bibliographic Notes

Proving lower bounds for decision trees using communication complexity was introduced explicitly in [Nisan 1993] and implicitly in [Groger and Turan 1991], where a slightly better bounds than those given in Example 9.3 and Exercise 9.4 are proven. The first hint of Exercise 9.4 is due to [Muroga 1971]. A proof can also be found in [Goldmann, Håstad, and Razborov 1992].

The first lower bounds for data structures, in the static case, were proven for the range-query problem in [Ajtai 1988]. Additional such proofs were given in [Xiao 1992, Miltersen 1994, Miltersen 1995]. The connection to communication complexity was discovered by [Miltersen 1995]. The dynamic case was discussed in [Miltersen et al. 1995], where, in particular, Examples 9.7 and 9.10 were given.

CHAPTER 10

Boolean Circuit Depth

In this chapter we present interesting connections between communication complexity and the depth of Boolean circuits. Using these connections, several results regarding circuits depth are proven.

10.1. Introduction

In this section we provide the definitions of Boolean circuits, the way these circuits compute functions, and their complexity measures.

Definition 10.1: *Let $z_1, \ldots, z_n$ be a set of variables. A* Boolean circuit *is a directed acyclic graph with two types of nodes*: (1) *nodes with in-degree 0, called the* input nodes, *each is labeled by either a variable z_i or a negated variable $\bar{z}_i$, and* (2) *nodes with in-degree 2, called* gates, *each is labeled by a Boolean operation–either $\vee$ (logical OR) or $\wedge$ (logical AND). There is a single node with out-degree 0 that is called the* output node.

A monotone circuit *is a circuit in which all input nodes are labeled by variables (and none is labeled by a negated variable $\bar{z}_i$).*

A circuit in which each node has out-degree 1 (except for the output node) is called a formula. *(Note that we allow many input nodes to have the same label).*

Definition 10.2: *The* function computed by a Boolean circuit *is defined inductively in the natural way: the function computed by an input node is $g(z_1, \ldots, z_n) = z_i$ if the node is labeled z_i and $g(z_1, \ldots, z_n) = \bar{z}_i$ if the node is labeled $\bar{z}_i$. For the gates: if one of the two nodes entering the gate computes the function $g_1(z_1, \ldots, z_n)$ and the other node computes the function $g_2(z_1, \ldots, z_n)$ then the gate computes the function*

$$g(z_1, \ldots, z_n) = g_1(z_1, \ldots, z_n) \vee g_2(z_1, \ldots, z_n)$$

if the gate is labeled $\vee$ and it computes

$$g(z_1, \ldots, z_n) = g_1(z_1, \ldots, z_n) \wedge g_2(z_1, \ldots, z_n)$$

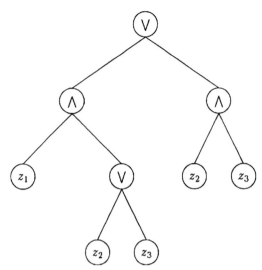

Figure 10.1: A circuit

if it is labeled $\wedge$. The function computed by the circuit is the function corresponding to its output node. (Note that in this definition we use the fact that the circuit is described by an acyclic directed graph.)

For example, in Figure 10.1 a circuit is presented whose input is 3 variables z_1, z_2, and z_3 (all edges are directed upward; the bottom nodes are the input nodes and the top node is the output node). The function computed by the circuit is 1 iff at least 2 of the 3 variables are 1s. Note that the circuit is monotone. In fact, it is also a formula.

Observe that for every Boolean function $f: \{0, 1\}^n \to \{0, 1\}$ there is a circuit computing it. For example, we can write f in disjunctive-normal-form and generate the corresponding circuit. In fact, the resulting circuit is even a formula. However, this circuit may be huge.

Exercise 10.3: For $x, y \in \{0,1\}^n$ we say that $x \leq y$ if for all i, $x_i \leq y_i$. A function $f: \{0,1\}^n \to \{0,1\}$ is called monotone if $x \leq y$ implies $f(x) \leq f(y)$. Prove that (1) the function computed by a monotone circuit is monotone, and (2) for every monotone function there is a monotone circuit computing it. Note: This does *not* say that a monotone function cannot be computed by a nonmonotone circuit.

Naturally, we are interested in finding small circuits. We now define (some of) the measures of complexity for circuits and functions:

Definition 10.4: *The depth of a circuit C, denoted $d(C)$, is the length of the longest path from the output node to an input node. The size of a formula F, denoted $L(F)$, is the number of input nodes.*

For a function f, the depth complexity $d(f)$ is the minimum depth of a circuit computing f and the size complexity $L(f)$ is the minimum size of a formula computing f.

For the special case of monotone circuits and monotone functions, the measures $d_m(C)$, $L_m(F)$, $d_m(f)$, and $L_m(f)$ are defined in a similar way.

The definition given here assumes that circuits contain only $\vee$, $\wedge$ gates. Allowing other types of gates, for example $\oplus$-gate (exclusive-or), usually have only a small influence on the complexity of the circuits (particularly their depth) for a given function f. Also, the (nonmonotone version of the) definition allows using negations only on the input variables. Once again, circuits that use negations in internal nodes can be converted to circuits with negations only on the variables without changing the complexity significantly.

10.2. The Connection to Communication Complexity

We now present a connection between Boolean circuits and the communication complexity of relations (see Chapter 5). To define the connection, it is useful to think of Boolean circuits not as a tool to compute functions but rather as a tool to separate between two sets (by outputting 0 on elements of one set and 1 on the elements of the other set). We will associate with every Boolean function $f: \{0, 1\}^n \to \{0, 1\}$ a relation R_f. We will show that there is an isomorphism between Boolean circuits that compute f and communication protocols that compute R_f. This isomorphism has some nice properties, in particular, the depth of the circuit and the number of bits exchanged in the corresponding protocol are equal. This will imply that $d(f) = D(R_f)$. Formally:

Definition 10.5: *For a Boolean function $f: \{0, 1\}^n \to \{0, 1\}$ let $X = f^{-1}(1)$ (that is, the set of all xs such that $f(x) = 1$) and $Y = f^{-1}(0)$. Let $R_f \subseteq X \times Y \times \{1, \ldots, n\}$ consist of all triples (x, y, i) such that $x_i \neq y_i$. If, in addition, f is monotone we also define $M_f \subseteq X \times Y \times \{1, \ldots, n\}$ as all triples (x, y, i) such that $x_i = 1$ and $y_i = 0$.*

Observe that, both in the definition of R_f and in the definition of M_f, for all (x, y) there is always an i such that (x, y, i) satisfies the relation (in the case of R_f because $f(x) = 1$ and $f(y) = 0$, then $x \neq y$; in the case of M_f, if no such i exists, then $y \geq x$. Hence, because $f(x) = 1$ by the monotonicity also $f(y) = 1$ –a contradiction). As an example, consider the parity function $\oplus(z_1, \ldots, z_n)$. The corresponding relation $R_\oplus$ is exactly the relation defined in Example 5.8.

Lemma 10.6: *For every circuit C for f there is a corresponding protocol $\mathcal{P}$ for R_f in which at most $d(C)$ bits are exchanged.*

PROOF: The idea of the protocol is the following: Alice and Bob traverse the nodes of the circuit C, starting from the output node and continuing toward the input nodes, while maintaining the following invariant: the function g computed by the current node satisfies $g(x) = 1$ and $g(y) = 0$.
    Because $x \in f^{-1}(1)$ and $y \in f^{-1}(0)$, the invariant is true at the beginning (that is, at the output node). Suppose that the current node is an OR-gate computing a function g.

Let g_1 and g_2 be the functions corresponding to the nodes entering the current node. By definition,

$$g(z_1, \ldots, z_n) = g_1(z_1, \ldots, z_n) \vee g_2(z_1, \ldots, z_n).$$

Hence, because $g(y) = 0$, also $g_1(y) = g_2(y) = 0$. In addition, because $g(x) = 1$, either $g_1(x) = 1$ or $g_2(x) = 1$ (or both). Alice, who knows x, sends a single bit indicating for which i ($i \in \{1, 2\}$) $g_i(x) = 1$ (if both are 1 she chooses, say, g_1) and they both proceed to the corresponding node, which obviously satisfies the invariant. Symmetrically, if the current node is an AND-gate computing a function g, and g_1 and g_2 are the functions corresponding to the nodes entering the current node, then because $g(x) = 1$ we get $g_1(x) = g_2(x) = 1$. In addition, because $g(y) = 0$, either $g_1(y) = 0$ or $g_2(y) = 0$ (or both). This time Bob sends a single bit indicating for which i ($i \in \{1, 2\}$) $g_i(y) = 0$ and they both proceed to the corresponding node.

Finally, when the players reach an input node, labeled by either z_i or $\bar{z}_i$ they both know that i is an appropriate output. This is because, if the node is labeled z_i, then by the invariant $x_i = 1$ and $y_i = 0$, and if the node is labeled $\bar{z}_i$, then by the invariant $x_i = 0$ and $y_i = 1$.

The number of bits exchanged in the protocol is bounded by the length of the longest path from the output node to an input node, that is $d(C)$. ☐

Figure 10.2 shows the protocol (and the corresponding partition into monochromatic rectangles) obtained by applying Lemma 10.6 to the circuit of Figure 10.1. The relation corresponding to the function f of Figure 10.1 is defined by $X = \{101, 111, 110, 011\}$ and $Y = \{100, 000, 001, 010\}$. Note, that the 5 input nodes of the circuit correspond to the 5 monochromatic rectangles induced by the protocol.

Lemma 10.7: *For every protocol $\mathcal{P}$ for R_f there is a corresponding circuit C for f such that $d(C)$ is at most the communication complexity of $\mathcal{P}$.*

PROOF: Given the protocol $\mathcal{P}$, consider the corresponding protocol tree (as in Definition 1.1). Convert this tree into a circuit as follows: each internal node in which Alice sends a bit (that is, a node labeled by a function of x) is labeled by $\vee$ and each internal

	100	000	001	010
101	3	1	1	1
111	2	1	1	1
110	2	1	1	1
011	2	2	2	3

Figure 10.2: The protocol (and partition) induced by Lemma 10.6

node in which Bob sends a bit is labeled by $\wedge$. In addition, each leaf of the tree is a monochromatic rectangle $A \times B$ with whom an output i is associated. We claim that either (1) for all $x \in A$, $x_i = 1$ and for all $y \in B$, $y_i = 0$, in which case this leaf is labeled by z_i; or (2) for all $x \in A$, $x_i = 0$ and for all $y \in B$, $y_i = 1$, in which case this leaf is labeled by $\bar{z}_i$. To see this, take any $x \in A$ and let $x_i = \sigma$. Because for all $y \in B$ the value i is a legal output on (x, y), then this implies that for all $y \in B$, $y_i = \bar{\sigma}$. This in turn implies that for *all* $x \in A$, $x_i = \sigma$.

Obviously, the depth of the circuit equals the depth of the protocol tree; that is, the worst case number of bits exchanged in the protocol. It remains to prove that the circuit computes the function f. It is sufficient to prove that for every node of the circuit, the function g corresponding to that node satisfies $g(z) = 1$ for all $z \in A$ and $g(z) = 0$ for all $z \in B$, where $A \times B$ are the inputs that reach the corresponding node of the protocol. This immediately implies that the function computed by the output node is f, because it is 1 for all inputs in $f^{-1}(1)$ and 0 for all inputs in $f^{-1}(0)$.

The claim is proved by induction starting from the input nodes toward the output node. It is true in the input nodes because this is the way in which the labels of these nodes are defined. Now, consider an internal node computing a function g such that the claim was already proved for its two children (computing the functions g_1 and g_2). Let $A \times B$ be the inputs reaching this node in the protocol tree. Assume, without loss of generality, that Alice sends a bit in this node (the case that Bob sends a bit is symmetric). Her bit partitions A into A_1 and A_2. By the induction hypothesis, for all $y \in B$, $g_1(y) = g_2(y) = 0$; for all $x \in A_1$, $g_1(x) = 1$; and for all $x \in A_2$, $g_2(x) = 1$. By the construction,

$$g(z_1, \ldots, z_n) = g_1(z_1, \ldots, z_n) \vee g_2(z_1, \ldots, z_n).$$

Hence, g satisfies $g(y) = 0$ for all $y \in B$ and $g(x) = 1$ for all $x \in A = A_1 \cup A_2$. $\square$

Note that applying the transformation of Lemma 10.7 on the protocol described by Figure 10.2 gives the circuit of Figure 10.1.

Applying Lemma 10.6 and Lemma 10.7 to the optimal circuit and to the optimal protocol (respectively) we get:

Theorem 10.8: $d(f) = D(R_f)$.

Recall that we proved in Lemma 2.8 that $D(R) = \Theta(\log C^P(R))$ (in fact this was proved in the context of functions but extends as it is to relations). A similar proof can be applied to formulae proving that $d(f) = \Theta(\log L(f))$ (one direction, showing that $d(f) \geq \log L(f)$ is trivial). Hence, we get that $L(f) = \Theta(C^P(R_f))$. This connection can be made even tighter:

Exercise 10.9: Prove that $L(f) = C^P(R_f)$. Hint: The above constructions have the desired properties.

Exercise 10.10: Let f be a monotone function. Prove that $d_m(f) = D(M_f)$ and $L_m(f) = C^P(M_f)$. Hint: The above constructions have the desired properties.

With this connection between communication complexity and circuits we can now use the examples presented in Chapter 5. In particular, from Lemma 5.9 we get the so-called Khrapchenko's Bound:

Corollary 10.11: *Let $f: \{0, 1\}^n \rightarrow \{0, 1\}$ be any Boolean function. Let $X \subseteq f^{-1}(1)$, $Y \subseteq f^{-1}(0)$, and $C = \{(x, y): x \in X, y \in Y, d(x, y) = 1\}$. Then $L(f) \geq \frac{|C|^2}{|X||Y|}$.*

From Example 5.8 and the discussion following Lemma 5.9 we get

Corollary 10.12: *The parity function $\oplus(z_1, \ldots, z_n)$ satisfies $d(\oplus) = 2 \log n$ and $L(\oplus) = n^2$.*

Exercise 10.13: The *majority* function, MAJ: $\{0,1\}^n \rightarrow \{0,1\}$ is defined to be 1 iff the number of 1s among the input variables is larger than the number of 0s. Prove that $d(\text{MAJ}) = O(\log n)$. Hint: Use Exercise 5.10.

10.3. Matching and *ST*-Connectivity

The question of proving good bounds ($\omega(\log n)$) on $d(f)$ for any explicit function f is a long standing open problem in computational complexity that goes back to Shannon. We do know however to prove such lower bounds on the depth of *monotone* circuits. In this section, we show two such proofs that use lower bounds on the communication complexity of the corresponding relations M_f.

▶ **Example 10.14:** A *matching* in a graph $G = (V, E)$ is a set of edges in the graph such that no pair of them has a common vertex. The function MATCH is the following: Given a graph G on n vertices, represented by $n' = \binom{n}{2}$ Boolean variables (each indicating whether a certain edge (i, j) appears in the graph or not), MATCH$(G) = 1$ if there is a matching of size at least $n/3$ in G and MATCH$(G) = 0$ if no such matching exists. Note that MATCH is a monotone function. Assume, without loss of generality, that n is divisible by 3, that is $n = 3m$. We will prove a lower bound on $d_m(\text{MATCH})$ of $\Omega(n) = \Omega(\sqrt{n'})$ by proving such a lower bound on $D(M_{\text{MATCH}})$. Recall, that the relation M_{MATCH} is defined by letting X be the set of all graphs with a matching of size m, and Y be the set of all graphs with no such matching. Alice is given $x \in X$, Bob is given $y \in Y$, and they have to find an edge that is in the graph x but is not in the graph y (that is, an index i such that $x_i = 1$ and $y_i = 0$).

The first step is to concentrate on a relation M' that is the same as M_{MATCH} but on a restricted domain $X' \times Y'$, where $X' \subset X$ and $Y' \subset Y$. Clearly, $D(M') \leq D(M_{\text{MATCH}})$. Let X' be the set of all graphs on n vertices that are matchings of size m (that is, the graph consists only of m, mutually disjoint edges). The set Y' consists of all graphs in which the vertices are partitioned into two sets S of size $m - 1$ and T of size $2m + 1$, and the edges are all the pairs in which at least one vertex is in S (in other words, every vertex in S is connected to all vertices in the graph, whereas the set T is an independent set). Such a graph cannot contain a matching of size m because every edge has at least one vertex in S and there are only $m - 1$ such vertices. Hence, $Y' \subset Y$.

Next we show how a protocol for M' can be used to solve the pair–disjointness relation defined in Section 5.2. Alice, given a list P of m mutually disjoint pairs (of elements in $\{1, \ldots, 3m\}$), transforms it into a matching of size m (in a graph with $n = 3m$ vertices), hence obtaining $x \in X'$. Bob, given a set S of $m-1$ elements (in $\{1, \ldots, 3m\}$), transforms it into the graph $y \in Y'$ corresponding to this set S. They use the protocol for M' to find an edge that is in x but not in y. By the definition of graphs in Y', the only missing edges in y are those in which both elements are not in S. Hence, the output of the protocol determines a pair of P that contains no elements of S. Finally, Alice sends the index of this pair in the list P ($\log m$ bits). Hence we get $D(M) \leq D(M') + \log m$. By Section 5.2, $D(M) = \Omega(m)$. All together we have

$$d_m(\text{MATCH}) = D(M_{\text{MATCH}}) \geq D(M') \geq D(M) - \log m = \Omega(m) = \Omega(n).$$

▶ **Example 10.15:** The s-t-connectivity function STCON is defined as follows: Given a *directed* graph G on n nodes, two of which are marked as s (source) and t (target), STCON$(G) = 1$ if there is a directed path in the graph G connecting s and t and otherwise STCON$(G) = 0$ (without loss of generality assume that $s = 1$ and $t = n$). Note that STCON is a monotone function. The corresponding monotone relation M_{STCON} is defined by letting X be all the directed graphs with a directed path from vertex 1 to vertex n, Y be all the directed graphs with no directed path from vertex 1 to vertex n, and the task of Alice and Bob is given $x \in X$ and $y \in Y$ to find an edge that appears in x but not in y.

Once again, our first step will be restricting the domain of the relation to some $X' \subset X$ and $Y' \subset Y$. We define a relation M that is identical to M_{STCON} on $X' \times Y'$, hence $D(M) \leq D(M_{\text{STCON}})$. The domains X' and Y' are obtained by restricting our attention to layered graphs that consist of $\ell + 2$ layers $0, 1, \ldots, \ell, \ell + 1$ each of them with w vertices, where $\ell + 2 = w = \sqrt{n}$. Each edge connects a vertex in some layer i to a vertex in the adjacent layer $i + 1$, where the source (vertex 1) belongs to layer 0 and the target (vertex n) belongs to layer $\ell + 1$.

Finally, we prove that $D(M) \geq D(\text{FORK})$, where FORK is the relation defined in Section 5.3. Suppose we are given a protocol for M, then Alice and Bob can solve the relation FORK as follows: Alice considers her string $a \in \{1, \ldots, w\}^\ell$ as a directed path from s to t (this will be her graph x) by choosing from each layer i the vertex a_i and connecting them (for example, in Figure 10.3 the solid edges show the path Alice

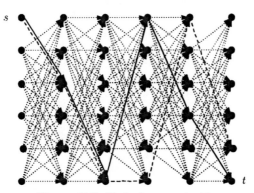

Figure 10.3: Reducing FORK to M

constructs on input $a = 3614$). Bob considers his string $b \in \{1, \ldots, w\}^\ell$ as a path p from s to another vertex in the last layer (say $n - 1$), and constructs a graph $y \in Y'$ that contains this path (the dashed edges in Figure 10.3 denote the path corresponding to $b = 3661$) and, in addition, edges connecting each vertex *not* in the path to all the vertices in the next layer (these are the dotted edges in Figure 10.3). Observe that the path corresponding to b does not reach t and hence s is not connected to t in the graph y, as desired (the only vertices connected to s in the graph y are those on the path). Now Alice and Bob use the protocol for M on x and y and get as an output an edge (u, v) that appears in x but not in y. In addition, u belongs to some layer i and v belongs to layer $i + 1$. We claim that i is a legal output for the FORK relation. This is because (u, v) belongs to the path a (those are the only edges in x) and in addition u belongs to b but v does not (because these are the only edges missing in y). Since this is a protocol for FORK we have

$$d_m(\text{STCON}) = D(M_{\text{STCON}}) \geq D(M) \geq D(\text{FORK}) = \Omega(\log^2 n).$$

Exercise 10.16: Recall the undirected s-t-connectivity function USTCON (Exercise 7.15). This function is similar to STCON but with respect to *undirected* graphs. That is, given an *undirected* graph G on n nodes, two of which are marked as s and t, we define USTCON(G) $= 1$ iff there is a path connecting s and t. Prove that $d_m(\text{USTCON}) = \Omega(\log^2 n)$. Hint: Use the relation FORK' (Exercise 5.21).

10.4. Set Cover

In this section we present a general technique that allows using any function $g: \{0, 1\}^n \times \{0, 1\}^n \to \{0, 1\}$ whose (deterministic) communication complexity $D(g)$ is significantly larger than its nondeterministic communication complexity $N(g)$ to construct a function $f: \{0, 1\}^l \to \{0, 1\}$ for which a nontrivial lower bound on the size of monotone circuits can be given. Using this technique, we prove such a lower bound on the set-cover problem (to be defined). Functions that may serve as g are given, for example, in Examples 2.12 and 4.13.

Let g be a function as above, and let $R_1, \ldots, R_t$ be a cover (possibly with intersections) of the matrix corresponding to g, M_g, with monochromatic rectangles. Clearly, this implies that $N(g) \leq \log t$. We define a relation $M \subseteq \{0, 1\}^n \times \{0, 1\}^n \times \{1, \ldots, t\}$ that consists of all triples (x, y, i) such that $(x, y) \in R_i$. Note that because we started with a cover of the matrix M_g, then for every (x, y) there exists such an i but because the rectangles in the cover may intersect, there may be more than a single i that satisfies the relation. Obviously $D(g) \leq D(M)$ because given (x, y) Alice and Bob can compute M and get as an output a name of a monochromatic rectangle to which (x, y) belongs. The value in this rectangle is $g(x, y)$.

The next step is to construct a function $f: \{0, 1\}^l \to \{0, 1\}$ such that $D(M_f) \geq D(M)$. We can think of the input to f as a subset of $R_1, \ldots, R_t$. Let $f(z_1, \ldots, z_t)$ be 1 if there exists a row x of the matrix M_g such that for all i if $x \in R_i$, then $z_i = 1$. If no such row exists, then $f(z_1, \ldots, z_t) = 0$. Obviously f is monotone. We now show

how M can be solved using a protocol for the relation M_f. Alice, given $x \in \{0, 1\}^n$, constructs $x' \in \{0, 1\}^t$ by assigning $x'_i = 1$ if the row x belongs to R_i and 0 otherwise. By the definition, $f(x') = 1$ (because x is a row of the matrix M_g as required). Bob, given $y \in \{0, 1\}^n$, constructs $y' \in \{0, 1\}^t$ by assigning $y'_i = 0$ if the column y belongs to R_i and 1 otherwise. We get that $f(y') = 0$ because for every row x the entry (x, y) is uncovered (all the rectangles that cover it were assigned $y'_i = 0$). Now, Alice and Bob use the protocol for the relation M_f on (x', y') and get as an output an index i such that $x'_i = 1$ and $y'_i = 0$. This implies, by the definitions of x' and y', that both the row x and the column y intersect R_i. Therefore, i is a legal output for the relation M as well. So if we start, for example, with a function g such that $D(g) = N^2(g)$, then the function f has $t = 2^{N(g)}$ variables and $d_m(f) = D(M_f) \geq D(g) = \log^2 t$. Similarly $L(f) = \Omega(t^{\log t})$. Note that we can write the function f as:

$$f(z_1, \ldots, z_t) \equiv \exists x \in \{0, 1\}^n : [(x \in R_1) \Rightarrow (z_1 = 1)] \wedge \cdots \wedge [(x \in R_t) \Rightarrow (z_t = 1)].$$

If deciding "$x \in R_i$" can be done in time polynomial (in t), then this implies that f is a function in NP (also note that $x = x_1 x_2 \cdots x_n$ can be thought of as a collection of n Boolean variables). In such a case, f can be translated in a standard way to a 3-CNF form. Namely, it can be written as

$$f(z_1, \ldots, z_t) \equiv \exists x_1 \cdots x_p : \phi_1 \wedge \phi_2 \wedge \cdots \wedge \phi_s,$$

where $x_{n+1}, \ldots, x_p$ are auxiliary variables, each of $\phi_1, \ldots, \phi_s$ is a disjunction of 3 literals on the variables $x_1, \ldots, x_p$, and both p and s are polynomial in t.

Before going any further consider, for example, the function $\text{LNE}_{\sqrt{n}, \sqrt{n}}$ (Example 4.13) and the "simple" cover for it. It consists of the $2^{O(\sqrt{n})}$ 0-rectangles R_{j, x^j} that contain all the pairs (x, y) such that the j-th block of both x and y is x^j, and the $2^{O(\sqrt{n} \log n)}$ 1-rectangles $R_{i_1, b_1, \ldots, i_{\sqrt{n}}, b_{\sqrt{n}}}$ that contain all the pairs (x, y) such that, for all k, in the k-th block of x the i_k-th bit is b_k, whereas in the k-th block of y the i_k-th bit is $\bar{b}_k$. This cover is *not* the optimal cover (see Example 4.5) but it is convenient to work with these rectangles because for each of them testing whether "$x \in R_i$" is very simple.

Now consider a function f in NP as above, we will show that it can be reduced to the set-cover problem. This, again, is a standard fact that appears here for the sake of completeness. The set-cover problem is the following: given a collection of m sets over a universe of ℓ elements and a number d, is there a subcollection of d sets that cover the whole universe. The reduction from f to the set-cover problem is done by letting the universe be of size $s + p$. One element corresponding to each of $\phi_1, \ldots, \phi_s$ and an additional p element are associated with the terms $x_i \vee \bar{x}_i$. Define a set $A_{x_i=1}$ that consists of all the terms in which x_i appears (out of the above $s + p$ terms) and similarly a set $A_{x_i=0}$ that consists of all the terms in which $\bar{x}_i$ appears. Finally, set $d = p$. We claim that if f is 1, then there exists an assignment for $x_1, \ldots, x_p$ that satisfies all the terms. It is easy to verify that the corresponding p sets form a cover. On the other hand, if there is a cover, note that for each i at least one of $A_{x_i=1}$ and $A_{x_i=0}$ is in the cover (because we have to cover the term $x_i \vee \bar{x}_i$) and because $d = p$ this implies that actually exactly one of these two sets is in the cover. Therefore, the cover induces an assignment that is a satisfying assignment by the construction.

Finally, if the reduction itself can be performed in a small (for example, $O(\log t)$) depth, which is the case with the function LNE (due to the simplicity of its rectangles), then this implies that monotone circuits for set-cover also require $\Omega(\log^2 t)$ depth. This is because a circuit for f can be constructed by combining a circuit for set-cover with circuits for the reduction. Hence,

$$d_m(\text{set-cover}) \geq d(f) - O(\log t) = \Omega(\log^2 t).$$

10.5. Monotone Constant-Depth Circuits

The connection between Boolean circuits and communication complexity can be further extended using the same isomorphism presented in Section 10.2. In particular, we want to examine unbounded fan-in circuits (in oppose to the (bounded) fan-in 2 circuits considered so far). Note that definitions like $d(C)$ and $L(F)$ still hold. We will keep using the notations $d(f)$ and $L(f)$, although in this section we mean the best circuit over all unbounded fan-in circuits. It is still the case that $L(F)$, the size of a formula F, translates to the protocol partition number $C^P(f)$. The depth however is not equal to the communication complexity anymore but rather to the *rounds* complexity of the protocol (Section 4.2). This is because now at each step, if the players are at node v, it is not enough to send one bit to indicate which child of v they should continue with, but rather they need $\log(\text{fan-in}(v))$ bits.

The following example shows a function that has a "small" monotone circuit of depth k, but any depth $k - 1$ monotone circuit for it has an exponential size.

▶ **Example 10.17:** Let $n = m^k$. We start by defining a function $f: \{0, 1\}^n \to \{0, 1\}$. We do so by describing an appropriate depth k formula. The formula consists of a complete m-ary tree of depth k. Each of its m^k leaves is given a distinct label out of $\{x_1, \ldots, x_n\}$. The gates in odd levels (including the root at level 1) are labeled $\wedge$, and the gates in even levels are labeled $\vee$. Obviously, by the way we define it, f has a depth k monotone formula of size $n = m^k$. To give a lower bound on the size of a $k - 1$ depth formula for f we consider the relation M_f and show that $C^{P,k-1}(M_f)$ is large (that is, the partition induced by any $k - 1$ round-protocol for M_f is large). Note that if we prove that $D^{k-1}(M_f)$ is at least some value b, then the number of rectangles in the protocol partition is $\Omega(2^{b/(k-1)})$, because this implies that in some node of the protocol at least $b/(k - 1)$ bits must be sent.

To prove a lower bound on the communication complexity of M_f, we use the lower bound for the tree problem, T_k, of Example 4.30. Namely, we show that $D^{k-1}(T_k) \leq D^{k-1}(M_f)$ (recall that $D^{k-1}(T_k) = \Omega(m/polylog(m))$). To do so, we show how Alice and Bob can compute T_k using a protocol for M_f. Recall that in the problem T_k there is a complete depth-k m-ary tree. Bob has the labeling of each node in an odd level by a number in $\{1, \ldots, m\}$ (that can be interpreted as a pointer to one of its m children), and similarly Alice has the labeling of each node in an even level by a number in $\{1, \ldots, m\}$. These labels define a unique path from the root to one of the leafs. The goal is to find this leaf. Now, Alice computes a sequence of sets $S_1, \ldots, S_k$ inductively as follows: S_1

contains only the root of the tree. If i is even, then for each node $v \in S_i$ include in S_{i+1} the child of v defined by the labeling given to Alice. If i is odd, then for each node $v \in S_i$ include in S_{i+1} all the children of v. Hence, each set S_i is just a subset of the nodes in level i. Symmetrically, Bob computes a sequence of sets $Q_1, \ldots, Q_k$ as follows: Q_1 contains only the root of the tree. If i is even, then for each node $v \in Q_i$ include in Q_{i+1} all children of v. If i is odd, then for each node $v \in Q_i$ include in Q_{i+1} the child of v defined by the labeling given to Bob. Alice computes a string x of length n by putting 1 in all coordinates j for $j \in S_k$ and 0 elsewhere and Bob computes a string y of length n by putting 0 in all coordinates j for $j \in Q_k$ and 1 elsewhere (all this is done without any communication). Finally, Alice and Bob use the protocol for M_f on (x, y) and output the result.

To prove the correctness of the above protocol, we first claim that $f(x) = 1$ and $f(y) = 0$. To prove $f(x) = 1$, it is enough to prove (inductively) that if each node in S_{i+1} computes the value 1, then so do all nodes in S_i. This is enough because we start with an x in which all nodes in S_k are assigned 1 and applying this claim k times we get that the nodes in S_1 (which is just the root of the circuit) compute 1, then the value of S_1 is exactly the value of the circuit. The claim itself follows from the definition of the sets: for each node v in S_i if it is marked by $\vee$ (that is, i is even), then one of its children is in S_{i+1}, hence it is assigned 1 and so is v. If v is marked $\wedge$ (that is, i is odd), then all of its children are in S_{i+1}, hence because all of them are assigned 1 then so is v. In a symmetric way we prove $f(y) = 0$ by proving that if each node in Q_{i+1} computes 0, then so do all nodes in Q_i. Finally, we will prove that there is exactly one place where $x_j = 1$ and $y_j = 0$ and this is the variable corresponding to the leaf that the path defined by the input T_k reaches. To see this, it is enough to prove that for all i, $S_i \cap Q_i$ includes a single node v_i, which is the node in level i that the path from the root reaches. It is obviously true for $i = 1$. Also, if it is true for i, then in one of the sets, say S_{i+1}, we put all the children of nodes in S_i, whereas in Q_{i+1} we put only those that are defined by the labeling. Therefore because $v_i \in S_i \cap Q_i$, then the next node on the path v_{i+1} is in $S_{i+1} \cap Q_{i+1}$. In addition, if v is a node in $S_{i+1} \cap Q_{i+1}$, then its father is in $S_i \cap Q_i$, which means that it can only be v_i and hence that $v = v_{i+1}$.

To conclude, for any constant k, the size of any depth $k - 1$ formula for f is

$$C^{P,k-1}(M_f) = \Omega\left(2^{D^{k-1}(M_f)/(k-1)}\right) = \Omega\left(2^{D^{k-1}(T_k)/(k-1)}\right) = \Omega\left(2^{m/polylog(m)}\right).$$

10.6. Bibliographic Notes

Boolean circuits are widely used in practice and hence understanding their complexity is of great importance. Although there has been a lot of success by hardware designers in developing efficient circuits, the lower bounds achieved thus far for unrestricted circuits (for example, nonmonotonic) seem somewhat pathetic (for excellent sources of various results see [Wegener 1987, Dunne 1988, Håstad 1986, Boppana and Sipser 1990, Karchmer 1989] and the references therein). It appears that Boolean circuits induce complicated combinatorial structures and that new approaches are required.

The approach presented here, which uses communication complexity of relations, is due to [Karchmer and Wigderson 1988]. They showed the isomorphism between circuits and communication complexity of the appropriate relations, proved most of the basic results and the lower bound for STCON. The proof presented here is simpler than their original proof and is based on a paper of [Gringi and Sipser 1991]. Khrapchenko's Bound (Corollary 10.11) was first proved, without using communication complexity arguments, in [Khrapchenko 1971]. The lower bound for MATCH is due to [Raz and Wigderson 1990] and the lower bound for Set-Cover is due to [Razborov 1990b] (for some standard facts about the complexity class *NP* such as translation of *NP* functions into 3-CNF form, and reductions from 3-CNF to Set-Cover, see for example [Garey and Johnson 1979]). Separations in monotone constant-depth circuits were first shown in [Klawe et al. 1984] and later in [Nisan and Wigderson 1991] and by Yannakakis (unpublished).

Related results were proved in [Håstad and Wigderson 1993, Karchmer et al. 1991, Edmonds et al. 1991].

CHAPTER 11

More Boolean Circuit
Lower Bounds

In this chapter we describe several other ways to use communication complexity for proving various results on Boolean circuits. These results differ from those in Chapter 10 in that they do not use the connection between the circuit complexity of f and the communication complexity of the corresponding relation R_f and in that the circuits considered here are not restricted to use only $\vee$ and $\wedge$ gates but instead use richer families of gates.

11.1. Small Circuits

A Q-circuit is a directed acyclic graph whose gates are taken from a fixed family of gates Q. Each of the gates in the family takes as an input a sequence of bits that are either inputs of the circuit or outputs of previously computed gates and its output is also a bit. The circuit defines a function over $\{0, 1\}^m$ in the natural way. The cost of a circuit here is its size (the number of gates). The results proved in this section can be thought of as an extension of the results proven in Section 9.1 for decision trees (Q-circuits are different than decision trees over Q in that decision trees only apply functions from Q on the input variables). In particular, we get lower bounds for the size of threshold circuits.

Definition 11.1: *The Q-circuits complexity of a function f, denoted $S_Q(f)$, is the minimum cost of a Q-circuit computing f.*

Recall the definition of the measure D^{worst} (Definition 7.1).

Lemma 11.2: *Denote $c_Q = max_{q \in Q} D^{worst}(q)$. Then, for all f, $S_Q(f) \geq D^{worst}(f)/c_Q$.*

PROOF: The proof is similar to the proof of Lemma 9.2. Fix an arbitrary partition of the input bits into two disjoint sets. To compute f with respect to this partition, Alice and Bob agree on a "bottom-up" order of the gates (that is, an order in which the inputs for each gate come from previous gates or from the input variables). Alice and Bob

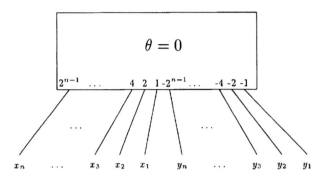

Figure 11.1: A threshold gate for the "greater than" function

simulate the Q-circuit for f according to this order; each time they encounter a gate q, there are some inputs for q that are the results of previous gates (both players know these values) and some input variables. They compute the value of q using the best protocol for computing q with respect to any partition that has all the inputs to the gate that are Alice's variables in one set, all the inputs to the gate that are Bob's variables in the other set, and all the other inputs (that both players know) are partitioned in an arbitrary way. Thus, to simulate each gate, c_Q bits of communication are sufficient. Because the circuit is of size $S_Q(f)$, the whole simulation uses at most $c_Q \cdot S_Q(f)$ bits.

$\square$

Below we modify Example 9.3 for the case of circuits with threshold gates. Exercise 9.4 and Exercise 9.5 can be modified in a similar way.

▶ **Example 11.3:** Consider a circuit with "threshold gates." That is, each gate computes a weighted sum of the edges entering the gate and outputs 1 iff this sum is larger than some integer θ (that is, the gate has t edges entering it, $z_1, \ldots, z_t$, and there are $t + 1$ integers associated with the gate $w_1, \ldots, w_t$ and θ; the gate computes the result of the comparison "$\sum_{i=1}^{t} w_i \cdot z_i > \theta$"). Threshold gates may be very powerful. For example, the gate in Figure 11.1 computes the "greater than" function $GT(x, y)$ where $x = x_n \cdots x_1$ and $y = y_n \cdots y_1$ are two n bit numbers. This is so because

$$\sum_{i=1}^{n} 2^{i-1} x_i + \sum_{i=1}^{n} -2^{i-1} y_i = x - y$$

so comparing the weighted sum to $\theta = 0$ gives exactly the answer to the question whether $x > y$ or not. An important parameter of a threshold circuit is W, the *total weight* of the gate; that is, the maximum (over all gates in the circuit) of $\sum |w_i|$. In the example of Figure 11.1

$$W = 2 \cdot \sum_{i=1}^{n} 2^{i-1} = 2^{n+1} - 2.$$

We will show that an exponential weight, $W \geq 2^n$, is necessary for computing GT with a single gate. More generally, any circuit of threshold gates with total weight W to compute the function GT requires size at least $(n + 1)/(\log W + 1)$. This is because in this case

$c_Q \leq \log W + 1$: For any partition $S : T$ of the input bits, Alice computes $\sum_{z_i \in S} w_{z_i} z_i$, where w_{z_i} is the weight corresponding to z_i (and each z_i is either a bit of x or a bit of y) and sends the result (a number between $-W$ to W; that is, $\log W + 1$ bits) to Bob. Now, Bob computes $\sum_{z_i \in T} w_{z_i} z_i$, adds the result to the number received from Alice, and compares the sum with θ to get the output (a single bit which he sends to Alice). All together, $\log W + 2$ bits (one bit can be saved by letting the player whose sum of weights in absolute value is at most $W/2$ to take the first step). Because $D^{worst}(\text{GT}) = D(\text{GT})$ $= n + 1$ (Exercise 1.22), then by Lemma 11.2 the size is at least $(n + 1)/(\log W + 1)$, as claimed. For example, if $W = poly(n)$, then we get a lower bound of $\Omega(n/\log n)$. Similar lower bounds apply to other functions f for which $D^{worst}(f)$ is large, such as the inner product function, IP, or the equality function, EQ.

11.2. Depth 2 Threshold Circuits

Threshold circuits are circuits whose gates are threshold elements (as defined in Example 11.3 above). The size of such a circuit is the number of gates, and the depth is the number of gates on the longest path from the input gates to the output gate. As shown in Example 11.3, W, the *total weight* of the gate, is also a very important parameter. Using the technique of the previous section we can prove at most linear lower bounds on the size of such circuits (even if W is small). Here we present a different approach that allows using two-party communication complexity (and multiparty communication complexity) to prove *exponential* lower bounds on the size of certain types of small depth, threshold circuits. Again, the method uses the total weight W.

Lemma 11.4: *Assume that a function $f : \{0, 1\}^m \rightarrow \{0, 1\}$ can be computed by a depth 2 threshold circuit, where the total weight of each gate is bounded by W. Then,*

$$R^{pub,worst}_{\frac{1}{2} + \frac{1}{4W}}(f) \leq \log W + 1.$$

PROOF: Consider a circuit for f. It can be converted into another circuit C, which still computes f but its top gate is a threshold gate whose threshold θ' equals 0. This is done by feeding the gate with the constant 1 with weight $-\theta$. Moreover, by multiplying each weight by two and increasing the weight of the constant 1 by -1, we do not change the function computed by the gate but we guarantee that the weighted sum computed by the gate is either positive or negative but it never equals 0. The new total weight of the top gate after these transformations, W', is at most four times larger than the original total weight (that is, $W' \leq 4W$). Denote by $f_1, \ldots, f_t$ the functions that are the inputs to the top gate and $w_1, \ldots, w_t$ their weights. These functions are either constants or input variables of the circuit or threshold gates. In each case, $D^{worst}(f_i) \leq \log W + 1$ (see Example 11.3).

Now consider the following randomized protocol for f (with respect to any partition of the input, and in the public coin model): Alice and Bob choose at random an index $1 \leq i \leq t$ (no communication), where each i is chosen with probability $|w_i|/W'$. They run the deterministic protocol for f_i with respect to this partition and get some output b.

If $b = 0$ the output is chosen at random to be 0 or 1 with equal probability (that is, $1/2$). If $b = 1$ the output is 1 if $w_i > 0$ and the output is 0 if $w_i < 0$. Consider an input for which $f(x) = 1$. Let α be the probability that the randomly chosen index i satisfies $f_i(x) = 0$. The contribution of these indices to the probability that the output is 1 is $\alpha/2$. With probability $1 - \alpha$ the index i chosen satisfies $f_i(x) = 1$. In this case, by the correctness of C, $\sum_{i:f_i(x)=1} w_i > 0$ and because all the weights are integers the contribution of these indices to the probability that the output is 1 is at least $\frac{1-\alpha}{2} + \frac{1}{W'}$. Therefore the total success probability is at least $\frac{1}{2} + \frac{1}{W'}$. The case of inputs for which $f(x) = 0$ is similar, where here it is important to note that $\sum_{i:f_i(x)=1} w_i < 0$ (in particular, we ensured that $\sum_{i:f_i(x)=1} w_i \neq 0$). To summarize, in both cases we get the correct answer with probability at least $\frac{1}{2} + \frac{1}{W'} \geq \frac{1}{2} + \frac{1}{4W}$. Because $D^{worst}(f_i) \leq \log W + 1$, we are done. $\square$

▶ **Example 11.5:** Consider the IP function (see Example 3.29). By Exercise 3.30, we know that $R^{pub,worst}_{\frac{1}{2}+\frac{1}{4W}}(\text{IP}) \geq m - O(\log W)$. Combining this with the above lemma we get that any depth 2 threshold circuit for IP requires gates with total weight $W = 2^{\Omega(m)}$.

A more natural complexity measure is the *size* of the circuit. Assume that all weights in the circuit (the w_is and the θs) are bounded by some value w. Clearly, the total weight satisfies $W \leq s \cdot w$. Therefore, we get that any depth 2 threshold circuit for IP has size $s = 2^{\Omega(m)}/w$. That is, as long as the weights are sufficiently small the size must be exponential.

In fact, the proof of Lemma 11.4 implies the following general lemma:

Lemma 11.6: *Let Q be a family of functions, and denote $c_Q = \max_{q \in Q} D^{worst}(q)$. Assume that f can be computed by a depth 2 circuit with a threshold gate at the top level that has total weight of W and arbitrary gates from Q in the bottom level. Then $R^{pub,worst}_{\frac{1}{2}+\frac{1}{4W}}(f) \leq c_Q$.*

Exercise 11.7: Let Q be a family of functions, and denote $r_Q = \max_{q \in Q} R^{pub,worst}_{\frac{1}{8W}}(q)$. Assume that f can be computed by a depth 2 circuit with a threshold gate at the top level whose total weight is W and arbitrary gates from Q in the bottom level. Then $R^{pub,worst}_{\frac{1}{2}+\frac{1}{8W}}(f) \leq r_Q$. Conclude that if Q is the class of all threshold functions, then still any circuit for IP is of exponential size, hence strengthening Example 11.5. Hint: See Example 9.3.

Exercise 11.8: Assume that f can be computed by a depth 3 circuit where the top two levels contain threshold gates (with total weight bounded by W) and the third level contains AND gates with in-degree at most k. Prove that $R^{pub,(k+1)-worst}_{\frac{1}{2}+\frac{1}{4W}}(f) \leq (k+1)\log W$ (Hint: Lemma 6.20). Conclude that such a circuit for the function GIP^{k+1}_n (see Example 6.16) must have total weight $W = 2^{\Omega(\frac{n}{k4^k})}$. Moreover, if each weight is bounded by w, then the size of the circuit is $s = 2^{\Omega(\frac{n}{k4^k})}/w$.

11.3. Size–Depth Tradeoffs: An Approach

In this section we present an approach that would allow using certain multiparty communication complexity lower bounds (once such bounds are proven) to prove size–depth tradeoffs. Particularly, to prove that for certain functions there is no circuit that is simultaneously of $O(\log n)$ depth and $O(n)$ size.

Consider a function $f(x, j, i)$ (for $x \in \{0, 1\}^n$ and $i, j \in \{1, \ldots, n\}$). We will show that any Boolean circuit C (as in Definition 10.1) that on input (x, j) (that is, $n + \log n$ bits) outputs n values $y_1 = f(x, j, 1), \ldots, y_n = f(x, j, n)$ (that is, the circuit has n output gates) cannot have both shallow depth and small size, provided that f is "hard" for 3-party communication complexity in a sense specified below. We first need the following lemma:

Lemma 11.9: *For any circuit C with m edges and depth d, there are $km/\log d$ edges (wires) whose removal yields a circuit of depth less than $d/2^{k-1}$ (recall that the depth is simply the number of edges in the longest directed path of the circuit).*

PROOF: Mark each node v by a $\lceil \log d \rceil$ bit number, $h(v)$, indicating its height (the length of the longest directed path from a leaf ending at v). That is, for each leaf h gets the value 0 and $h(\text{root})$ equals d, the depth of the circuit. Mark each edge $e = (u, v)$ by the index i of the most significant bit in which $h(u)$ and $h(v)$ differ. For some value j ($1 \leq j \leq \log d$) the set of edges marked by j is of size at most $m/\log d$. Omit these edges from the circuit and consider a new marking h' of the nodes, where $h'(v)$ is obtained from $h(v)$ by omitting the j-th bit. We claim that $h'(v)$ is a monotone function (and clearly it still gets the value 0 on the leaves) and hence $h'(\text{root})$ is a bound on the new depth (after the omission).

For this, we consider any (directed) edge $e = (u, v)$ that remained in the circuit and verify that $h'(u) < h'(v)$. Consider the index i of the most significant bit in which $h(u)$ and $h(v)$ differ (in this case the i-th bit of $h(u)$ is 0 and the i-th bit of $h(v)$ is 1 since we know that $h(u) < h(v)$). If $i = j$, then this edge would be omitted. If $i < j$, then the omission of the j-th bit does not matter and still $h'(u) < h'(v)$. If $i > j$, then it must be that the j-th bit of $h(u)$ and $h(v)$ are the same, and again the omission of the j-th bit does not matter and $h'(u) < h'(v)$.

Repeating this process k times we get that by omitting $km/\log d$ edges the depth can be represented by $\lceil \log d \rceil - k$ bits instead of $\lceil \log d \rceil$ bits. The result follows. □

The following lemma shows that if 3-party protocols for f, with certain communication constraints, do not exist, then a circuit C as described above cannot have linear size and logarithmic depth simultaneously. Recall the definition of simultaneous protocols (Definition 6.18).

Lemma 11.10: *Let C be a circuit as above of depth $c \log n$, size $c'n$ (with fan-in 2) and $f(x, j, i)$ the corresponding three-argument function (as defined above). Then f can be computed using a 3-party simultaneous protocol in which*

1. *the player holding x, j sends $O(n/\log\log n)$ bits;*

2. *the player holding x, i sends $O(n^\varepsilon)$ bits, for a fixed constant ε (in fact, the bits he sends are just a subset of the bits of x); and*

3. *the player holding i, j sends $O(\log n)$ bits.*

PROOF: First, apply Lemma 11.9 on the circuit C with $k = \log(c/\varepsilon) + 1$ (that is, k is a constant depending on the constants c and ε). This implies that there are $O(n/\log\log n)$ edges that can be omitted from C (we use here the assumption that the depth is $c\log n$ and that the number of edges is bounded by the size of the circuit) so that the depth remains at most $\varepsilon\log n$. This implies that if we are given the values on all omitted edges, and in addition the values of all input variables that remained connected to y_i, we can compute the value of y_i. Note that for each i this set of variables may be different, however because we remained with a fan-in 2 circuit of depth $\varepsilon\log n$, then for each value of i the number of these variables is at most n^ε.

With this in mind the protocol is as follows: the player holding x, j knows the computation of the circuit $C(x, j)$, hence he can send the values of all omitted edges; the player holding x, i knows what the set of n^ε important variables is and what their values are and can send these values; the player holding i, j sends these values. By the above, this information is enough to determine $f(x, j, i)$ and the communication is as guaranteed. □

▶ **Example 11.11:** Consider a circuit C as above that on input (x, j) outputs n bits $y_i = x_{j\oplus i}$ (where $\oplus$ here denotes bitwise exclusive-or). Observe that the corresponding function $f(x, j, i)$ is exactly the function SUM-INDEX of Example 6.26 for which a protocol with total communication $O(n^{0.92})$ was given. Note that this still does not give the desired tradeoff for the function $C(x, j)$ since we should be able to show that the second player (holding x, i) can send $O(n^\varepsilon)$ bits for any fixed ε. Also note that the $\Omega(\sqrt{n})$ lower bound on the total communication, given for the function SUM-INDEX, does not eliminate this possibility since we are willing to allow the first player (holding x, j) to send even $O(n/\log\log n)$ bits.

Open Problem 11.12: Let $C(x, j)$ be as in the Example 11.11. Prove that there is no circuit to compute $C(x, j)$ with $O(n)$ size and $O(\log n)$ depth.

11.4. ACC Circuits

ACC circuits are polynomial size, unbounded fan-in circuits that in addition to the OR, AND, and NOT gates allow MOD_m gates (that is, gates that for some fixed m output 1 iff the number of input bits that are 1 is divisible by m). ACC^0 are ACC circuits that are of constant depth. SYM^+ circuits are depth-2 circuits whose top gate is a symmetric gate (that is, a gate whose output depends only on the number of input bits that are 1) of fan-in s, and each of the gates in the bottom level is an AND gate of fan-in at most d. The importance of the class SYM^+ stems from the fact that such circuits can simulate ACC^0

circuits. More precisely, it is known that ACC^0 circuits can be transformed into SYM^+ circuits with $s = 2^{polylog(n)}$ and $d = polylog(n)$. Recall the definition of simultaneous protocols (Definition 6.18).

Lemma 11.13: *If a function f belongs to SYM^+ (with parameters s and d), then there exists a $(d + 1)$-party simultaneous protocol with $D^{\|}(f) = O(d \log s)$.*

PROOF: Similar to the proof of Lemma 6.20. Namely, because each AND gate of the circuit contains at most d variables and because there are $d + 1$ parties, then the value of each gate can be computed by some party (with no communication). The protocol will first fix a partition of the AND gates into $d + 1$ sets, with set i only containing AND gates that can be computed by the i-th party. Each party evaluates all the AND gates assigned to it and broadcasts the number of gates that evaluated to 1 ($\log s$ bits). Because the top gate is a symmetric one, this information is enough to determine the output. □

▶ **Example 11.14:** Consider the function GIP_n^d (Example 6.16). By Lemma 11.13, together with the lower bound proved for the function GIP_n^d (Section 6.4.1), it follows that any SYM^+ circuit for GIP_n^d with top fan-in s (and bottom fan-in at most $d - 1$) requires $s \geq 2^{n/4^d}$.

From Lemma 11.13 it follows that lower bounds of $D^{\|}(f) = \omega(polylog(n))$ for $d = polylog(n)$ for some function f would show that f does not belong to SYM^+ with parameter $s = 2^{polylog(n)}$ and $d = polylog(n)$. This, by the discussion preceding the lemma, implies that $f \notin ACC^0$. No explicit function $f \notin ACC^0$ is currently known. Note that Open-Problem 6.21 is a step in this direction.

11.5. Bibliographic Notes

Lower bounds similar to those presented in Section 11.1 were found by [Smolensky 1990]. The applicability of communication complexity for these kind of bounds was formalized by [Nisan 1993, Roychowdhury, Orlitsky, and Siu 1994]. See also [Siu, Roychowdhury, and Kailath 1995].

Example 11.5 is from [Hajnal et al. 1987]. Exercise 11.7 is from [Nissan 1993]. Exercise 11.8 is from [Håstad and Goldmann 1990]. See [Goldmann 1994] for a survey on lower bounds for threshold circuits using communication complexity.

The approach described in Section 11.3 is the communication complexity variant of a method proposed by [Valiant 1977]. In particular, Valiant proved Lemma 11.9 and suggested considering the function of Example 11.11. The communication complexity version of the approach is according to [Nisan and Wigderson 1991]. The original approach they suggested was to look only at the *total* amount of communication; however, Example 11.11, that is based on [Babai et al. 1995], as well as an example in [Pudlák and Rödl 1993] shows that for some of the problems of the type discussed here the total communication may be too small. Hence, we present here a refined approach.

[Yao 1990, Beigel and Tarui 1991] show how to transform ACC^0 circuits to SYM^+ circuits. Lemma 11.3 is due to [Håstad and Goldmann 1990]. For a survey on small depth circuits see [Beigel 1993].

CHAPTER 12

Time and Space

In many models of computation it is possible to imagine communication between different stages of the computation. This communication is usually realized by one part of the computation leaving the computing device in a certain state and other part of the computation starting from this state. The amount of information "communicated" this way can often be quantified as the "space" of this model; and the number of times such a communication takes place relates to the "time" of the model. We then usually get time–space tradeoffs by utilizing communication complexity lower bounds. In this chapter we discuss several lower bounds concerning *time* and *space* in several models of computations. Particularly, certain types of *Turing machines, finite automata*, and *branching programs*.

12.1. Time–Space Tradeoffs for Turing Machines

In this section we discuss the standard model of multi-tape Turing machines; these are finite automata with an arbitrary but fixed number k of read/write tapes. The input for the machine is provided on another read-only tape, called the *input tape*. The cells of the read/write tapes are initiated with a special blank symbol, b. At each step the finite control reads the symbols appearing in the $k + 1$ cells (on the $k + 1$ tapes) to which its heads are pointing. Based on these $k + 1$ symbols and the state of the finite control, it decides what symbols (out of a finite set of symbols) to write in the k read/write tapes (in the same locations where it reads the symbols from), where to move the $k+1$ heads (one cell to the left, one cell to the right, or stay on the same cell), and what is the new state of the finite control (out of a finite set of states). There are two special states, "accept" and "reject," in which the machine halts. Figure 12.1 sketches a Turing machine with 3 tapes (an input tape and two additional read/write tapes). A Turing machine has time complexity $T(m)$ if for all inputs of length m the machine halts within $T(m)$ steps, and space complexity $S(m)$ if for all inputs of length m the *total* number of cells on the k read/write tapes that are used is bounded by $S(m)$.

We can find a communication bottleneck in this model by considering how information can flow between the two sides of the (read-only) input tape. Such information

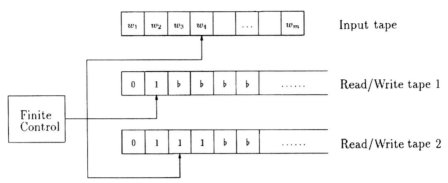

Figure 12.1: A Turing machine

can be passed only by the movement of the input head from one side to the other. The information that can be "carried" by the head must all be stored on the read/write tapes (other than the state of the finite control that can "carry" a constant number of bits), and thus is bounded in quantity by the space used by the algorithm. Formally, we can get lower bounds using the following simulation.

Lemma 12.1: *Let* $f: \{0, 1\}^n \times \{0, 1\}^n \rightarrow \{0, 1\}$ *be a function. Let M be a multi-tape Turing machine that runs simultaneously in time $T(n)$ and space $S(n)$ on inputs of size $m = 3n$, accepts all inputs in*

$$\{x0^n y \mid |x| = |y| = n, f(x, y) = 1\}$$

and rejects all inputs in

$$\{x0^n y \mid |x| = |y| = n, f(x, y) = 0\}.$$

Then $D(f) = O(T(n)S(n)/n)$.

PROOF: Alice and Bob, on input (x, y), jointly simulate the execution of the Turing machine M on input $x0^n y$. They output 1 or 0 depending on whether the machine accepts or rejects this input. At each point in time, the head of the Turing machine on the read-only input tape is either in the x-region (that is, the first n bits of the input tape), in the y-region (that is, the last n bits of the input tape), or in the 0-region (that is, the middle n bits of the input tape). In the first case Alice simulates the machine; in the second case Bob simulates the machine; and in the third case the simulation is done by the last player in whose region the head was before entering the 0-region. In other words, the player who is simulating the machine at any given time will continue the simulation by himself until the head moves into the region of the other player.

Notice that the player who is simulating the machine at any single point knows the contents of the cell of the read-only tape to which the head points. We still need to make sure that this player has the rest of the information needed for carrying out the simulation. Therefore, whenever the players change roles, all the information needed is sent from the player who was responsible for the simulation until this time to the player that has to continue the simulation. This information includes the state of the finite control and the contents of all the read/write tapes (only the used cells of each tape, separated by some delimiter, including the location of the head on each of the tapes). All together $O(S(n))$ bits of information. Now, because the head on the read-only tape can move at most one position in any step, there must be at least n steps between the times where the simulation switches from Alice to Bob and vice versa. It follows that there can be at most $T(n)/n$ such steps during the $T(n)$ steps of computation. All together at most $O(S(n)T(n)/n)$ bits of communication are exchanged while simulating the Turing machine. $\qquad\square$

This allows proving time–space tradeoff lower bounds for many simple functions.

▶ **Example 12.2:** Consider the language of palindromes $L = \{ww^R\}$, and concentrate on the special case where the last third of w is all 0s. Let M be any Turing machine for L that runs in time $T(n)$ and space $S(n)$ on inputs of length $m = 3n$. Finally, let $f(x, y) = 1$ iff $x = y^R$. Observe that such a machine accepts all inputs in

$$\{x0^n y \,|\, |x| = |y| = n, \, f(x, y) = 1\}$$

and rejects all inputs in

$$\{x0^n y \,|\, |x| = |y| = n, \, f(x, y) = 0\}.$$

Also note that f is equivalent to the equality function, EQ, and thus $D(f) = n + 1$ (Example 1.21). Therefore, any Turing machine recognizing palindromes requires a time–space tradeoff of $T(n) \cdot S(n) = \Omega(n^2)$.

It is not difficult to see that this language can be recognized in linear time using linear space (by copying the first half of the input to one of the read/write tapes and then checking that the first half matches the second half) and in quadratic time using logarithmic space (by verifying for each i that the i-th bit matches the $(m - i)$-th bit). Thus, this tradeoff is essentially tight.

Because for every function f, $D(f) \le n + 1$, the best time–space tradeoff that we can prove, using this method, is quadratic. Although this may seem very weak, we note that this is essentially the only technique known for proving such bounds.

Exercise 12.3: Prove that recognizing palindromes requires $\Omega(\log n)$ space. Namely, we can get space lower bounds and not only time–space tradeoffs.

Exercise 12.4: Show that a co-nondeterministic Turing machine can recognize the language of palindromes in logarithmic space and linear time but that a nondeterministic one still requires a quadratic time–space tradeoff. (A nondeterministic Turing machine is a Turing machine that makes nondeterministic steps; each input not in the language is always rejected, whereas for each input in the language there is a sequence of steps in which the machine accepts.)

Exercise 12.5: Consider a model of Turing machines that have two heads on the input tape. Use multiparty communication complexity to prove a time–space tradeoff for such machines.

Exercise 12.6: In this exercise we are concerned with finite automata. Those are similar to Turing machines but they have only an input tape (and no read/write tapes) and the head is only allowed to move one cell to the right at each step. It is well known that any nondeterministic automaton with k states can be transformed into a deterministic one that has 2^k states. For some constant c, consider the (finite) language $L_c = \{ww|w \in \{0,1\}^c\}$. (1) Prove that there is a co-nondeterministic automaton with $O(c)$ states that accepts the language L_c. (2) Use communication complexity to prove that any deterministic automaton that accepts the language L_c requires at least 2^c states. Conclude that the above-mentioned transformation from deterministic automata to nondeterministic automata is optimal.

12.2. One-tape Turing Machines

In this section we show how to prove time lower bounds for Turing machines. There is of yet no known super-linear time lower bound on an "explicit" function for general Turing machines, as defined in the previous section. What we show here is a lower bound for one-tape Turing machines (that is, these are machines that have a single tape; at the beginning, the input is written on this tape and this time the machine is allowed to overwrite this tape). A naive use of (deterministic) communication complexity, that argues about the flow of information between the part before the middle of the input and the part after the middle, can only be used to prove $T(n) \leq D(f)$. This is of no interest because for all f, $D(f)$ is at most $n+1$ (and n steps are required by the machine just to read its input). The following lemma enables us to achieve better lower bounds (at most quadratic):

Lemma 12.7: *Let* $f: \{0, 1\}^n \times \{0, 1\}^n \to \{0, 1\}$ *be a function. Let M be a one-tape Turing machine that runs in time $T(n)$ on inputs of size $m = 3n$, accepts all inputs in*

$$\{x0^n y\,|\,|x| = |y| = n,\ f(x, y) = 1\}$$

and rejects all inputs in

$$\{x0^n y\,|\,|x| = |y| = n,\ f(x, y) = 0\}.$$

Then $R_0^{pub}(f) = O(T(n)/n)$.

PROOF: Alice and Bob, on input (x, y), simulate the Turing machine M on input $x0^n y$ using a public coin randomized (zero error) protocol. They output 1 or 0 depending on whether the machine accepts or rejects this input. Alice and Bob first choose together, uniformly at random, a location in the 0-region of the tape (without any communication). Alice simulates the machine whenever the head is to the left of this location, and Bob simulates the machine whenever the head is to the right of this location. Each time the head crosses this location only the state of the finite control ($O(1)$ bits) needs to be sent. Because the total running time of the machine M on the input is at most $T(n)$, the expected number of times the machine crosses this location (which is chosen at random among n different possibilities) is at most $T(n)/n$. Thus, the expected total communication is $O(T(n)/n)$. $\qquad\square$

► **Example 12.8:** Consider the language of palindromes $\{ww^R\}$. As in Example 12.2, concentrate on the special case where the last third of w is all 0s. Let M be any one-tape Turing machine for L that runs in time $T(n)$ on inputs of length $m = 3n$. Finally, let $f(x, y) = 1$ iff $x = y^R$. Note again that f is equivalent to the equality function, EQ, and that such a Turing machine accepts all inputs in

$$\{x0^n y \,|\, |x| = |y| = n, \, f(x, y) = 1\}$$

and rejects all inputs in

$$\{x0^n y \,|\, |x| = |y| = n, \, f(x, y) = 0\}.$$

We also know that $R_0(\text{EQ}) = \Theta(n)$ (Example 3.9) which implies, by Exercise 3.15, that $R_0^{pub}(\text{EQ}) = \Theta(n)$. Using Lemma 12.7, we get that any one-tape Turing machine recognizing this language requires $\Omega(n^2)$ time.

As remarked in Example 12.2, the language of palindromes can be recognized in linear time on a two-tape Turing machine. There is a simple quadratic simulation of k-tape Turing machines by one-tape Turing machines. Combining the linear upper bound for the language of palindromes on two-tape Turing machines with the quadratic lower bound for one-tape Turing machines, we get that this simulation is optimal. Also note that it is possible to recognize the language of palindromes on a one-tape Turing machine in $O(n^2)$ time. Hence, for this language, the lower bound it tight.

It is not known whether the simulation in Lemma 12.7 can be made deterministic. On the other hand, Lemma 12.7 can be extended in various ways. For example, it extends almost as it is to zero error randomized one-tape Turing machines (the time complexity is measured according to the expected running time). A more interesting version is the following:

Exercise 12.9: Let $f: \{0,1\}^n \times \{0,1\}^n \to \{0,1\}$ be a function. Let M be a one-tape non-deterministic Turing machine with the same properties as in Lemma 12.7. That is, the machine M accepts all inputs in $\{x0^n y \,|\, |x| = |y| = n, f(x,y) = 1\}$, rejects all inputs in $\{x0^n y \,|\, |x| = |y| = n, f(x,y) = 0\}$, and runs in time $T(n)$ (where the time of a nondeterministic Turing machine is defined as the maximum over all inputs in $\{0,1\}^n$ and all possible nondeterministic choices). Then, $N^1(f) = O((T(n)/n) + \log n)$. Conclude that such a nondeterministic Turing machine for the language of palindromes requires $\Omega(n^2)$ time.

Open Problems 12.10: *Prove any super-linear lower bound for computing an explicit function on two-tape Turing machines.*

12.3. Ordered Binary Decision Diagrams (OBDDs)

The *branching program* model is a model of computation that is very useful in studying issues related to space. Many variants of this model are studied in the literature. Here we are interested in leveled branching programs of various types. A *leveled branching program* is a directed, leveled graph with $\ell + 1$ levels. Each node in the first ℓ levels is

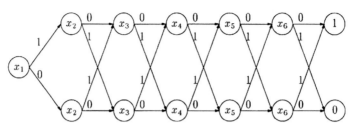

Figure 12.2: A branching program

labeled by a variable in $x_1, \ldots, x_m$; level 1 contains a single node (the root) and level $\ell + 1$ contains two nodes labeled 0 and 1. From each node in level i ($1 \le i \le \ell$) there are two outgoing edges connected to (not necessarily distinct) nodes in level $i + 1$. One of these two edges is labeled 0 and the other is labeled 1. A branching program computes a function $f(x_1, \ldots, x_m)$ in a natural way: start at the root; at each level look at the current node whose label is some variable x_j; check the value of x_j in the assignment and depending on its value (0 or 1) choose the corresponding edge going out of this node, and proceed from the node reached. When level $\ell + 1$ is reached the label of the node reached (0 or 1) is the value of f. For example, Figure 12.2 shows a leveled branching program that computes $\oplus(x_1, \ldots, x_6)$.

Let w be the maximal number of nodes in any level; we call w the *width* of the program, and ℓ the *length* of the program.

Exercise 12.11: Let $f: \{0,1\}^m \to \{0,1\}$ be any function. Show that there is a branching program for f of length m and width 2^m and branching program of width 3 and length $O(m2^m)$.

The above exercise shows that for every function f we can make the width or the length of the branching program to be "small." An important question is, given a function f, whether there is a branching program that has both "small" width and "small" length. In this section (and the following one) we prove lower bounds of this kind for certain types of branching programs.

A branching program is called *oblivious* if for each level i all the nodes in level i are labeled by the same variable x_j (for example, the branching program of Figure 12.2 is oblivious). Note that every branching program can be made oblivious by increasing its length by a factor of w (and not changing its width). Oblivious branching programs are discussed in the next section. An even more restricted type of branching program includes those that are oblivious and, in addition, each variable appears in at most one level. In other words, we can think of the variables as ordered in some order and the program has m levels (or less) that are labeled according to this order. This kind of branching programs is referred to as an *OBDD (Ordered Binary Decision Diagram)*. The branching program of Figure 12.2 is in fact an OBDD. The following lemma shows how to derive lower bounds on the width of such programs. Recall the definition of D^{best} (Section 7.2).

Lemma 12.12: *Let* $f: \{0, 1\}^m \to \{0, 1\}$ *be a function that can be computed using an OBDD of width* w, *then* $D^{best}(f) \le \log w + 1$.

PROOF: Given the OBDD, let S be the variables that appear in the first $\ell/2$ levels and T be the variables that appear in the last $\ell/2$ levels (variables that do not appear in the program are partitioned between S and T; because each variable appears at most once, $S : T$ is indeed a partition of the variables). Now Alice can simulate the first $\ell/2$ levels of the OBDD, she then sends the name of a node in level $\ell/2 + 1$ from which the simulation should continue ($\log w$ bits), and Bob can finish the simulation and compute the output. We get $D^{best}(f) \leq D^{S:T}(f) \leq \log w + 1$, as needed. □

▶ **Example 12.13:** Consider the "shifted equality" function (SEQ) for which we proved (Example 7.9) that $D^{best}(\text{SEQ}) = \Omega(m)$. By Lemma 12.2, any OBDD for this function has width $w = 2^{\Omega(m)}$.

12.4. Width–Length Tradeoff for Branching Programs

In this section we give a width–length tradeoff for oblivious branching programs, in which there is no restriction on the number of levels in which each variable appears. The main difficulty is that, in opposition to the case of OBDDs, it is not clear how to partition the variables between the two players. We overcome this by using the measure $D^{n-best}(f)$, introduced in Section 7.3.

Lemma 12.14: *Let $f: \{0, 1\}^m \to \{0, 1\}^m$ be a function that can be computed using an oblivious branching program of width w and length $\ell \leq m(\log m - 4)/8$. Then,*

$$D^{\sqrt{m}-best}(f) = O(\ell \log w/m).$$

PROOF: Because the branching program is oblivious, we can think of its labels as a string $z \in \{1, \ldots, m\}^\ell$. Suppose that we can find two sets $S, T \subset \{1, \ldots, m\}$ and a number s such that

1. $|S| = |T| = \sqrt{m}$; and

2. z is (s, S, T)-*good*; that is, z can be partitioned into s substrings $z_1 z_2 \cdots z_s$, where each z_i consists of elements of either S or T but not both (in addition to elements which are neither in S nor in T).

In such a case we can show that $D^{S:T}(f) = O(s \cdot \log w)$. This is because Alice can simulate the branching program in blocks of levels corresponding to z_is that use elements of S (and elements not in $S \cup T$) and similarly Bob can simulate the branching program in blocks of levels corresponding to z_is that use elements of T (and elements not in $S \cup T$). To carry out the simulation, the players need to tell each other, at the end of each of the s blocks, the name of the node in the next level from which the simulation should proceed; for this $\log w$ bits are sufficient. Hence the bound follows. Obviously, $D^{\sqrt{m}-best}(f) \leq D^{S:T}(f) = O(s \cdot \log w)$. To complete the proof, we will show the existence of such sets S and T for which the partition of z uses only $s = 4\ell/m$ substrings. For this we need the following claim: □

Claim 12.15: *Let $A, B \subset \{1, \ldots, m\}$ be two sets of size k. Let $z \in \{1, \ldots, m\}^\ell$ be a string such that each $a \in A$ appears in z at most t_A times and each $b \in B$ appears in z at most t_B times. Then there are $A' \subseteq A$ and $B' \subseteq B$ of size at least $k/2^t$ such that z is (t, A', B')-good, where $t = t_A + t_B$.*

PROOF (OF CLAIM): The proof goes by induction on t. If $t = 1$, then either t_A or t_B is 0, hence A and B already have the required properties. For the induction step, assume without loss of generality that z contains each element in $\{1, \ldots, m\}$ at least once (otherwise, extend z with the missing elements in an arbitrary way). Examine the letters of z one by one until reaching a location where you already have seen $k/2$ letters of one of A and B but less than $k/2$ of the other (such a location exists by the above assumption). Denote this prefix by z' and the rest of z by z''. Without loss of generality, assume that A is the set that $k/2$ of its letters appear in z'. Let A^* be those letters of A that appear in z' and B^* be those letters of B that do *not* appear in z'. It follows that both A^* and B^* have size of at least $k/2$. Consider, the string z''; each letter of A^* appears in z'' at most $t'_A = t_A - 1$ times. Hence, we can apply the induction hypothesis on z'' with respect to A^*, B^* and $t' = t - 1$. That is, z'' is $(t - 1, A', B')$ good with respect to some sets $A' \subseteq A^*$, $B' \subseteq B^*$ of sizes $|A'| \geq |A^*|/2^{t-1} \geq k/2^t$ and $|B'| \geq |B^*|/2^{t-1} \geq k/2^t$. Since z' contains only letters of A^* and none of B^*, it follows that z is (t, A', B') good, and A', B' are as required. This completes the proof of the claim. $\square$

To complete the proof of the lemma, consider the variables that appear in the branching program at least $2\ell/m$ times. The number of these variables is at most $m/2$. Hence, at least $m/2$ of the variables appear at most $2\ell/m$ times. Partition these variables into two sets A and B each of size $m/4$ in an arbitrary way. By Claim 12.15 (with $k = m/4$; $t_A = t_B = 2\ell/m$; and $t = 4\ell/m$), there are sets A' and B' of size $m/(4 \cdot 2^t)$ such that the string z corresponding to the program is $(4\ell/m, A', B')$-good. Because $\ell \leq m(\log m - 4)/8$, then $t \leq (\log m - 4)/2$ and hence the size of A' and B' is at least $\sqrt{m}$. These two sets give the sets S and T as required.

▶ **Example 12.16:** Consider the function MAJ_m of Example 7.13. It is shown there, in particular, that $D^{\sqrt{m}-best}(\text{MAJ}_m) = \Omega(\log m)$. It follows from the above lemma that any constant width oblivious branching program to compute MAJ_m has length $\ell = \Omega(m \log m)$. By the discussion in Section 12.3, any constant width (non-oblivious) branching program can be made oblivious in the cost of increasing the width to a larger constant. Hence, the same lower bound holds for non-oblivious programs as well.

Exercise 12.17: Consider the element distinctness function, ED, of Example 7.14. Prove that any oblivious branching program for ED requires either $\Omega(m \log m)$ length or exponential width.

12.5. Bibliographic Notes

For rigorous definitions of languages, Turing machines (of various types), and finite automata see, for example, [Hopcroft and Ullman 1979]. In particular, the simulation of k-tape Turing machines on one-tape Turing machines, mentioned in Example 12.8, appears in [Hopcroft and Ullman 1979, Chapter 7].

Time–space tradeoffs for Turing machines were first proved by [Cobham 1966] and then by many others. The simulation of Lemma 12.1, and thus the lower bounds obtained by using it, only apply to standard Turing machines with a *single* head on the read-only input tape. [Babai et al. 1989] show the extension presented in Exercise 12.5; more generally, they show a simulation of Turing machines with k heads on the input tape by $k + 1$ player multiparty protocols. This way lower bounds for these types of machines may be obtained from multiparty communication complexity lower bounds.

The branching program model and many variants of it have been widely studied; see [Razborov 1991] for a survey of known results concerning branching programs. OBDDs were introduced by [Bryant 1986]. They are widely used in logic design, formal verification, and other fields. Lower bounds for them were given, for example, in [Hosaka, Takenaga, and Yajima 1994, Wegener 1993].

Width–length tradeoffs for oblivious branching programs were proved in the work of [Chandra et al. 1983, Alon and Maass 1986, Babai et al. 1990]. The method was further generalized to use multiparty communication complexity in [Babai et al. 1989]. The technique presented in Section 12.4 is due to [Alon and Maass 1986].

CHAPTER 13

Randomness

In Chapter 3 we considered randomized communication complexity, where Alice and Bob are allowed to use randomness during the execution of protocols. In this chapter we apply various communication complexity measures and results to the study of randomness in other areas.

13.1. Quasirandom Graphs

Randomly chosen graphs have many nice properties. It is an interesting question whether we can *construct* a graph with some of the basic properties of random graphs. The following definition captures one family of such interesting properties.

Definition 13.1: *Let* $G = (V, E)$ *be a graph on* N *vertices.* G *is a* k-quasirandom *to within* ε *if, when choosing at random* k *vertices* $v_1, \ldots, v_k$ *from* V, *the induced subgraph* H *is distributed to within statistical distance of at most* ε *from the uniform distribution on the* $2^{\binom{k}{2}}$ k-vertex *graphs (if* $v_i = v_j$ *there is no edge connecting them).*

The intuition is that if G was a truly random graph (that is, for every two vertices $v_1, v_2 \in V$ the edge (v_1, v_2) is in E with probability $1/2$), then each k vertex graph is equally likely to appear in G. It turns out that the distributional communication complexity of a certain function associated with the graph is closely related to its being quasirandom.

Definition 13.2: *Let* G *be a graph on* $N = 2^n$ *vertices. The function* $\text{EDGE}_G(x, y)$ *on two* n-bit strings x and y is defined to be 1 iff there is an edge between the vertices x and y in the graph G.*

Lemma 13.3: *If* $D_{\frac{1}{2}+\frac{\varepsilon}{2}}^{uniform}(\text{EDGE}_G) \geq k$, *then* G *is* k-quasirandom *to within* $\binom{k}{2} \cdot \varepsilon$.

PROOF: Enumerate the $\binom{k}{2}$ possible edges of the randomly chosen $H = (v_1, \ldots, v_k)$ according to some fixed order, say, $e_{1,2}, \ldots, e_{1,k}, e_{2,1}, \ldots, e_{k-1,k}$ (that is, those are bits $e_{i,j}$ indicating whether the edge between v_i and v_j is present in H or not). For $1 \leq i \leq \binom{k}{2}$, let D_i be the distribution induced on the first i edges (D_0 contains the empty string with probability 1). To prove the lemma, we show, by induction on i, that D_i is within statistical distance $i \cdot \varepsilon$ from the uniform distribution on $\{0, 1\}^i$. This is obviously true for D_0. For the induction step, it is enough to show that the statistical distance between $D_{i-1} \times U$ and D_i is at most ε, where U denotes the uniform distribution on a single bit (because by induction hypothesis $D_{i-1} \times U$ is within statistical distance of at most $(i-1)\varepsilon$ from the uniform distribution on $\{0, 1\}^i$). Assume toward a contradiction that the statistical distance is larger than ε; we present a $(k-1)$-bit deterministic protocol that computes the function EDGE$_G$ with probability at least $\frac{1}{2} + \frac{\varepsilon}{2}$ (with respect to the uniform distribution) contradicting the assumption of the lemma. We start with a *public coin (randomized)* protocol $\mathcal{P}_i$ for EDGE$_G$ that succeeds with probability $\frac{1}{2} + \frac{\varepsilon}{2}$, where now the probability is taken over the input (with uniform distribution) and the common random string.

The protocol goes as follows: Alice gets as her input x a uniformly chosen vertex of G. Similarly, Bob gets as his input y a uniformly chosen vertex of G. They treat x and y as the two end-points of the i-th edge, e_i and choose at random, using their public coin, $k - 2$ additional vertices. At this point they have obtained a uniformly chosen k-vertex subgraph H of G. The existence or nonexistence, in H, of each possible edge that does not involve x or y is immediately known by both parties. The edges involving x are known by Alice, and she sends this information ($k - 2$ bits) to Bob. The edges involving y are already known to Bob, which now knows all the subgraph H except the existence of the edge $e_i = (x, y)$, which is what should be computed. Bob's guess for e_i is a value b such that $D_i(e_1, \ldots, e_{i-1}, b) \geq D_i(e_1, \ldots, e_{i-1}, \bar{b})$. He sends this bit to Alice as the output.

We now compute $\Pr[\mathcal{P}_i \text{ succeeds}] - \Pr[\mathcal{P}_i \text{ fails}]$, where the probability is over the input to the protocol and the random choices made. As remarked, these random choices are equivalent to choosing a k-vertex subgraph H over all Hs with uniform distribution. Fix some values to $e_1, \ldots, e_{i-1}$ and let b be the corresponding output. The contribution of Hs that agree with $e_1, \ldots, e_{i-1}$ to the success probability is $D_i(e_1, \ldots, e_{i-1}, b)$, whereas the contribution of such Hs to the failure probability is $D_i(e_1, \ldots, e_{i-1}, \bar{b})$. Also note that

$$D_{i-1}(e_1, \ldots, e_{i-1}) = D_i(e_1, \ldots, e_{i-1}, b) + D_i(e_1, \ldots, e_{i-1}, \bar{b}).$$

Hence, we have

$$\Pr[\mathcal{P}_i \text{ succeeds}] - \Pr[\mathcal{P}_i \text{ fails}]$$
$$= \sum_{e_1, \ldots, e_{i-1}} (D_i(e_1, \ldots, e_{i-1}, b) - D_i(e_1, \ldots, e_{i-1}, \bar{b})).$$

By simple manipulation this is equal to

$$\sum_{e_1, \ldots, e_{i-1}, e_i} \left| (D_i(e_1, \ldots, e_{i-1}, e_i) - \frac{1}{2} D_{i-1}(e_1, \ldots, e_{i-1}) \right|.$$

The last sum is simply the statistical distance between D_i and $D_{i-1} \times U$, which by assumption is greater than ε. This implies that the success probability of $\mathcal{P}_i$ is at least $\frac{1}{2} + \frac{\varepsilon}{2}$. Finally, a deterministic protocol with the same success probability follows, as in Theorem 3.20. $\qquad\square$

▶ **Example 13.4:** Consider the inner product function, IP. Let G_{IP} be the $N = 2^n$-vertex graph defined by the IP function (vertices in G_{IP} have an n-bit name, and x is connected to y iff $\langle x, y \rangle = 1$). By the distributional lower bound for IP (Example 3.29) with $\varepsilon = 2 \cdot 2^{k-n/2}$) we get that G_{IP} is k-quasirandom to within $k(k-1)2^{k-n/2}$.

13.2. Deterministic Amplification

The pseudorandom generators for communication complexity, described in Section 4.4, may be used as building blocks for constructing pseudorandom generators that "fool" other classes of algorithms. We give here a simple example.

Definition 13.5: *A function* $G \colon \{0, 1\}^m \to (\{0, 1\}^n)^k$ *is an ε-pseudo-independent generator if for every sequence of sets* $A_1, \dots, A_k \subseteq \{0, 1\}^n$,

$$|\Pr[G(x) \in A_1 \times \cdots \times A_k] - \rho(A_1) \cdot \ldots \cdot \rho(A_k)| \leq \varepsilon,$$

where the probability is taken over a random choice of $x \in \{0, 1\}^m$ and $\rho(A_i)$, the density of the set A_i, is $|A_i|/2^n$.

Intuitively, this means that the k output strings of a pseudo-independent generator behave almost as if they are independent. Obviously, the challenge is to construct a pseudo-independent generator, for given n and k, with m as small as possible (relative to the trivial kn). Note that a pseudorandom generator for communication complexity $c \geq 2$ (Definition 4.40) is also a pseudo-independent generator for $k = 2$ (because if there were sets A_1 and A_2 for which the condition is not satisfied, then a 2-bit protocol can be derived in which Alice and Bob test whether $x \in A_1$ and $y \in A_2$ and output 1 iff both tests succeed). For general k, we will construct pseudo-independent generators recursively.

Define $n_1 = n$ and for each $1 \leq i \leq \log k$, let $g_i \colon \{0, 1\}^{n_{i+1}} \to \{0, 1\}^{n_i} \times \{0, 1\}^{n_i}$ be a pseudorandom generator for communication complexity 2 with parameter ε; denote the two outputs of the generator by g_i^{left} and g_i^{right}. Thus, using the construction of Section 4.4, $n_{i+1} = n_i + O(\log \varepsilon^{-1})$. Also denote $k_i = 2^i$.

The Generator

$G_1 \colon \{0, 1\}^{n_2} \to \{0, 1\}^{n_1} \times \{0, 1\}^{n_1}$ is defined by

$$G_1(x) = g_1(x).$$

For $i > 1$, $G_i \colon \{0, 1\}^{n_{i+1}} \to (\{0, 1\}^n)^{k_i}$ is defined by

$$G_i(x) = G_{i-1}\big(g_i^{left}(x)\big) \circ G_{i-1}\big(g_i^{right}(x)\big),$$

where $\circ$ denotes concatenation.

Lemma 13.6: G_i *is an* ε'*-pseudo-independent generator, where* $\varepsilon' = k_i \varepsilon$.

PROOF: We prove, by induction on i, that G_i is in fact a $(k_i - 1)\varepsilon$-pseudo-independent generator. For $i = 1$ this, as already mentioned, follows from the definitions. For the induction step, let $A_1, \ldots, A_{k_i} \subseteq \{0, 1\}^n$ be any sets and denote

$$A = \{y \in \{0, 1\}^{n_i} \mid G_{i-1}(y) \in A_1 \times \cdots \times A_{k_{i-1}}\}$$

and

$$B = \{y \in \{0, 1\}^{n_i} \mid G_{i-1}(y) \in A_{k_{i-1}+1} \times \cdots \times A_{k_i}\}.$$

Notice that

$$\Pr[G_i(x) \in A_1 \times \cdots \times A_{k_i}] = \Pr[g_i(x) \in A \times B].$$

Hence, we can write the following inequalities.

$$\left| \Pr[G_i(x) \in A_1 \times \cdots \times A_{k_i}] - \rho(A_1) \cdot \ldots \cdot \rho(A_{k_i}) \right|$$

$$\leq \left| \Pr[g_i(x) \in A \times B] - \frac{|A|}{2^{n_i}} \frac{|B|}{2^{n_i}} \right| + \left| \frac{|A|}{2^{n_i}} \frac{|B|}{2^{n_i}} - \rho(A_1) \cdot \ldots \cdot \rho(A_{k_i}) \right|$$

$$\leq \left| \Pr[g_i(x) \in A \times B] - \frac{|A|}{2^{n_i}} \frac{|B|}{2^{n_i}} \right| + \left| \frac{|A|}{2^{n_i}} - \rho(A_1) \cdot \ldots \cdot \rho(A_{k_{i-1}}) \right|$$

$$+ \left| \frac{|B|}{2^{n_i}} - \rho(A_{k_{i-1}+1}) \cdot \ldots \cdot \rho(A_{k_i}) \right|.$$

The first summand is at most ε, because otherwise a 2-bit communication protocol that distinguishes the output of g_i from random is just testing whether $g_i^{left}(x) \in A$ and $g_i^{right}(x) \in B$ (two bits) – a contradiction to the fact that g_i is a pseudorandom generator for communication complexity 2 (with parameter ε). Each of the second and third summands are at most $(k_{i-1} - 1)\varepsilon$, by the induction hypothesis, because by the definition of A (and similarly for B)

$$\frac{|A|}{2^{n_i}} = \Pr[G_{i-1}(x) \in A_1 \times \cdots \times A_{k_{i-1}}].$$

Hence, G_i is $\varepsilon + 2(k_{i-1} - 1)\varepsilon = (k_i - 1)\varepsilon$-pseudo-independent. $\qquad\square$

A particularly simple application of pseudo-independent generators is for, so-called, "deterministic amplification" – reducing the error probability of randomized algorithms, with a small penalty in the number of random bits used.

▶ **Example 13.7:** Suppose that we are given a randomized algorithm A to recognize a language L, which uses n random bits on inputs of length ℓ (the relation between n and ℓ may be arbitrary) and has one-sided error probability $1/2$ (i.e, the algorithm may err only for inputs $x \in L$). We construct another randomized algorithm A' that uses $O(n)$ random bits and has error probability $2^{-n/\log n}$. For this, we use an ε-pseudo-independent generator $G : \{0, 1\}^m \rightarrow (\{0, 1\}^n)^k)$, where $k = n/\log n + 1$, $\varepsilon = 2^{-k}$, and thus using our construction (with $i = \log k$) we get $m = O(n)$. The new algorithm A' first flips m random bits and feeds them to G to produce k strings of length n. The original algorithm A is then run k times, each time using a different output string of G instead of truly random bits. A' accepts iff some run of A accepts.

If $x \notin L$, then clearly all runs of A reject (since error is one-sided) and so A' always rejects. To see what happens for $x \in L$, denote $A_1 = A_2 = \cdots = A_n = R$ to be the set of random strings that make A reject (mistakenly). Thus $\rho(R) \leq 1/2$. The new algorithm A' rejects only if all outputs of G_i are in R. Because G is an ε-pseudo-independent generator, this happens with probability at most $\varepsilon + \rho(A_1) \cdots \rho(A_k) = 2/2^k = 2^{-n/\log n}$.

Exercise 13.8: Obtain a similar deterministic amplification for algorithms with two-sided error.

13.3. Slightly Random Sources

A randomized algorithm assumes that it has a source of truly random bits: each bit is unbiased and, moreover, independent of all other bits. In practice though, this is probably too optimistic. Even when we have a physical source of randomness (for example, a zener diode), this source probably does have some correlation between the different bits produced. We may model such a source of randomness as a distribution where each bit is not completely determined by the previous ones.

Definition 13.9: *A probability distribution D on $\{0, 1\}^m$ is δ-slightly random if for all $1 \leq i \leq m$ and for all $\alpha_1, \ldots, \alpha_{i-1} \in \{0, 1\}$,*

$$\delta \leq \Pr[x_i = 1 | x_1 = \alpha_1, \ldots, x_{i-1} = \alpha_{i-1}] \leq (1 - \delta),$$

where $x_1 \ldots x_m$ are chosen according to D.

A truly random source satisfies the above definition with $\delta = 1/2$. Note that the definition implies that in a δ-slightly random source, the probability of all $x \in \{0, 1\}^m$ satisfies $D(x) \leq (1 - \delta)^m$. It turns out that such a source suffices for simulating any randomized algorithm. Such a simulation may be obtained using any function whose discrepancy is sufficiently small (see Section 3.5). The following lemma, which is required for the proof, may shed some light on how a function with small discrepancy may be used to "gain" a little randomness.

Lemma 13.10: *Let $f: \{0, 1\}^n \times \{0, 1\}^n \rightarrow \{0, 1\}$ be a function. Let C be a distribution on $\{0, 1\}^n$ such that $C(x) \leq v$ for all $x \in \{0, 1\}^n$. Choose x at random according to C and choose y uniformly at random in $\{0, 1\}^n$. Then the distribution of $y \circ f(x, y)$ is within statistical distance of at most $2^{n+1} \cdot v \cdot Disc_{uniform}(f)$ from the uniform distribution on $\{0, 1\}^{n+1}$.*

PROOF: The statistical distance between $y \circ f(x, y)$, constructed as above, and the uniform distribution is given by

$$\sum_{y}\sum_{b}\left|\Pr[y \circ b] - \frac{1}{2^{n+1}}\right| = \frac{1}{2^n}\sum_{y}\left|\Pr[f(x, y) = 0|y] - \frac{1}{2}\right|$$

$$+ \left|\Pr[f(x, y) = 1|y] - \frac{1}{2}\right|$$

which by a simple manipulation is equal to

$$2\frac{1}{2^n}\sum_{y}\left|\sum_{x}C(x)\left(f(x, y) - \frac{1}{2}\right)\right|.$$

Partition the ys into two sets according to the sign of $\sum_x C(x)(f(x, y) - 1/2)$. Let B_1 be the set of ys such that $\sum_x C(x)f(x, y) \geq 1/2$, and B_2 be the set of ys such that $\sum_x C(x)f(x, y) < 1/2$. Hence, the statistical distance equals to

$$2\frac{1}{2^n}\left(\sum_{y \in B_1, x}C(x)\left(f(x, y) - \frac{1}{2}\right) + \sum_{y \in B_2, x}C(x)\left(\frac{1}{2} - f(x, y)\right)\right).$$

Let A_1 be the set of xs such that $\sum_{y \in B_1}(f(x, y) - 1/2) \geq 0$, and A_2 be the set of xs such that $\sum_{y \in B_2}(1/2 - f(x, y)) \geq 0$. The statistical distance is bounded from above by

$$2\frac{1}{2^n}\nu\left(\sum_{y \in B_1, x \in A_1}\left(f(x, y) - \frac{1}{2}\right) + \sum_{y \in B_2, x \in A_2}\left(\frac{1}{2} - f(x, y)\right)\right).$$

Finally, note that for every rectangle R, $\sum_{(x, y) \in R}(f(x, y) - 1/2)$ is exactly $2^{2n}/2$ times its discrepancy, that is, bounded by $(2^{2n}/2) \cdot Disc_{uniform}(f)$. All together, the statistical distance is at most $2^{n+1} \cdot \nu \cdot Disc_{uniform}(f)$. $\qquad\square$

We now return to the simulation of randomized algorithms using a δ-slightly random source D. Let A be a randomized algorithm that asks for k (truly) random bits and is correct on every input with probability of at least 2/3. Choose $n = O(\log k)$ and let $f : \{0, 1\}^n \times \{0, 1\}^n \to \{0, 1\}$ be a function with "small" discrepancy. Fix $m = nk$, and view the string $x \in \{0, 1\}^m$ (chosen according to D) as composed of k blocks of length n each: $b_1, \ldots, b_k$.

The Simulation

Choose $x = b_1, \ldots, b_k$ according to the distribution D on $\{0, 1\}^m$
For all $y \in \{0, 1\}^n$ do
    For $i = 1, \ldots, k$ do
        $z_i \leftarrow f(b_i, y)$
    Run A using $z = z_1, \ldots, z_k$ as its k random bits
Output the majority answer of all 2^n A's runs

Note that $n = O(\log k)$ so if f can be computed in time polynomial in k, then the whole simulation time is a polynomial in k times the running time of A. The correctness of this simulation follows directly from the following lemma.

Lemma 13.11: *Let $x = b_1, \ldots, b_k$ be chosen according to a δ-slightly random source and y be chosen uniformly in $\{0, 1\}^n$. Then the distribution of $z_1, \ldots, z_k$ (where $z_i = f(b_i, y)$) is within statistical distance of $k2^{n+1}(1 - \delta)^n Disc_{uniform}(f)$ from the uniform distribution on k-bit strings.*

Note that the lemma deals with a truly random y, though the whole motivation for studying slightly random sources is that truly random bits are hard to achieve. However, since y is "short" ($O(\log k)$ bits), the simulation overcomes this by enumerating all the possible values of y. It follows that the simulation is correct as long as the parameters satisfy $k2^{n+1}(1 - \delta)^n Disc_{uniform}(f) < 1/6$. Taking f to be the inner product function, IP, for which $Disc_{uniform}(\text{IP}) = 2^{-n/2}$ (Example 3.29), this is achieved as long as $\delta > 1 - \sqrt{1/2} \approx 0.3$.

PROOF (OF LEMMA): We prove the following claim for all i: for every $\beta_1, \ldots, \beta_{i-1} \in \{0, 1\}^n$, the distribution of $y \circ z_i, \ldots, z_k$ conditioned upon $b_1 = \beta_1, \ldots, b_{i-1} = \beta_{i-1}$ is within statistical distance of at most $(k + 1 - i)\varepsilon$ from the uniform distribution on $\{0, 1\}^{n+k+1-i}$, where $\varepsilon = 2^{n+1}(1 - \delta)^n Disc_{uniform}(f)$. Start with $i = k + 1$ for which the claim is clearly true (because y is chosen uniformly at random in $\{0, 1\}^n$ so the two distributions are identical), and continue by induction for smaller values of i.

For the induction step, fix the conditioning $b_1 = \beta_1, \ldots, b_{i-1} = \beta_{i-1}$ and denote the induced distribution on b_i by D'. Now for each fixed value β_i, we have by induction hypothesis that even conditioned on $b_i = \beta_i$, the distribution of $y \circ z_{i+1}, \ldots, z_k$ is within statistical distance $(k - i)\varepsilon$ from uniform. It follows that the distribution of $b_i \circ y \circ z_{i+1}, \ldots, z_k$ is also within statistical distance $(k-i)\varepsilon$ from $D' \times U$, where U denotes the uniform distribution (on strings of length $n+k+2-i$). This implies, by substituting $z_i = f(b_i, y)$, that the distribution of $y \circ z_i, \ldots, z_k$ in our construction is within statistical distance $(k - i)\varepsilon$ from what it would have been if $b_i, y, z_{i+1}, \ldots, z_k$ were chosen from $D' \times U$. By Lemma 13.10, because $D'(b_i) \leq (1 - \delta)^n$ for all b_i, if $y, z_i, \ldots, z_k$ is chosen from $D' \times U$ (and substituting $z_i = f(b_i, y)$) it is within statistical distance $2^{n+1}(1 - \delta)^n Disc_{uniform}(f) = \varepsilon$ from the uniform distribution and the lemma follows.

$\square$

Exercise 13.12: Prove that the above simulation, using the inner product function, IP, in fact works for every fixed $\delta > 0$. Hint: Exercise 3.30.

13.4. Bibliographic Notes

Quasirandom graphs were studied, for example in [Chung, Graham, and Wilson 1989, Chung 1990] (see also [Alon and Spencer 1992]). In particular, several alternative definitions that can be given for this notion were proven equivalent. The relation between communication complexity and quasirandomness was presented in [Chung and Tetali 1993].

The connection between pseudorandom generators for communication complexity and deterministic amplification as well as its applicability in constructing pseudorandom generators for certain types of computations (for example, space-bounded computations) was exhibited in [Impagliazzo et al. 1994a]. For better deterministic amplification than the one presented here, see [Cohen and Wigderson 1989, Impagliazzo and Zuckerman 1989].

Various types of slightly random sources were considered in [von Neumann 1963, Blum 1986, Santha and Vazirani 1984, Chor and Goldreich 1985, Zuckermann 1991]. The treatment given here is similar to the one given in [Chor and Goldreich 1985] applied to the sources of [Santha and Vazirani 1984].

CHAPTER 14

Further Topics

In this chapter, we briefly mention several relevant topics not covered in this book.

14.1. Noisy Channels

[Schulman 1992, Schulman 1993] present a variant of the two-party model, in which Alice and Bob are communicating using a *noisy* channel. That is, each bit that is sent by either Alice of Bob is flipped with some probability $\lambda < 1/2$ (which is independent from what happens in other transmissions). Say, a player may send the bit 0 but the other player will receive 1. The question is what is the communication complexity of computing a function f in such a model.

Note that if Alice and Bob use a protocol $\mathcal{P}$ that was designed for the standard (noiseless) model, each such flip may lead the two players to be in different places in the protocol tree, and hence all subsequent communication may be meaningless. A naive approach would be to send each bit ℓ times instead of only once, and let the receiver, upon receiving a block of ℓ bits, take the majority of these ℓ bits. Because the bits are flipped independently, we can see that if $\ell = O(\log t)$, where t is the communication complexity of the original protocol $\mathcal{P}$ (and λ is fixed), then there is a good probability that all the t bits will arrive correctly. This solution uses $O(t \log t)$ bits. Schulman presented transformations that result in an $O(t)$ protocol $\mathcal{P}'$ (either randomized [Schulman 1992] or deterministic [Schulman 1993]) that fails in simulating $\mathcal{P}$ with exponentially small probability in t (and again, λ is fixed). For extensions, see [Rajagopalan and Schulman 1994]. These results generalize results of [Shannon 1948] for *one-way* communication.

14.2. Communication–Space Tradeoffs

An interesting question is what is the communication complexity of functions when space limits are put on the processors. This kind of problem was studied, for example, in [Lam, Tiwari, and Tompa 1989, Beame, Tompa, and Yau 1990]. The first issue that we need to address is the definition of the amount of "space" used by each of the processors. Intuitively, each player has a place to store its input, which is not counted as part of the space, and some additional space for the sake of making the computations. Note that in any reasonable definition of "space" the proof that for every function n bits of communication are enough, is no longer true. This is because the proof is based on the trivial protocol in which, say, Alice sends x to Bob, who computes $f(x, y)$. The problem is that now, with a restricted space $o(n)$, Bob cannot store x in order to use it in the computation of $f(x, y)$. Indeed, there are proofs that show that limiting the space requires higher communication complexity. For example, if Alice holds an $n \times n$ matrix, and Bob has an n-bit vector, then computing the matrix-vector product with space that is $o(n/\log n)$ requires $\Omega(n^2)$ bit [Beame et al. 1990], whereas without the space restriction, obviously $O(n)$ bits suffice.

14.3. Privacy

There are several scenarios in which the optimal protocol for computing a function f cannot be used. One example, discussed in Section 14.1, is in case that the communication channel is noisy. A different reason for not being able to use the optimal protocol is that in many cases the optimal protocols do not satisfy certain *privacy* constraints. [Orlitsky and El-Gamal 1984, Modiano and Ephremides 1992] consider a model in which Alice and Bob wish to compute $f(x, y)$ while preventing an eavesdropper from obtaining information on their input. In [Kushilevitz 1989] a different model is discussed where both players wish to compute $f(x, y)$ in a way that Alice will not have any information about y (other than what follows from her input x and the computed value $f(x, y)$) and Bob will not have any information about x (other than what follows from his input y and the computed value $f(x, y)$). It is shown that not for every function f this is possible, and even for functions that do have such protocols, n bits are not necessarily sufficient (in fact, $\Omega(2^n)$ bits may be necessary for certain functions). In some cases, communication complexity can be used for proving impossibility results in privacy [Chor, Geréb-Graus, and Kushilevitz 1990].

The following example shows that protocols developed in the study of communication complexity can sometimes be used to solve privacy problems. Consider the case where a user U wishes to obtain the k-th bit of a database x of $n = 2^\ell$ bits. However, the user wishes to get the bit x_k without the database knowing in which k he is interested. It is not difficult to prove that the only way of doing this is essentially by asking for a copy of the whole database x (that is, the communication complexity of solving this problem is $\Omega(n)$). Now, suppose that copies of the database x are stored in two sites D_1 and D_2 (as is the case with distributed databases). Now the problem can be solved much more efficiently. The best known upper bound is $O(n^{1/3})$ [Chor et al. 1995]. Here we present an inferior solution, yet a nontrivial one, based on the 3-party protocol for the function SUM-INDEX, given in Example 6.26. The user chooses uniformly at random a $\log n$ bit string i and computes $j = i \oplus k$ (i.e., the bitwise exclusive or of i and k). The user sends i to one of the databases (who now knows x and i) and j to the other database (who now knows x and j). The user obviously knows both i and j and so the three of them can use the protocol for SUM-INDEX (with messages sent only from the databases to the user). At the end of the protocol, the user can compute the output $x_{i \oplus j} = x_k$ as desired. The query to the first database, i, is obviously distributed uniformly at random in $\{0, 1\}^\ell$, and so is the query to the second database $j = i \oplus k$. This implies that the privacy of the user is maintained, while the communication complexity is now only $O(n^{0.92})$.

14.4. Algebraic Communication Complexity

The standard two-party model views the input given to each player as a vector of bits. In practice, it is sometimes useful to view the input as a vector of real numbers. The players are allowed to send messages that are also real numbers and naturally the functions of interest have an algebraic nature. The model should be defined carefully to avoid the possibility of encoding many real numbers into a single real number. This can be done, for example, by requiring that every message is a continuous function of the input and previous messages. This line of research was initiated by [Abelson 1978] and further studied, for example, in [Tsitsiklis and Luo 1987, Luo and Tsitsiklis 1991a, Luo and Tsitsiklis 1991b, Chen 1994]. The main motivation for this model is that, in practice, we would expect that if the real numbers will be sent within some finite precision, and if the function computed by the protocol is "smooth," then the computed result should be close to the true value.

14.5. Two-Sided Cards

Reviewing the definition of the protocol tree (Definition 1.1) in the standard two-party model, we see that it allows at each node v to evaluate a function that depends either on $x_1, \ldots, x_n$ (nodes corresponding to Alice) or on $y_1, \ldots, y_n$ (nodes corresponding to Bob). [Edmonds and Impagliazzo 1994] consider a generalization of this scenario in which at each node v we are allowed to evaluate a function w_v depending on n bits $z_1, \ldots, z_n$, where $z_i \in \{x_i, y_i\}$. Pictorially, we can think of n two-sided cards where on the front of the i-th card the value x_i is written and on the back of the i-th card the value y_i is written. In the standard two-party model Alice always transmits bits that depend on the front side of all of the cards and Bob transmits bits that depend on the back side of all of the cards. In the new model, we have a player that at each step sees from each card either its front or its back (the combination is specified by the protocol in the same way that in the two-party model the protocol specifies which player speaks next); the player transmits a bit depending on this combination of the cards; at the end the communication should determine the value of the function that we wish to compute. For example, the equality function, EQ, in this terminology is to check for each of these cards whether the same value appears on its front and on its back.

[Edmonds and Impagliazzo 1994] showed that good lower bounds on the communication complexity of such a game would give good width–length tradeoffs for oblivious branching programs (see Section 12.4). So far, however, such results were not obtained.

Consider, for example, the function EQ. It may seem that because we are not allowed to view x_i and y_i at the same time, then computing $EQ(x, y)$ should be difficult. Unfortunately, this intuition is wrong and surprising upper bounds were shown in [Edmonds and Impagliazzo 1994, Pudlák 1994] and finally by [Pudlák and Sgall 1995]. We describe below a protocol to compute the function EQ in this model with $O(\log^2 n)$ bits.

Note that x and y are equal if and only if $\sum_{i=1}^{n}(x_i - y_i)^2 = 0$ (this can be viewed as measuring the Euclidean distance between two vectors x and y in R^n). Now, we can write

$$\sum_{i=1}^{n}(x_i - y_i)^2 = \sum_{i=1}^{n}(x_i^2 + y_i^2 - 2x_i y_i)$$

$$= \sum_{i=1}^{n} x_i^2 + \sum_{i=1}^{n} y_i^2 - 2\left[\left(\sum_{i=1}^{n} x_i\right) \cdot \left(\sum_{i=1}^{n} y_i\right) - \sum_{i \neq j} x_i y_j\right].$$

Each of the terms $\sum_{i=1}^{n} x_i^2$ and $\sum_{i=1}^{n} x_i$ can be computed based on $x_1, \ldots, x_n$ and communicated with $\log n$ bits. Similarly, each of the terms $\sum_{i=1}^{n} y_i^2$ and $\sum_{i=1}^{n} y_i$ can be computed based on $y_1, \ldots, y_n$ and communicated with $\log n$ bits. Therefore, the only term missing is $\sum_{i \neq j} x_i y_j$. For this, look at each index $1 \leq i \leq n$ in its binary representation (that is, an index is represented by $\log n$ bits). For each $1 \leq k \leq \log n$ consider two combinations of the cards: (1) for each i whose k-th bit is 0 we view x_i and for each i whose k-th bit is 1 we view y_i; and (2) for each i whose k-th bit is 0 we view y_i and for each i whose k-th bit is 1 we view x_i. Note that for all $i \neq j$ there is a k for which the k-th bits in the binary representations of i and j differ. Hence, there is a combination in which we view x_i and y_j at the same time and can add $x_i y_j$ to the sum. In other words, with the $2 \log n$ combinations we can compute $2 \log n$ partial sums ($O(\log n)$ bits each), which together give us $\sum_{i \neq j} x_i y_j$. All together, we get an $O(\log^2 n)$-bit protocol.

Index of Notation

In this appendix we briefly go over some of the notations present throughout this book. We concentrate on notations that are not used locally but appear in at least two chapters of the book. Figure A.1 summarizes various complexity measures.

For a finite set Σ and an integer m, denote by Σ^m the set of all strings consisting of m characters from the set Σ. Most often we use the special case $\{0, 1\}^n$, which is the set of all binary strings of length n. We also use Σ^* to denote the collection of all finite strings over the set Σ. That is, $\Sigma^* = \cup_{m \geq 0} \Sigma^m$.

When we use "$\log t$" (where t is a number or a more complicated term), it should usually be interpreted as $\lceil \log_2 t \rceil$. This is often the case where $\log t$ denotes the number of bits transmitted by one of the players.

Notation	Defined in ...	Remarks
$B_\mu(f)$	Definition 2.14	μ-rectangle size bound
$B^1_*(f)$	Definition 2.14	Rectangle size bound
$C(f)$	Definition 2.1	Cover Number
$C^D(f)$	Definition 2.1	Partition Number
$C^P(f)$	Definition 2.1	Protocol partition Number
$D(f)$	Definition 1.2	Deterministic communication complexity
	Definition 5.2	Extended to relations
	Definition 6.2	Extended to multiparty protocols
$D^k(f)$	Definition 4.23	k-round (deterministic) communication complexity
$D^\mu_\epsilon(f)$	Definition 3.19	(μ, ϵ)-distributional communication complexity
$D^{||}(f)$	Definition 6.18	Simultaneous communication complexity
$D^{S:T}(f)$	Definition 7.1	Fixed partition communication complexity
$D^{worst}(f)$	Definition 7.1	Worst partition communication complexity
$D^{best}(f)$	Definition 7.7	Best partition communication complexity
$D^{n-best}(f)$	Definition 7.12	n-best partition communication complexity
$Disc_\mu(f)$	Definition 3.27	discrepancy (often used with $\mu = uniform$)
	Definition 6.14	Extended to multiparty protocols
$N(f)$	Definition 2.3	$\log C(f)$
$N^1(f)$	Definition 2.3	Nondeterministic communication complexity
$N^0(f)$	Definition 2.3	Co-nondeterministic communication complexity
$R(f)$	Definition 3.3	Randomized communication complexity
$R_\epsilon(f)$	Definition 3.3	ϵ-error randomized communication complexity
$R_0(f)$	Definition 3.3	Zero error randomized communication complexity
$R^1(f)$	Definition 3.3	One sided error randomized communication complexity
$R^1_\epsilon(f)$	Definition 3.3	One sided ϵ-error communication complexity
$R^{pub}(f)$	Definition 3.12	Public coin (randomized) communication complexity
$R^{pub}_\epsilon(f)$	Definition 3.12	ϵ-error public coin communication complexity
$R^{pub}_0(f)$	Definition 3.12	Zero error public coin communication complexity

Figure 0.1: Summary of Notations

Mathematical Background

In this section we give some mathematical background that is related to the topics of this book. We do not attempt to give a detailed description of any of the subjects that we mention. Rather, we mention some definitions and facts and refer the reader to appropriate books for further reading.

A.1. Asymptotics

Usually, when a solution to some problem P is analyzed, we are not interested in the amount of resources that are used on some particular input; rather, we want to know how the amount of resources grows with the size of the input. Hence, we usually think of P as a sequence of problems $P_1, P_2, P_3, \ldots$ where each P_n is the restriction of P to inputs of size n. For example, to analyze the number of bits Alice and Bob need to exchange in order to tell whether two input strings are equal, we make the analysis as a function of n, the length of the input strings. Hence, a complexity function is a function $f(n)$ that depends on n, the size of the input.

It is most important to be able to compare such complexity functions. The difficulty is that it is possible that some functions f and g on input size n_1 satisfy $f(n_1) < g(n_1)$, whereas on input size n_2 they satisfy $f(n_2) > g(n_2)$. Hence it is useful to consider the asymptotic behavior of the complexity functions. That is, to see which function is larger for sufficiently large values of n. The following relations between f and g are of interest. Intuitively they say that "f grows at most as fast as g," "f grows at least as fast as g," "f grows as fast as g," "f grows strictly slower than g," and "f grows strictly faster than g" (respectively):

$f(n) = O(g(n))$ – if there exist positive constants c and n_0 such that for all
$\qquad n \geq n_0$, $f(n) \leq c \cdot g(n)$.

$f(n) = \Omega(g(n))$ – if there exist positive constants c and n_0 such that for all
$\qquad n \geq n_0$, $f(n) \geq c \cdot g(n)$(alternatively, if $g(n) = O(f(n))$).

$f(n) = \Theta(g(n))$ – if there exist positive constants c_1, c_2 and n_0 such that for

all $n \geq n_0, c_1 \cdot g(n) \leq f(n) \leq c_2 \cdot g(n)$ (alternatively, if both $f(n) = O(g(n))$
and $g(n) = O(f(n))$).

$f(n) = o(g(n))$ – if for all positive constant $c > 0$, there exists a constant n_0
such that for all $n \geq n_0$, $f(n) < c \cdot g(n)$.

$f(n) = \omega(g(n))$ – if for all positive constant $c > 0$, there exists a constant n_0
such that for all $n \geq n_0$, $f(n) > c \cdot g(n)$ (alternatively, if $g(n) = o(f(n))$).

The reader who is not familiar with these notations is referred to almost any book on
algorithms or complexity. For example, [Cormen, Leiserson, and Rivest 1990] has an
excellent discussion of these notions and a lot of exercises.

A.2. Linear Algebra

A *group* $(G, +)$ consists of a non-empty set of elements and an operation $+$ defined on
them such that the following properties hold:

- Associativity: $(a + b) + c = a + (b + c)$, for every a, b, and c in G.

- There exists an element $0 \in G$ such that $a + 0 = 0 + a = a$, for every $a \in G$. This
  element is called the *identity element*.

- There exists an *inverse* for every $a \in G$. That is, an element $-a$ that satisfies $a + (-a) = (-a) + a = 0$.

The group is called *Abelian* if in addition it satisfies:

- Commutativity: $a + b = b + a$, for every a and b in G.

A *field* $(F, +, \cdot)$ is a set of elements F with two operations $+$ and $\cdot$ such that the
following holds:

- $(F, +)$ is an Abelian group.

- Commutativity of $\cdot$: $a \cdot b = b \cdot a$, for every a and b in F.

- Distributive law: $a \cdot (b + c) = (a \cdot b) + (a \cdot c)$, for every a, b, and c in F.

- There exists an identity element $1 \neq 0$, with respect to $\cdot$, such that $a \cdot 1 = 1 \cdot a = a$, for
  every $a \in F$.

- For every $a \in F$ different than 0 there exists an *inverse*. That is, an element a^{-1} that
  satisfies $a \cdot a^{-1} = 1$.

A *vector space* V over a field F is a set of elements, called vectors, with two operations:

- $+$ such that $(V, +)$ is an Abelian group.

- multiplication of elements in F and elements in V (which is also denoted by $\cdot$) that satisfies the following properties (for all $a, b \in F$ and $v, w \in V$): (1) $(ab) \cdot v = a \cdot (b \cdot v)$;
  (2) $a \cdot (v + w) = (a \cdot v) + (a \cdot w)$; (3) $(a + b) \cdot v = (a \cdot v) + (b \cdot v)$; and (4) $1 \cdot v = v$,
  where 1 is the identity element of F (with respect to $\cdot$).

—— 163 ——

Usually we will use vector spaces V, which are n-tuples of elements of F (that is $V = F^n$). In this case $+$ is defined by applying in each coordinate the $+$ operation of F. The operation $\cdot$ is also defined coordinate-wise. That is, if $v = (v_1, \ldots, v_n)$, $u = (u_1, \ldots, u_n)$, and $a \in F$, then $v + u = (v_1 + u_1, \ldots, v_n + u_n)$ and $a \cdot v = (a \cdot v_1, \ldots, a \cdot v_n)$. For example, the 0 element of $(V, +)$ in this case is a vector containing in each coordinate the 0 element of F. We denote this vector by $\vec{0}$.

Let $v_1, \ldots, v_k$ be k vectors in a vector space V over a field F. A vector $w \in V$ is a *linear combination* of $v_1, \ldots, v_k$ if there exist k scalars $a_1, \ldots, a_k$ in F such that

$$w = a_1 \cdot v_1 + \ldots + a_k \cdot v_k.$$

The vectors $v_1, \ldots, v_k$ are *linearly independent* if the only way to get $\vec{0}$ as a linear combination of $v_1, \ldots, v_k$ is by taking $a_1 = \cdots = a_k = 0$. The (*linear*) *dimension* of V, denoted $dim(V)$, is the cardinality of the largest set of vectors that are linearly independent. The (linear) span of k vectors $v_1, \ldots, v_k \in V$ is the collection of all vectors w that are linear combinations of $v_1, \ldots, v_k$ (using scalars from F). It can be verified that this collection forms a vector space. We will often be interested in $Z_2^n = GF[2]^n$, the vector space of all n-dimensional binary vectors (over the field $GF[2]$). If $v_1, \ldots, v_k$ are linearly independent vectors in Z_2^n, then the size of the spanned vector space is exactly 2^k.

Below are some additional topics that are of interest for the reader of this book. For additional text see, for example, [Lang 1993] or [Babai and Frankl 1988].

Rank of Matrices

Let F be a field, and $M = (m_{i,j})$ be a $k \times n$ matrix whose elements belong to the field F. The *row rank* of M is the maximal number of rows of M that are linearly independent (over the field F). Similarly, the *column rank* of M is the maximal number of columns of M that are linearly independent (over the field F). It is a known fact that for every matrix M (and any field F) the row rank and the column rank are always equal. This common value is called the *rank* of the matrix and is denoted $\text{rank}_F(M)$. If F is omitted we refer to the rank over the *reals* (unless other field is specified). It is known that, for every F, $\text{rank}_F(M)$ is no more than the rank of M over the reals.

Let F be any field, and let A and B be any two matrices over F. The following are known facts:

- $\text{rank}_F(c \cdot A) = \text{rank}_F(A)$, for any scalar $c \in F$ different than 0 (where $c \cdot A$ is a matrix whose (i, j) entry is $c \cdot a_{i,j}$).

- $\text{rank}_F(A + B) \leq \text{rank}_F(A) + \text{rank}_F(B)$ (where A and B are two matrices of the same dimensions and $A + B$ is a matrix whose (i, j) entry is $a_{i,j} + b_{i,j}$).

- $\text{rank}_F(AB) \leq \min\{\text{rank}_F(A), \text{rank}_F(B)\}$ (where A is a $k \times n$ matrix, B is an $n \times \ell$ matrix, and AB is a $k \times \ell$ matrix whose (i, j) entry is $\sum_{p=1}^{n} a_{i,p} \cdot b_{p,j}$).

- $\text{rank}_F(A \otimes B) = \text{rank}_F(A) \cdot \text{rank}_F(B)$, where $A \otimes B$ denotes the *Kronecker product*. Namely, if A is a $k \times n$ matrix and B is a $k' \times n'$ matrix, then $A \otimes B$ is a $(k \cdot k') \times (n \cdot n')$

matrix obtained by

$$
\begin{matrix}
a_{1,1} \cdot B & a_{1,2} \cdot B & \ldots & a_{1,n} \cdot B \\
a_{2,1} \cdot B & a_{2,2} \cdot B & \ldots & a_{2,n} \cdot B \\
\vdots & \vdots & \ddots & \vdots \\
a_{k,1} \cdot B & a_{k,2} \cdot B & \ldots & a_{k,n} \cdot B
\end{matrix}
$$

Inner Product

In what follows we define the notion of *inner product*. Although this notion is very general, in this book we use it only over the space Z_2^n, hence we consider the definition for this case only. Let u and v be two binary vectors in $\{0, 1\}^n$. The inner product of u and v is defined by

$$
\langle u, v \rangle = \sum_{i=1}^{n} u_i \cdot v_i \bmod 2.
$$

It follows immediately from the definition of the inner product that $\langle u, v \rangle = \langle v, u \rangle$ and that $\langle u + u', v \rangle = \langle u, v \rangle + \langle u', v \rangle \bmod 2$. A useful property of the inner product is that, for every $u \neq \vec{0}$,

$$
\Pr[\langle u, v \rangle = 1] = 1/2,
$$

where the probability is taken over $v \in \{0, 1\}^n$ with uniform distribution. The reason is that if $u \neq \vec{0}$, then for some coordinate j, $u_j = 1$. Hence we can partition the space $\{0, 1\}^n$ into 2^{n-1} pairs v, v' that differ only in their j-th coordinate. For each of these pairs, $\langle u, v \rangle \neq \langle u, v' \rangle$ hence with probability exactly $1/2$ the inner product of u with a random vector is 1. It follows from the above property that for every $u \neq u'$,

$$
\Pr[\langle u, v \rangle = \langle u', v \rangle] = 1/2,
$$

where the probability is taken over $v \in \{0, 1\}^n$ with uniform distribution. The reason is that $\Pr[\langle u, v \rangle = \langle u', v \rangle] = \Pr[\langle u - u', v \rangle = 0]$ and because $u \neq u'$, then $u - u' \neq \vec{0}$ so by the previous property this probability is exactly $1/2$. In a similar way, for every pair of distinct vectors u and u' that are both different than $\vec{0}$,

$$
\Pr[\langle u, v \rangle = \langle u', v \rangle = 1] = 1/4,
$$

where the probability, again, is taken over $v \in \{0, 1\}^n$ with uniform distribution.

Two vector spaces V and W in Z_2^n such that for all $v \in V$ and $w \in W$, $\langle v, w \rangle = 0$ are called orthogonal. The dimensions of these spaces satisfy $dim(V) + dim(W) \leq n$.

Norms

Let $v = (v_1, \ldots, v_n)$ be a vector over the reals. The (*Euclidean*) *norm* of v, is defined by

$$
\|v\| = \sqrt{\sum_{i=1}^{n} v_i^2}.
$$

Let A be a real matrix. The *norm* of A, denoted $\|A\|$, is defined as

$$\max_{v:\|v\|=1} \|Av\|.$$

A real number λ is called an *eigenvalue* of a matrix B if there exists a vector w such that $Bw = \lambda w$. Using this definition, a known characterization of the norm of a matrix is given by:

$$\|A\| = \max\{\sqrt{\lambda} : \lambda \text{ is an eigenvalue of } B = AA^T\},$$

where A^T denotes the *transpose* of the matrix A; that is, if A is a $k \times \ell$ matrix, then A^T is an $\ell \times k$ matrix such that $A^T_{i,j} = A_{j,i}$. The *Cauchy–Schwartz* inequality relates the scalar-product of v and w to their norms:

$$(vw) \leq \|v\| \cdot \|w\|.$$

Written differently it says:

$$\left(\sum_{i=1}^n v_i w_i\right)^2 \leq \sum_{i=1}^n v_i^2 \cdot \sum_{i=1}^n w_i^2.$$

The Cauchy–Schwartz inequality implies the following useful inequality:

$$vAw \leq \|v\| \cdot \|A\| \cdot \|w\|.$$

A.3. Probability Theory

In what follows we present several definitions and inequalities from probability theory. The reader is referred to [Alon and Spencer 1992] for further information, including proofs. The simplest inequality, is the so-called *Markov inequality* that states that for every nonnegative random variable X,

$$\Pr[X \geq \alpha] \leq \frac{E[X]}{\alpha},$$

where $E[X]$ denotes the expected value of X. Equivalently, the inequality can be stated as

$$\Pr[X \geq \beta \cdot E[X]] \leq 1/\beta.$$

The basic laws of probability say that if a random variable is sampled many times, then the average value converges to the expected value of the random variable. The following inequalities give bounds on the rate of this convergence. Let $X_1, \ldots, X_n$ be n independent 0-1 random variables with $\Pr[X_i = 1] = p \leq 1/2$ (that is, $E[X_i] = p$). Then, the *Chernoff inequality* says that for all δ ($0 < \delta \leq p(1-p)$)

$$\Pr\left[\left|\frac{\sum_{i=1}^n X_i}{n} - p\right| \geq \delta\right] \leq 2e^{-\frac{\delta^2 n}{2p(1-p)}}.$$

It can be generalized to get the so-called *Hoeffding inequality*: Let $X_1, \ldots, X_n$ be n independent random variables with identical probability distribution over the real interval $[a, b]$ that have expected value p. Then,

$$\Pr\left[\left|\frac{\sum_{i=1}^n X_i}{n} - p\right| \geq \delta\right] \leq 2e^{-\frac{2n\delta^2}{b-a}}.$$

Let D be a probability distribution over a set S. The *support* of D is defined as the set of all elements in S with positive probability (that is, all $s \in S$ such that $D(s) > 0$). For two probability distributions D_1 and D_2 over a set S it is sometimes required to measure how different they are. The *statistical distance* (or variation distance) between D_1 and D_2, denoted $\|D_1 - D_2\|$, is defined by

$$\|D_1 - D_2\| = \frac{1}{2} \sum_{s \in S} |D_1(s) - D_2(s)|.$$

This measure gets values between 0 (when $D_1 = D_2$) to 1 (when the supports of D_1 and D_2 are disjoint). An equivalent formulation is $\|D_1 - D_2\| = \max_{A \subseteq S} |D_1(A) - D_2(A)|$.

The *entropy* of a random variable X that takes values in $\{x_1, \ldots, x_t\}$, is defined by

$$H(X) = \sum_{i=1}^{t} \Pr(X = x_i) \cdot \log \frac{1}{\Pr(X = x_i)}.$$

It can be verified that $H(X) \leq \log t$, where equality holds for the uniform distribution. Also $H(X, Y) \leq H(X) + H(Y)$, with equality in the case that X and Y are independent. In the special case of random variables that take values in $\{0, 1\}$ we denote by $H(p)$ the entropy of a random variable that gets the value 1 with probability p (and the value 0 with probability $1 - p$). In this case $H(p) \leq 1$, with equality in the case that $p = 1/2$.

Many times, while analyzing the probability of certain events, we get expressions that involve binomial coefficients. For making estimates of these probabilities it is useful to use the following bounds (which hold for all $1 \leq s \leq n$):

$$\left[\frac{n}{s}\right]^s \leq \binom{n}{s} \leq \left[\frac{en}{s}\right]^s.$$

Better estimates can be derived using the Stirling formula, which states that

$$n! = (n/e)^n \sqrt{2\pi n}(1 + o(1)).$$

In particular, for $0 < \alpha < 1$,

$$\binom{n}{\alpha n} = \frac{1 + o(1)}{\sqrt{2\pi n \alpha(1 - \alpha)}} \cdot 2^{H(\alpha) \cdot n}.$$

Answers to Selected Problems

In this appendix we provide solutions for some of the exercises given throughout this book.

Solution for Exercise 1.7: We start by giving an $O(\log^2 n)$ bit solution for the median problem, MED, which is different than the one given in Example 1.6. Then we modify this solution to get the improved communication complexity. Assume, without loss of generality, that x and y have the same size and that this size is a power of 2 (they can reach this situation by exchanging the sizes of their inputs ($O(\log n)$ bits) and padding them with the appropriate numbers of the minimal element (1) and the maximal element (n)). The protocol works in stages. During the protocol Alice maintains a set x' consisting of all elements in her input set x that may still be the median (initially, $x' = x$) and Bob maintains a set $y' \subseteq y$ of all elements in y that may still be the median (initially, $y' = y$). At each stage, Alice sends Bob the value a, which is the median of x', and Bob sends the value b, which is the median of y'. If $a < b$, then Alice omits from x' the half smallest numbers and Bob omits from y' the half largest numbers. If $b < a$, then Alice omits from x' the half largest numbers and Bob omits from y' the half smallest numbers. Note that in both cases this omission maintains the median of $x' \cup y'$ and that the size of $x' \cup y'$ is reduced by a factor of 2. If $a = b$, then this value is obviously the median, and if $|x'| = |y'| = 1$, then the smaller number is the median. To conclude, the number of stages is $O(\log n)$ and in each of these stages the number of bits exchanged is $O(\log n)$ so the communication complexity is $O(\log^2 n)$.

To reduce the communication complexity to $O(\log n)$, we make two observations. First, in each stage the players only need to know which of a and b is the larger. For this, it is enough that they will exchange these numbers in a bit-by-bit manner (starting from the most significant bit) and stop immediately when they find a coordinate j in which $a_j \neq b_j$. Second, note that if a and b were the medians in a certain stage and, say, $a < b$, then in the next stage (and on) the remaining numbers in $x' \cup y'$ are in the range between a and b. Therefore, all the medians exchanged in the next stages must agree with the coordinates in which a and b agreed (that is, $1, \ldots, j-1$) and therefore the values in these coordinates need not be sent. This implies that each of the $\log n$ coordinates will not be exchanged more than once and the communication complexity of the modified protocol is therefore $O(\log n)$.

Solution for Exercise 1.8: For every graph G, we describe an appropriate protocol $\mathcal{P}_G$. The protocol works in stages, where the number of stages is at most $\log n$ and in each stage $O(\log n)$ bits are exchanged. All together this proves that $D(CIS_G) = O(\log^2 n)$. The players maintain a set of vertices $V' \subseteq V$ such that if C and I intersect, then the intersection is in V'. Initially $V' = V$. In each stage the players do the following:

- Alice looks for a vertex u in $C \cap V'$ such that the number of vertices in u's neighborhood (that is, u and the vertices adjacent to it according to G) that also belong to V' is at most $|V'|/2$. She sends the bit "0" if no such vertex exists; otherwise, she sends the bit "1" followed by the name of u ($\log n$ bits).

- If Alice sends a name of a vertex u, then Bob checks whether $u \in I$. If so, he outputs "1" (that is, there is an intersection). Otherwise, both players update V' (in their own memories) to be the intersection of V' with the neighborhood of u and they start a new stage. If Alice does not find a vertex u as needed, then Bob looks for a vertex w in $I \cap V'$ such that the number of vertices in w's neighborhood that also belong to V' is greater than $|V'|/2$. If there is no such vertex, Bob outputs "0" (that is, C and I are disjoint) and the protocol terminates. If there is such a vertex, w, then Bob sends its name to Alice.

- Alice checks whether $w \in C$. If so, she outputs "1" (that is, there is an intersection). Otherwise, both players update V' so that it contains only w and its nonneighbors that appeared in V' before the current stage.

For the correctness of the protocol, we claim that if C and I intersect in some vertex v then, by induction, $v \in V'$. This obviously holds when the protocol starts. There are two places in which V' is modified: (1) If Alice sends a name of a vertex u that is different than v. In this case, because C is a clique, v is a neighbor of u, and because it was in V' before the stage started (by the induction hypothesis) it also remains in V' when it is modified. (2) If Bob sends a name of a vertex w that is different than v. In this case, because I is an independent set, v is a nonneighbor of u, and because it was in V' before the stage started it also remains in V' when V' is modified. If the protocol outputs "1" then C and I clearly intersect. By the above claim, because the neighborhood of all vertices in $C \cap V'$ is of size at most $|V'|/2$ and the neighborhood of all vertices in $I \cap V'$ is of size greater than $|V'|/2$, then C and I are disjoint (otherwise, the intersection vertex v has neighborhood of size at most $|V'|/2$ and greater than $|V'|/2$ at the same time).

As for the complexity, it follows immediately from the protocol that the size of V' decreases by a factor of 2 in each stage and hence the number of stages is at most $\log_2 n$, and the communication complexity is $O(\log^2 n)$ as desired.

Solution for Exercise 2.18: The proof utilizes the *probabilistic method* (for an introduction to the probabilistic method the reader is referred to [Alon and Spencer 1992]). Choose at random a function $f : \{0, 1\}^n \times \{0,1\}^n \to \{0,1\}$. By this, we mean that for every input pair $(x, y) \in \{0,1\}^n \times \{0,1\}^n$ the value $f(x,y)$ is chosen to be 0 or 1 each with probability $1/2$. In addition, the choices for different input pairs are independent. The expected number of 1s in f is $2^{2n}/2$. By Chernoff inequality, the probability that f has less than $2^{2n}/4$ 1s can be bounded by $\epsilon_1 = 2e^{-n/8}$. Now we show that the probability that $N^1(f) = \Omega(n)$ is large. For this it is enough to show that with high probability f has no 1-monochromatic rectangle of size $10 \cdot 2^n$ (obviously, this also implies that there are no larger monochromatic 1-rectangles). In such a case, to cover the 1s of f at least $\frac{2^{2n}}{4 \cdot 10 \cdot 2^n} = \frac{2^n}{40}$ 1-monochromatic rectangles are needed and therefore $N^1(f) = \Omega(n)$.

To prove this, note that the probability of a particular rectangle of size $10 \cdot 2^n$ to be 1-monochromatic is $2^{-10 \cdot 2^n}$ and that the number of rectangles is clearly bounded by $2^{2^n} \cdot 2^{2^n} = 2^{2 \cdot 2^n}$. Therefore, the probability that there exists a 1-monochromatic rectangle of size $10 \cdot 2^n$ is at most $\epsilon_2 = 2^{2 \cdot 2^n} \cdot 2^{-10 \cdot 2^n} = 2^{-8 \cdot 2^n}$.

Next, we prove that with high probability f has no fooling set of size $10n$ (therefore clearly, f cannot have a larger fooling set). The probability of a particular set of size $10n$ to be a fooling set is not larger than 2 (the number of choices for the value b that f gets on the fooling set pairs) times 2^{-10n} (the probability that for all pairs in the fooling sets b is chosen as the value of f) times $(3/4)^{\binom{10n}{2}}$ (the probability that, for each two distinct pairs (x_1, y_1) and (x_2, y_2) in the fooling set, for at least one of (x_1, y_2) and (x_2, y_1) the complement value $\bar{b}$ was chosen). This is bounded by 2^{-50n^2}. Now the number of possible fooling sets of size $10n$ is $\binom{2^{2n}}{10n} < 2^{20n^2}$. All together, the probability that a fooling set of size $10n$ exists for f is bounded by $\epsilon_3 = 2^{20n^2} \cdot 2^{-50n^2} = 2^{-30n^2}$.

To conclude, with very high probability (that is, at least $1 - \epsilon_1 - \epsilon_2 - \epsilon_3$) a randomly chosen function f satisfies $N^1(f) = \Omega(n)$ and it has no fooling set of size $10n$.

Solution for Exercise 3.18: Assume that $x \neq y$ (as shown in Example 3.13, this can be checked with $O(1)$ communication in the public coin model). The idea is that the two players will do a binary search for i_0, the most significant bit in which x and y differ. This bit i_0 clearly determines which of the numbers, x or y, is larger. We start by an $O(\log n \log \log n)$ solution and then modify it to get an $O(\log n)$ solution.

Suppose that Alice and Bob have a subprotocol $TEST(i, j)$ ($i \leq j$) that tests whether the two substrings $x_i, \ldots, x_j$ and $y_i, \ldots, y_j$ are equal. The players maintain two borders i and j ($i \leq j$) for the search (initially, $i = 1$ and $j = n$). In each stage, if $i = j$, then the players exchange their i-th bits to see which number is larger. If $i < j$, then the players define $m = (i + j)/2$ and run the subprotocol $TEST(i, m)$. If the result of this subprotocol is "not equal," they set $j = m$, whereas if the result is "equal," they set $i = m + 1$. In each case the difference $j - i$ is divided by 2 and hence the number of stages is $\log n$. The only question remaining is the implementation of $TEST(i, j)$. Example 3.13 shows that equality can be tested in the public coin model with $O(1)$ bits and error probability $1/4$. Thus if we implement $TEST$ by repeating this protocol $O(\log \log n)$ times we can reduce the error probability to, say, $1/(4 \log n)$ while increasing the communication to $O(\log \log n)$. All together, because we use $TEST$ $\log n$ times, the communication complexity is only $O(\log n \log \log n)$ and with probability at most $\log n \cdot 1/(4 \log n) = 1/4$ any of them is wrong.

To improve the communication complexity, we use a more efficient $TEST$, with $O(1)$ bits (as in Example 3.13), but take into account that because $TEST$ fails with probability $1/4$ we may have to "fix" the search borders from time to time. However, because the protocol of Example 3.13 makes only one-sided error (that is, the only type of error is that it may say "equal" when actually the numbers are not equal), when j is updated then indeed $i_0 \leq j$, and only when i is updated an error can be made (that is, $i_0 < i$). The following protocol modifies the previous one by "fixing" the value of i from time to time.

1. Both players set $i = 1$ and $j = n$.

2. If $c \log n$ bits were already exchanged, then if $i < j$ stop with an arbitrary output (say, 0); otherwise, if $i = j$, Alice sends the bit x_i to Bob, who compares it with y_i and outputs 0 or 1 accordingly. If less than $c \log n$ bits were exchanged so far, then the players continue to the next step.

3. (FIXING) The players run $TEST(1, i-1)$. If the output is "equal" they proceed to the next step. If the output is "not equal" (this implies that $i_0 < i$) the players backtrack to the previous value of i and return to Step (2).

4. (SEARCH) If $i = j$, the players go to Step (2). Otherwise, if $i < j$, the players set $m = (i+j)/2$ and run $TEST(i,m)$. If the output is "equal" (this may be wrong), they store the current value of i and set $i = m+1$ and if the output is "not equal," they set $j = m$. In both cases they return to Step (2).

The complexity is easy, since the protocol is forced to stop (Step (2)) if more than $c\log n$ bits are exchanged. For the correctness, we need to prove that within this many stages the players indeed find (with high probability) the bit i_0. Consider the sequence of pairs (i,j) the players have in Step (2) of the protocol (between any two executions of Step (2) the subprotocol $TEST$ is used at most twice, hence each pair in the sequence corresponds to $O(1)$ bits of communication). A pair (i,j) in this sequence is *good* if i_0 is within the search borders (that is, $i \le i_0 \le j$) and, in addition, this is the first time that this pair appears in the sequence. As before, the difference $j - i$ is reduced by a factor of 2 each time that the borders are updated correctly. Hence, the number of good pairs is $\log n$. We will prove that the *expected* number of tests done between two consecutive *good* pairs is $O(1)$ and hence, by linearity of the expectation, an *expected* number of $O(\log n)$ tests is sufficient. This implies that stopping after $c\log n$ bits is also sufficient (with a constant increase in the error probability).

Consider a good pair (i,j). If i_0 is larger than $m = (i+j)/2$, then $TEST(i,m)$ always outputs "equal" and with a single test the players proceed to the next good pair. If however $i_0 \le m$, then with probability $3/4$ $TEST(i,m)$ outputs "not equal" and with a single test we are done, and with probability $1/4$ it outputs "equal" and we have a bad pair (i,j). In such a case, again, we have a probability $3/4$ of fixing i and probability $1/4$ of going deeper in the search (note that when we proceed with the wrong i any further updates of j still satisfy $i_0 \le j$ and any further updates of i still satisfy $i_0 < i$). In other words, at each step, with probability $3/4$ we take the right move and with probability $1/4$ we take the wrong move. We are interested in the expected number of steps until the number of right moves becomes larger than the number of wrong moves (at this point we will be in the next good pair). The probability that we will make exactly k steps is smaller than the probability that we will not finish within the first $k-1$ steps. By Chernoff inequality, this probability is smaller than α^{k-1} for some constant $\alpha < 1$. Hence the expected number of steps needed is at most $\sum_{k=1}^{\infty} \alpha^{k-1} \cdot k$. This sum, by simple calculation, equals $(1/(1-\alpha))^2 = O(1)$.

Solution for Exercise 4.8 (Part (1)): A linear program is just an optimization problem that consists of a collection of linear inequalities that a solution should satisfy and an objective function to be maximized (or minimized). More precisely, let A be a $k \times \ell$ real matrix, let $\vec{b}$ be a length ℓ real vector, and let $\vec{c}$ be a length k real vector. Then a linear program has the form:

$$\max_{\vec{v}=v_1,\dots,v_\ell} \vec{b}\cdot\vec{v} \quad \text{such that} \quad A\vec{v} \le \vec{c},\ \vec{v} \ge \vec{0}.$$

(In fact the definition can be made even more general but this form is enough for our purposes.) The duality theorem of linear programming states that the solution for this program (that is, the maximum value $\vec{b}\cdot\vec{v}$ as above) equals the solution of the following minimization problem (sometimes referred to as the *dual* program):

$$\min_{\vec{u}=u_1,\dots,v_k} \vec{c} \cdot \vec{u} \quad \text{such that} \quad A^T\vec{u} \geq \vec{b}, \vec{u} \geq \vec{0}.$$

(For a background on linear programming see, for example, [Karloff 1991].)

To represent $B^1_*(f)$ by a linear program, let k be the number of 1-monochromatic rectangles with respect to f, and let ℓ be the number of input pairs (x, y) such that $f(x,y) = 1$. Let A be a $k \times \ell$ matrix such that each row corresponds to a 1-monochromatic rectangle R and each column corresponds to an input (x,y) such that $f(x,y) = 1$. The entry $(R,(x,y))$ of the matrix A equals 1 if (x,y) belongs to R and 0 otherwise. Consider the following linear program:

$$\max_{\vec{v}=v_1,\dots,v_\ell} \vec{1} \cdot \vec{v} \quad \text{such that} \quad A\vec{v} \leq \vec{1}, \vec{v} \geq \vec{0}.$$

We claim that α, the optimal solution for this program, equals $B^1_*(f)$ (it can be easily seen that $\alpha \geq 1$). On one hand, if $\vec{v}$ is a vector for which α is obtained, we can define a probability distribution μ on the 1s of f by $\mu(x,y) = \frac{v_{(x,y)}}{\alpha}$. Because $\vec{v}$ satisfies $\vec{v} \geq \vec{0}$ then, for every (x,y), $\mu(x,y) \geq 0$. Moreover, $\sum_{(x,y)} \mu(x,y) = \sum_{(x,y)} \frac{v_{(x,y)}}{\alpha} = \frac{\alpha}{\alpha} = 1$. Therefore μ is indeed a probability distribution. In addition, for every 1-monochromatic rectangle R, by the fact that $A\vec{v} \leq \vec{1}$ it follows that $\mu(R) \leq \frac{1}{\alpha}$. Thus, $B^1_*(f) \geq B_\mu(f) \geq \alpha$.

On the other hand, let μ be probability distribution on the 1s of f such that $B^1_*(f) = B_\mu(f)$. Define a vector $\vec{v}$ by $v_{(x,y)} = B_\mu(f) \cdot \mu(x,y)$. Because μ is a probability distribution, $\vec{v} \geq \vec{0}$. In addition, for every 1-monochromatic rectangle R, when multiplying the R row of A by $\vec{v}$ we get $B_\mu(f) \cdot \mu(R)$, which is at most $\frac{B_\mu(f)}{B_\mu(f)} = 1$, so $A\vec{v} \leq \vec{1}$. Therefore, $\alpha \geq \vec{1} \cdot \vec{v} = \sum_{(x,y)} B_\mu(f) \cdot \mu(x,y) = B_\mu(f) = B^1_*(f)$. All together, $\alpha = B^1_*(f)$. Finally, we can write the corresponding dual program:

$$\min_{\vec{u}=u_1,\dots,v_k} \vec{1} \cdot \vec{u} \quad \text{such that} \quad A^T\vec{u} \geq \vec{1}, \vec{u} \geq \vec{0}.$$

Solution for Exercise 5.10: For the lower bound, we use Lemma 5.9 with X restricted to the set of all strings x such that $\#_1(x) = (n/2) + 1$ (where, for a string w, $\#_1(w)$ denotes the number of 1s in w) and Y restricted to the set of all strings y such that $\#_1(y) = n/2$. For these sets X and Y, the set C satisfies $|C| = |Y| \cdot (n/2)$ (for every $y \in Y$ every 0-bit that is changed to 1 gives $x \in X$) and also $|C| = |X| \cdot ((n/2) - 1)$ (for every $x \in X$ every 1-bit that is changed to 0 gives $y \in Y$). Hence

$$C^D(R_{\text{MAJ}}) \geq \frac{|C|^2}{|X||Y|} = \frac{|Y| \cdot (n/2) \cdot |X| \cdot ((n/2) - 1)}{|X||Y|} = n^2/4 - n/2.$$

That is, $D(R_{\text{MAJ}}) \geq 2 \log n - O(1)$.

For the upper bound, we start with an $O(\log^2 n)$ protocol. At stage $i + 1$ Alice views her current string $x(i)$ as consisting of two (equal-sized) halves x_L and x_R (that is, $x(i) = x_L \circ x_R$). She sends Bob $\#_1(x_L)$ and $\#_1(x_R)$ ($O(\log n)$ bits). Bob compares these numbers with $\#_1(y_L)$ and $\#_1(y_R)$. He tells Alice (using a single bit) in which half the numbers of 1s differ (if this holds in both halves he chooses one of them arbitrarily). Alice and Bob set $x(i+1)$ and $y(i+1)$ (respectively) to this half of their strings. By induction, there is always a half with different number of 1s (because we start with $\#_1(y) \leq n/2 < \#_1(x)$). After $\log n$ stages, the players have substrings of length 1 in which x and y differ. The index of this bit is the desired output. The total communication is $O(\log^2 n)$.

To get an $O(\log n)$ protocol, we modify the above protocol as follows. In the above protocol, the only aim was to make sure that $\#_1(x(i)) \neq \#_1(y(i))$. Here, Alice and Bob at the end of the i-th stage will also have a number d_i such that $|\#_1(x(i)) - \#_1(y(i))| \geq 2^{d_i}$ $(0 \leq d_i \leq \log n)$. The intuition is that if d_i is large the players probably sent many bits so far but will be able to save bits in the next stages. The $i + 1$ stage of the protocol goes as follows. We know that in (at least) one of the halves, say the left, the difference in the number of 1s is at least 2^{d_i-1} (the players do not know which of the halves is this, so they will do the following in each of the two halves in parallel). Let $a_{\log n} \cdots a_2 a_1$ be the binary representation of $\#_1(x_L)$ and $b_{\log n} \cdots b_2 b_1$ the binary representation of $\#_1(y_L)$. The players exchange these numbers in a bit-by-bit manner, going from the least significant bits toward the most significant bits. However, they start from position $d_i - 1$, ignoring the $d_i - 2$ least significant bits in positions $1, \ldots, d_i - 2$ (when d_i is very small we may refer to positions that are smaller than 1; think of this positions as containing 0s). If $\#_1(x_L)$ and $\#_1(y_L)$ differ by at least 2^{d_i}, this implies that the truncated numbers (i.e, $a' = a_{\log n} \cdots a_{d_i-1}$ and $b' = b_{\log n} \cdots b_{d_i-1}$) differ by at least 2. The players stop exchanging their bits in a position ℓ according to these rules:

1. If $a_{d_i-1} = b_{d_i-1}$, then ℓ is the first position in which the bits differ (there must be such a position because $a' \neq b'$). That is, $a_\ell \neq b_\ell$ and for all $d_i - 1 \leq \ell' < \ell$, $a_{\ell'} = b_{\ell'}$.

2. If $a_{d_i-1} \neq b_{d_i-1}$ but $a_{d_i} = b_{d_i}$, then ℓ is the next position in which the bits differ (there must be such a position because a' and b' differ by at least 2).

3. If both $a_{d_i-1} \neq b_{d_i-1}$ and $a_{d_i} \neq b_{d_i}$, then if in one of the numbers both bits are 1s and in the other number both are 0s, stop in position $\ell = d_i$. Otherwise, the bits in one of the numbers are 10 and in the other 01. Again, because a' and b' differ by at least 2 (and $10 - 01$ is 1), we let ℓ be the next position in which the bits differ.

Let $k_{i+1} = \ell - d_i + 1$ and $d_{i+1} = d_i + k_{i+1} - 3$. The number of bits transmitted in stage $i + 1$ is $4k_{i+1}$ (Alice and Bob exchange the positions $d_i - 1, \ldots, \ell$ in the 4 numbers $\#_1(x_L)$, $\#_1(x_R)$, $\#_1(y_L)$, and $\#_1(y_R)$). We now prove that the difference at the end of stage $i + 1$ is indeed at least $2^{d_{i+1}}$. Because the proof for all stopping rules is similar we prove it only for case (1), leaving the details of the other cases to the reader. Assume, without loss of generality, that $a_\ell = 1$ and $b_\ell = 0$. There are two subcases depending on the bits in positions $\ell + 1, \ldots, \log n$. Let β_a be the number represented by $a_{\log n} \cdots a_{\ell+1}$ and β_b represented by $b_{\log n} \cdots b_{\ell+1}$. If $\beta_a \geq \beta_b$, then $a - b \geq 2^{\ell-1} - (2^{d_i-1} - 1)$, where the term $2^{\ell-1}$ is contributed by the ℓ-th position (and the more significant bits are either equal or larger in a which makes the difference only bigger) and we subtract $2^{d_i-1} - 1$ because we do not know anything about the content of positions $1, \ldots, d_i - 1$. Because $\ell \geq d_i + 1$ we get $a - b > 2^{\ell-2} = 2^{d_i+k_{i+1}-3}$. The second subcase is where $\beta_a < \beta_b$. In this case, using similar arguments,

$$b - a \geq (\beta_b - \beta_a) \cdot 2^\ell - 2^{\ell-1} - (2^{d_i-1} - 1) \geq 2^{\ell-1} - (2^{d_i-1} - 1) \geq 2^{d_i+k_{i+1}-3}.$$

We showed that $4 \cdot k_{i+1}$ bits are sent in the $i + 1$ stage and $d_{i+1} = d_i + k_{i+1} - 3$. This implies that the total communication is

$$4 \cdot \sum_{i=0}^{\log n - 1} k_{i+1} = 4 \cdot \sum_{i=0}^{\log n - 1} ((d_{i+1} - d_i) + 3) = 4 \cdot (3\log n + d_{\log n} - d_0) = O(\log n).$$

Solution for Exercise 7.11 (Part (2)): The idea is to use the technique of Example 7.9 (the "shifted equality" function, SEQ) by embedding the "shifted inner product" function into the function PROD as follows. Let $k = \log n$, $t = n/k$, and let $0 \leq s, r < k$ be two parameters (to be chosen). Given $x, y \in \{0,1\}^t$, we define $a, b \in \{0,1\}^n$ by assigning $a_{ki+s} = x_i$ and $b_{kj+r} = y_j$, for all $0 \leq i, j < t$, and fix all other entries of a and b to zero (that is, most of the entries of a and b contain 0s; and the 1s are separated by at least $k = \log n$ 0s). It can be verified that for $0 \leq \ell < 2t$,

$$\text{PROD}(a, b, k\ell + s + r) = \sum_{i=0}^{\ell} x_i y_{\ell-i} \bmod 2 = \langle x_0 \ldots x_\ell, y_\ell \ldots y_0 \rangle$$

(where for $i \geq t$, x_i and y_i are defined to be zero). This uses the fact that due to the sparseness of 1s in a and b there is no carry for more than k steps.

There are two minor technical problems to solve before we can emulate the proof of Example 7.9 using the lower bound for IP (instead of the lower bound for EQ). First, the bits of x and y are only a fraction of $1/\log n$ of the bits of a and b. Hence, in principle, it is possible that all of them are given to one player. Second, because the length of the inner product induced by a certain value of ℓ is $\ell + 1$, there is no complete symmetry for all shifts (values of ℓ). We overcome these difficulties as follows: as in the case of SEQ we may assume, without loss of generality, that Alice holds at least $n/2 - O(\log n)$ bits of a and Bob holds at least $n/2 - O(\log n)$ bits of b. Now we use the freedom to choose s and r. We look at Alice's bits and fix s to be such that Alice holds the largest number of bits of the form a_{ki+s}. Denote by A the set of $0 \leq i < t$ such that Alice holds the bit a_{ki+s}, and notice that $|A| \geq \frac{1}{k}(n/2 - O(\log n)) = \Omega(t)$. Similarly, fix r to be such that Bob holds the largest number of bits of the form b_{kj+r}. Denote by B the set of $0 \leq j < t$ such that Bob holds the bit b_{kj+r} (again, $|B| = \Omega(t)$). Fix all bits outside of A and B to zero.

Let $B_\ell = \{i \mid \ell - i \in B\}$. We now claim that there is a value for ℓ that satisfies $|A \cap B_\ell| = \Omega(t) = \Omega(m/\log m)$. This will conclude the proof due to the lower bound on the deterministic communication complexity of IP (Example 1.29). This again can be proven as in Example 7.9. We use here a somewhat different argument (which is essentially the same proof with a different terminology): consider the expected value for $|A \cap B_\ell|$, where ℓ is chosen at random in $0, \ldots, 2t - 1$. For an arbitrary $i \in A$, the probability that $0 \leq \ell - i < t$ is at least $1/2$. Conditioned on this happening, ℓ is uniformly distributed in $0, \ldots, t - 1$, and thus $\Pr[i \in B_\ell] \geq \alpha$, for some constant α (recall that $|A|$ and $|B|$ are $\Omega(t)$). It follows that the expected value for $|A \cap B_\ell|$ is $\Omega(t)$ and thus some value of ℓ achieves at least this.

Solution for Exercise 7.15: Consider the graph G_A consists of the n edges that are input to Alice and the graph G_B consists of the n edges that are input to Bob. Let $d = n/4\ell$. Let S_A be a set of d edges $(u_1, v_1), \ldots, (u_d, v_d)$ in G_A such that $v_1, \ldots, v_d$ are all distinct and they are different from $u_1, \ldots, u_d$ ($u_1, \ldots, u_d$ may not be distinct). Such a set of edges must exist because either there is a vertex u in G_A of degree at least d (in which case S_A is a set of d edges connected to u), or else, if all vertices are of degree at most $d - 1$, the graph G_A contains a matching of size at least d (in which case S_A is a matching of size d). The reason is that we can construct such a matching in a greedy way: at each step we pick an edge $e = (u, v)$, add it to the matching, and eliminate the edge e together with all other edges connected to u and v (at most $d - 2$ additional edges for each of the two vertices). All together, at most $2d - 3$ edges. Because $d(2d - 3) \leq n$ this can be repeated at least d times. Now consider the graph G_B. Remove from it all edges that have a joint vertex with any of the d edges in S_A. Because there are at most $2d$ vertices in S_A, the number of edges eliminated from G_B is at most $2d \cdot \ell \leq n/2$. In other words, in the modified graph G'_B, there are at least $n/2$ edges. Therefore, in a similar way, we can find in G'_B a set S_B of d edges $(u'_1, v'_1), \ldots, (u'_d, v'_d)$ such that $v'_1, \ldots, v'_d$ are all distinct and they are different from $u'_1, \ldots, u'_d$. (By the definition of G'_B, the vertices $u'_1, \ldots, u'_d, v'_1, \ldots, v'_d$ are all different from $u_1, \ldots, u_d, v_1, \ldots, v_d$.)

We now fix all input bits (that is, edges) not in S_A or S_B. We will show that the disjointness function DISJ on $\{0,1\}^d \times \{0,1\}^d$ can be reduced to the communication problem defined by S_A and S_B. This implies, by Example 1.23, that at least $d = \Omega(n/\ell)$ bits are required to solve USTCON, as needed. Connect every two distinct vertices u_i and u_j with an edge (that is, fix the input bit corresponding to the edge (u_i, u_j) to 1). Similarly, connect every two distinct vertices u'_i and u'_j with an edge. Also, connect vertex s of the graph to $u_1, \ldots, u_d$ and vertex t of the graph to $u'_1, \ldots, u'_d$ and put an edge connecting v_i to v'_i, for all $1 \leq i \leq d$. All other edges out of S_A and S_B do not exist (that is, fix the corresponding input bits to 0). The reader may now verify that vertices s and t of the graph are connected if and only if for some j the edge (u_j, v_j) (given to Alice) and the edge (u'_j, v'_j) (given to Bob) are both set to 1. Hence the problem that Alice and Bob need to solve in this case is the disjointness function.

Bibliography

H. Abelson, "Lower Bounds on Information Transfer in Distributed Computations," *Journal of the ACM* **27**(2), 1980, 384–392. (Early version in *Proc. of 19th IEEE Symposium on Foundations of Computer Science*, 1978, 151–158.)

F. Ablayev, "Lower Bounds for One-Way Probabilistic Communication Complexity," *Proc. of 20th International Colloquium on Automata, Languages, and Programming*, Lecture Notes in Computer Science (Springer) 700, Springer: Berlin, 1993, 241–252.

R. Ahlswede and N. Cai, "On Communication Complexity of Vector-Valued Functions," *IEEE Transactions on Information Theory* **40**(6), 1994, 2062–2067.

A. Aho, J. Ullman, and M. Yannakakis, "On Notions of Information Transfer in VLSI Circuits," *Proc. of 15th ACM Symposium on Theory of Computing*, 1983, 133–139.

M. Ajtai, "A Lower Bound for Finding Predecessors in Yao's Cell Probe Model," *Combinatorica* **8**, 1988, 235–247.

N. Alon and W. Maass, "Meanders and their Applications in Lower Bound Arguments," *Journal of Computer and System Sciences* **37**(2), 1988, 118–129. (Early version in *Proc. of 27th IEEE Symposium on Foundations of Computer Science*, 1986, 410–417.)

N. Alon and A. Orlitsky, "Repeated Communication and Ramsey Graphs," *IEEE Transactions on Information Theory* **41**(5), 1995, 1276–1289.

N. Alon and P. D. Seymour, "A Counterexample to the Rank-Coloring Conjecture," *J. Graph Theory* **13**, 1989, 523–525.

N. Alon and J. Spencer, "The Probabilistic Method," Wiley: New York, 1992.

N. Alon, P. Frankl, and V. Rödl, "Geometric Realization of Set Systems and Probabilistic Communication Complexity," *Proc. of 26th IEEE Symposium on Foundations of Computer Science*, 1985, 277–280.

A. Ambainis, "Upper Bounds on Multiparty Communication Complexity of Shifts," *Proc. of 13th STACS*, Lecture Notes in Computer Science 1046, Springer: Berlin, 1996, 631–642.

L. Babai and P. Frankl, "Linear Algebra Methods in Combinatorics (preliminary version)," 1988.

L. Babai, P. Frankl, and J. Simon, "Complexity Classes in Communication Complexity Theory," *Proc. of 27th IEEE Symposium on Foundations of Computer Science*, 1986, 337–347.

L. Babai and P. Kimmel, manuscript, 1996.

L. Babai, P. Kimmel, and S. V. Lokam, "Simultaneous Messages vs. Communication," *Proc. of 12th Symposium on Theoretical Aspects of Computer Science*, Lecture Notes in Computer Science (Springer) 900, Springer: Berlin, 1995, 361–372.

L. Babai, N. Nisan, and M. Szegedy, "Multiparty Protocols, Pseudorandom Generators for LOGSPACE, and Time–Space Trade-offs," *Journal of Computer and System Sciences* **45**(2), 1992, 204–232. (Early version in *Proc. of 21st ACM Symposium on Theory of Computing*, 1989, 1–11.)

L. Babai, P. Pudlák, V. Rödl, and E. Szemeredi, "Lower Bounds to the Complexity of Symmetric Boolean Functions," *Theoretical Computer Science* **74**, 1990, 313–323.

P. Beame and J. Lawry, "Randomized versus Nondeterministic Communication Complexity," *Proc. of 24th ACM Symposium on Theory of Computing*, 1992, 188–199.

P. Beame, M. Tompa, and P. Yan, "Communication–Space Tradeoffs for Unrestricted Protocols," *SIAM J. Computing* **23**(3), 1994, 652–661. (Early version in *Proc. of 31st IEEE Symposium on Foundations of Computer Science*, 1990, 429–438.)

R. Beigel, "The Polynomial Method in Circuit Complexity," *Proc. of the 8th Structure in Complexity Theory*, 1993, 82–95.

R. Beigel and J. Tarui, "On ACC," *J. of Computational Complexity* **4**(4), 1994, 350–366. (Early version in *Proc. of 32nd IEEE Symposium on Foundations of Computer Science*, 1991, 783–792.)

A. Björner, J. Karlander, and B. Lindström, "Communication Complexity of Two Decision Problems," *Discrete Applied Mathematics*, **39**, 1992, 161–163.

M. Blum, "Independent Unbiased Coin Flips from a Correlated Biased Source: A Finite State Markov Chain," *Combinatorica*, **6**, 1986, 277–280.

R. B. Boppana and M. Sipser, "The Complexity of Boolean Functions," in *Handbook of Theoretical Computer Science*, Elsevier: Amsterdam 1990, Vol. A, Chapter 14, 757–804.

R. E. Bryant, "Graph-Based Algorithms for Boolean Function Manipulations," *IEEE Transactions on Computers*, **35**, 1986, 677–691.

R. Canetti and O. Goldreich, "Bounds on Tradeoffs between Randomness and Communication Complexity," *J. Computational Complexity*, **3**, 1993, 141–167. (Early version in *Proc. of 31st IEEE Symposium on Foundations of Computer Science*, 1990, 766–775.)

A. K. Chandra, M. L. Furst, and R. J. Lipton, "Multy-party Protocols," *Proc. of 15th ACM Symposium on Theory of Computing*, 1983, 94–99.

P. Chen, "The Communication Complexity of Computing Differentiable Functions in Multicomputer Network," *Theoretical Computer Science* **125**, 1994, 373–383.

B. Chor and O. Goldreich, "Unbiased Bits from Sources of Weak Randomness and Probabilistic Communication Complexity," *SIAM J. Computing* **17**(2), 1988, 230–261. (Early version in *Proc. of 26th IEEE Symposium on Foundations of Computer Science*, 1985, 429–442.)

B. Chor, M. Geréb-Graus, and E. Kushilevitz, "Private Computations Over the Integers," *SIAM J. Computing* **24**(2), 1995, 376–386. (Early version in *Proc. of 31st IEEE Symposium on Foundations of Computer Science*, 1990, 335–344.)

B. Chor, O. Goldreich, E. Kushilevitz, and M. Sudan, "Private Information Retrieval," *Proc. of 36th IEEE Symposium on Foundations of Computer Science*, 1995, 41–50.

J. I. Chu and G. Schnitger, "The communication complexity of Several Problems in Matrix Computation," *J. Complexity* **7**, 1991, 395–407.

J. I. Chu and G. Schnitger, "The communication complexity of Matrix Computation over Finite Fields," *Mathematical Systems Theory* **28**(3), 1995, 215–228.

F. R. K. Chung, "Quasi-random Classes of Hypergraphs," *Random Structures and Algorithms* **1**(4), 1990, 363–382.

F. R. K. Chung and P. Tetali, "Communication Complexity and Quasi Randomness," *SIAM J. Discrete Mathematics* **6**(1), 1993, 110–123.

F. R. K. Chung, R. L. Graham, and R. M. Wilson, "Quasi-random Graphs," *Combinatorica* **9**, 1989, 345–362.

A. Cobham, "The Recognition Problem for the Set of Perfect Squares," Technical report RC-1704, IBM, 1966.

B. Codenotti, P. Gemmell, and J. Simon, "Average Circuit Complexity and Average Communication Complexity," *Proc. of 3rd European Symposium on Algorithms (ESA)*, Lecture Notes in Computer Science 979, Springer: Berlin, 1996, 102–112.

B. Codenotti, G. Manzini, and L. Margare, "Algebraic Techniques in Communication Complexity," *Information Processing Letters* **56**, 1995, 191–195.

A. Cohen and A. Wigderson, "Dispersers, Deterministic Amplification, and Weak Random Sources," *Proc. of 30th IEEE Symposium on Foundations of Computer Science*, 1989, 14–19.

T. H. Cormen, C. E. Leiserson, and R. L. Rivest, "Introduction to Algorithms," MIT Press: Cambridge, Mass., 1990.

C. Damm, S. Junka, and J. Sgall, "Some Bounds on Multiparty Communication Complexity of Pointer Jumping," *Proc. of 13th STACS*, Lecture Notes in Computer Science 1046, Springer: Berlin, 1996, 643–654.

C. Damm, M. Krause, C. Meinel, and S. Waack, "Separating Counting Communication Complexity Classes," *Proc. of Symposium on Theoretical Aspects of Computer Science*, Lecture Notes in Computer Science (Springer) 577, Springer: Berlin, 1992, 281–292.

M. Dietzfelbinger, J. Hromkovic, and G. Schnitger, "A Comparison of Two Lower Bound Methods for Communication Complexity," *Proc. of International Symposium on Mathematical Foundations of Computer Science 94*, Lecture Notes in Computer Science (Springer) 841, Springer: Berlin, 1994, 326–335.

D. Dolev and T. Feder, "Multiparty Communication Complexity," *Proc. of 30th IEEE Symposium on Foundations of Computer Science*, 1989, 428–433.

D. Dolev and T. Feder, "Determinism vs. Nondeterminism in Multiparty Communication Complexity," *SIAM J. Computing* **21**(5), 1992, 889–895.

P. E. Dunne, "The Complexity of Boolean Networks," Academic Press: London, 1988.

P. Ďuriš and Z. Galil, "On the Power of Multiple Reads in a Chip," *Information and Computation* **104**(2), 1993, 277–287. (Early version in *Proc. of 18th International Colloquium on Automata, Languages, and Programming*, Lecture Notes in Computer Science (Springer) 510, Springer: Berlin, 1991, 697–706.)

P. Ďuriš, Z. Galil, and G. Schnitger, "Lower Bounds on Communication Complexity," *Information and Computation* **73**(1), 1987, 1–22. (Early version in *Proc. of 16th ACM Symposium on Theory of Computing*, 1984, 81–91.)

P. Ďuriš and P. Pudlák, "On the Communication Complexity of Planarity," *Proc. of 7th International Conference on Fundamentals of Computation Theory*, Lecture Notes in Computer Science (Springer) 380, Springer: New York, 1989, 145–147.

J. Edmonds and R. Impagliazzo, unpublished manuscript, 1994.

J. Edmonds, S. Rudich, R. Impagliazzo, and J. Sgall, "Communication complexity towards lower bounds on circuit depth," *Proc. of 32nd IEEE Symposium on Foundations of Computer Science*, 1991, 249–257.

A. El-Gamal and A. Orlitsky, "Interactive Data Compression," *Proc. of 25th IEEE Symposium on Foundations of Computer Science*, 1984, 100–108.

A. El-Gamal and A. Orlitsky, "Average and Randomized Communication Complexity," *IEEE Transactions on Information Theory* **36**(1), 1990, 3–16.

U. Faigle, R. Schrader, and G. Turan, "The Communication Complexity of Interval Orders," *Discrete Applied Mathematics* **40**, 1992, 19–28.

T. Feder, E. Kushilevitz, M. Naor, and N. Nisan, "Amortized Communication Complexity," *SIAM J. Computing* **24**(4), 1995, 736–750. (Early version in *Proc. of 32nd IEEE Symposium on Foundations of Computer Science*, 1991, 239–248.)

R. Fleischer, "Communication Complexity of Multi-Processor Systems," *Information Processing Letters* **30**, 1989, 57–65.

R. Fleischer, H. Jung, and K. Mehlhorn, "A Communication-Randomness Tradeoff for Two-Processor Systems," *Information and Computation* **116**(2), 1995, 155–161. (Early version in *Proc. of 4th International Workshop on Distributed Algorithms*, Lecture Notes in Computer Science (Springer) 486, Springer: Berlin, 1990, 390–401.)

Fredman M., J. Komlòs, and E. Szemerèdi, "Storing A Sparse Table with O(1) Access Time," *Journal of the ACM* **31**, 1984, 538–544.

M. Fürer, "The Power of Randomness for Communication Complexity," *Proc. of 19th ACM Symposium on Theory of Computing*, 1987, 178–181.

M. R. Garey and D. S. Johnson, "Computers and Intractability–A Guide to the Theory of NP-Completeness," W. H. Freeman: New York, 1979.

M. Goldmann, "Communication Complexity and Lower Bounds for Threshold Circuits," in *Theoretical Advances in Neural Computation and Learning*, V. Roychowdhury, K. Y. Siu, and A. Orlitsky, Eds., Kluwer Academic: Boston, 1994, Chapter 3, 85–125.

M. Goldmann and J. Håstad, "A Simple Lower Bound for Monotone Clique Using A Communication Game," *Information Processing Letters* **41**, 1992, 221–226.

M. Goldmann, J. Håstad, and A. Razborov, "Majority Gates vs. General Weighted Threshold Gates," *Computational Complexity*, Vol. 2, 1992. (Early version in *Proc. of the 7th Structure in Complexity Theory*, 1992.)

R. L. Graham, B. Rothschild, and J. H. Spencer, "Ramsey Theory," Wiley: New York, Second edition, 1990.

M. Gringi and M. Sipser, "Monotone Separation of Logarithmic Space from Logarithmic Depth," *Journal of Computer and System Sciences* **50**, 1995, 433–437. (Early version in *Proc. of 6th Structure in Complexity Theory*, 1991, 294–298.)

H. D. Groger and G. Turan, "On Linear Decision Trees Computing Boolean Functions," *Proc. of 18th International Colloquium on Automata, Languages, and Programming*, Lecture Notes in Computer Science (Springer) 510, Springer: Berlin, 1991, 707–718.

V. Grolmusz, "Separating the Communication Complexities of MOD *m* and MOD *p* Circuits," *Proc. of 33rd IEEE Symposium on Foundations of Computer Science*, 1992, 278–287.

V. Grolmusz, "The BNS Lower Bound for Multi-Party Protocols is Nearly Optimal," *Information and Computation* **112**(1), 1994, 51–54.

V. Grolmusz, "Harmonic analysis, real approximation, and the communication complexity of Boolean functions," to appear in *Proc. of COCOON'96*, 1996.

A. Hajnal, W. Maass, P. Pudlák, M. Szegedy, and Gy. Turan, "Threshold Circuits of Bounded Depth," *Proc. of 28th IEEE Symposium on Foundations of Computer Science*, 1987, 99–110.

A. Hajnal, W. Maass, and Gy. Turan, "On the Communication Complexity of Graph Pro- perties," *Proc. of 20th ACM Symposium on Theory of Computing*, 1988, 186–191.

B. Halstenberg and R. Reischuk, "Different Modes of Communication," *SIAM J. Computing* **22**(5), 1993, 913–934. (Early version in *Proc. of 20th ACM Symposium on Theory of Computing*, 1988a, 162–172.)

B. Halstenberg and R. Reischuk, "Relations between Communication Complexity Classes," *Journal of Computer and System Sciences* **41**(3), 1990, 402–429. (Early version in *Proc. of 3rd Structure in Complexity Theory*, 1988b.)

J. Håstad, "Computational Limitations for Small Depth Circuits," MIT Press: Cambridge, Mass., 1986.

J. Håstad and M. Goldmann, "On the Power of Small-Depth Threshold Circuits," *Proc. of 31st IEEE Symposium on Foundations of Computer Science*, 1990, 610–618.

J. Håstad and A. Wigderson, "Composition of the Universal Relation," *DIMACS Series in Discrete Mathematics and Theoretical Computer Science* **13**, 1993, 119–134.

J. Håstad, S. Jukna, and P. Pudlák, "Top-Down Lower Bounds for Depth 3 Circuits," *Proc. of 34th IEEE Symposium on Foundations of Computer Science*, 1993, 124–129.

J. E. Hopcroft and J. D. Ullman, "Introduction to Automata Theory, Languages, and Computation," Addison-Wesley: Reading, Mass., 1979.

K. Hosaka, Y. Takenaga, and S. Yajima, "On the Size of Ordered Binary Decision Diagrams Representing Threshold Functions," *Proc. of International Symposium on Algorithms and Computation '94*, Lecture Notes in Computer Science (Springer) 834, Springer: Berlin, 1994, 584–592.

J. Hromkovic and G. Schnitger, "Nondeterministic Communication with a Limite Number of Advice Bits," *Proc. of 28th STOC*, 1996, 551–560.

R. Impagliazzo and D. Zuckerman, "How to Recycle Random Bits," *Proc. of 30th IEEE Symposium on Foundations of Computer Science*, 1989, 248–253.

R. Impagliazzo, N. Nisan, and A. Wigderson, "Pseudorandomness for Network Algorithms," *Proc. of 26th ACM Symposium on Theory of Computing*, 1994a, 88–96.

R. Impagliazzo, R. Raz, and A. Wigderson, "A Direct Product Theorem," *Proc. of 9th Structure in Complexity Theory*, 1994b, 356–364.

A. Itai, "The Communication Complexity of the Two List Problem," *Proc. of 5th International Workshop on Distributed Algorithms*, Lecture Notes in Computer Science (Springer) 579, Springer: Berlin, 1991, 193–199.

J. Ja'ja' and V. K. P. Kumar, "Information Transfer in Distributed Computing with Applications to VLSI," *Journal of the ACM* **31**(1), 1984, 150–162.

J. Ja'ja', V. K. P. Kumar, and J. Simon, "Information Transfer under Different Sets of Protocols," *SIAM J. Computing* **13**(4), 1984, 840–849.

B. Kalyanasundaram and G. Schnitger, "The Probabilistic Communication Complexity of Set Intersection," *SIAM J. Discrete Mathematics* **5**(4), 1992, 545–557. (Early version in *Proc. of 2nd Structure in Complexity Theory*, 1987, 41–49.)

M. Karchmer, "Communication Complexity: A New Approach to Circuit Depth," MIT Press: Cambridge, Mass., 1989.

M. Karchmer and A. Wigderson, "Monotone Circuits for Connectivity Require Super-Logarithmic Depth," *SIAM J. Discrete Mathematics* **3**(2), 1990, 255–265. (Early version in *Proc. of 20th ACM Symposium on Theory of Computing*, 1988, 539–550.)

M. Karchmer, R. Raz, and A. Wigderson, "On Proving Super-Logarithmic Depth Lower Bounds via the Direct Sum in Communication Complexity," *Proc. of 6th IEEE Structure in Complexity Theory*, 1991, 299–304.

M. Karchmer, E. Kushilevitz, and N. Nisan, "Fractional Covers and Communication Complexity," *SIAM J. Discrete Mathematics* **8**(1), 1995, 76–92. (Early version in *7th IEEE Structure in Complexity Theory*, 1992a, 262–274.)

M. Karchmer, I. Newman, M. Saks, and A. Wigderson, "Non-deterministic Communication Complexity with Few Witnesses," *Journal of Computer and System Sciences* **49**(2), 1994, 247–257. (Early version in *Proc. of 7th Structure in Complexity Theory*, 1992b.)

H. Karloff, "Linear Programming," Birkhäuser: Boston, 1991.

R. Karp, "Lecture Notes on Concrete Complexity," University of California, Berkeley, 1986.

V. Khrapchenko, "A Method of Determining Lower Bounds for the Complexity of π-Schemes," *Math. Notes Acad. Sci. USSR*, 1971, 474–479.

M. Klawe, W. J. Paul, N. Pippenger, and M. Yannakakis, "On Monotone Formulae with Restricted Depth," *Proc. of 26th ACM Symposium on Theory of Computing*, 1984, 480–487.

M. Krause and S. Waack, "Variation Ranks of Communication Matrices and Lower Bounds for Depth Two Circuits Having Symmetric Gates with Unbounded Fan-in," *Mathematical Systems Theory* **28**(6), 1995, 553–564. (Early version in *Proc. of 32nd IEEE Symposium on Foundations of Computer Science*, 1991, 777–782.)

I. Kremer, "Quantum Communication Complexity," Master Thesis, Hebrew University, 1995.

I. Kremer, N. Nisan, and D. Ron, "On Randomized One-Round Communication Complexity," *Proc. of 27th ACM Symposium on Theory of Computing*, 1995, 596–605.

E. Kushilevitz, "Privacy and Communication Complexity," *SIAM J. Discrete Mathematics* 5(2), 1992, 273–284. (Early version in *Proc. of 30th IEEE Symposium on Foundations of Computer Science*, 1989, 416–421.)

E. Kushilevitz, N. Linial, and R. Ostrovsky, "The Linear-Array Conjecture of Communication Complexity is False," *Proc. of 28th STOC*, 1996, 1–10.

T. Lam and W. L. Ruzzo, "Results on Communication Complexity Classes," *Journal of Computer and System Sciences* 44(2), 1992, 324–342. (Early version in *Proc. of 4th Structure in Complexity Theory*, 1989, 148–157.)

T. Lam, P. Tiwari, and M. Tompa, "Tradeoffs between Communication Complexity and Space," *Journal of Computer and System Sciences* 45(3), 1992, 296–315. (Early version in *Proc. of 21st ACM Symposium on Theory of Computing*, 1989, 217–226.)

S. Lang, "Algebra," Addison Wesley: Reading, Mass., Third edition, 1993.

F. T. Leighton, "Introduction to Parallel Algorithms and Architectures: Arrays, Trees, Hypercubes," Morgan-Kaufmann: San Mateo, Calif., 1991.

T. Lengauer, "VLSI Theory," in *Handbook of Theoretical Computer Science*, Elsevier:Amsterdam, 1990, Vol. A, Chapter 16, 835–868.

R. J. Lipton and R. Sedgewick, "Lower Bounds for VLSI," *Proc. of 13th ACM Symposium on Theory of Computing*, 1981, 300–307.

R. J. Lipton and R. E. Tarjan, "Applications of A Planar Separator Theorem," *SIAM J. Computing* 9, 1980, 615–627.

S. V. Lokam, "Spectral Methods for Matrix Rigidity with Applications to Size–Depth Tradeoffs and Communication Complexity," *Proc. of 36th IEEE Symposium on Foundations of Computer Science*, 1995, 6–15.

L. Lovász, "On the ratio of optimal integral and fractional covers," *Discrete Mathematics* 13, 1975, 383–390.

L. Lovász, "Communication Complexity: A Survey," in *Paths, Flows, and VLSI Layout*, B. H. Korte, Ed., Springer Verlag: Berlin 1990. (Early version in *Technical Report CS-TR-204-89*, Princeton University, 1989.)

L. Lovász and M. Saks, "Lattices, Möbius Functions and Communication Complexity," *Journal of Computer and System Sciences* 47, 1993, 322–349. (Early version in *Proc. of 29th IEEE Symposium on Foundations of Computer Science*, 1988, 81–90.)

A. Lubotzky, R. Philips, and P. Sarnak, "Explicit Expanders and the Ramanujan Conjecture," *Proc. of 18th ACM Symposium on Theory of Computing*, 1986, 240–246.

A. Lubotzky, R. Philips, and P. Sarnak, "Ramanujan Graphs," *Combinatorica* 8(3), 1988, 261–277.

Z. Q. Luo and J. N. Tsitsiklis, "Communication Complexity of Algebraic Computation," *Proc. of 31st IEEE Symposium on Foundations of Computer Science*, 1991a, 758–765.

Z. Q. Luo and J. N. Tsitsiklis, "On the Communication Complexity of Solving a Polynomial Equation," *SIAM J. Computing* 20(5), 1991b, 936–950.

L. A. McGeoch, "A Strong Separation between k and $k-1$ Round Communication Complexity for a Constructive Language," Technical Report CMU-CS-86-157, Carnegie Mellon University, 1986.

K. Mehlhorn and E. Schmidt, "Las-Vegas is better than Determinism in VLSI and Distributed Computing," *Proc. of 14th ACM Symposium on Theory of Computing*, 1982, 330–337.

C. Meinel and S. Waack, "The Möbius Function, Variation Ranks, and $\Theta(n)$-Bounds on the Modular Communication Complexity of the Undirected Graph Connectivity Problem," unpublished manuscript, 1994.

C. Meinel and S. Waack, "The "log Rank" Conjecture for Modular Communication Complexity," *Proc. of 13th STACS*, Lecture Notes in Computer Science 1046, Springer: Berlin, 1996, 619–630.

C. Meinel and S. Waack, "Lower Bounds for the Modular Communication Complexity of Various Graph Accessibility Problems," *Proc. of LATIN'95*, Lecture Notes in Computer Science (Springer) 911, Springer: Berlin, 1995, 427–435.

P. B. Miltersen, "Lower Bounds for Union-Split-Find Related Problems on Random Access Machines," *Proc. of 26th ACM Symposium on Theory of Computing,* 1994, 625–634.

P. B. Miltersen, "On the Cell Probe Complexity of Polynomial Evaluation," *Theoretical Computer Science* **143**(1), 1995, 167–174.

P. B. Miltersen, N. Nisan, S. Safra, and A. Wigderson, "On Data Structures and Asymmetric Communication Complexity," *Proc of 27th ACM Symposium on Theory of Computing*, 1995, 103–111.

E. H. Modiano and A. Ephremides, "Communication Complexity of Secure Distributed Computation in the Presence of Noise," *IEEE Transactions on Information Theory* **38**(4), 1992, 1193–1202.

S. Muroga, "Threshold Logic and its Applications," Wiley Interscience: New York, 1971.

M. Naor, A. Orlitsky, and P. Shor, "Three Results on Interactive Communication," *IEEE Transactions on Information Theory* **39**(5), 1993, 1608–1615.

I. Newman, "Private vs. Common Random Bits in Communication Complexity," *Information Processing Letters* **39**, 1991, 67–71.

I. Newman and M. Szegedy, "Public vs. Private Coin Flips in One Round Communication Games," *Proc. of 28th STOC*, 1996, 561–570.

N. Nisan, "The Communication Complexity of Threshold Gates," *Combinatorics, Paul Erdös is Eighty (Vol. 1)*, D. Miklós, V. T. Sós, and T. Szönyi, Eds., Janos Bolyai Math. Society: Budapest, Hungary, 1993, 301–315.

N. Nisan and A. Wigderson, "Rounds in Communication Complexity Revisited," *SIAM J. Computing* **22**(1), 1993, 211–219. (Early version in *Proc. of 23rd ACM Symposium on Theory of Computing*, 1991, 419–429.)

N. Nisan and A. Wigderson, "On Rank vs. Communication Complexity," *Combinatorica*, **15**(4), 1995, 557–566. (Early version in *Proc. of 35th IEEE Symposium on Foundations of Computer Science*, 1994, 831–836.)

A. Orlitsky, "Communication Issues in Distributed Communication," Ph.D. thesis, Stanford University, 1986.

A. Orlitsky, "Worst-Case Interactive Communication I: Two Messages are Almost Optimal," *IEEE Transactions on Information Theory* **36**, 1990, 1111–1126. (Early version in *Proc. of 9th ACM Symposium on Principles of Distributed Computing*, 1990, 219–232.)

A. Orlitsky, "Worst-Case Interactive Communication II: Two Messages are not Optimal," *IEEE Transactions on Information Theory* **37**, 1991a, 995–1005.

A. Orlitsky, "Interactive Communication: Balanced Distributions, Correlated Files, and Average-Case Complexity," *SIAM J. Discrete Mathematics* **6**(4), 1993, 548–564. (Early version in *Proc. of 32nd IEEE Symposium on Foundations of Computer Science*, 1991b, 228–238.)

A. Orlitsky, "Average-Case Interactive Communication," *IEEE Transactions on Information Theory* **38**, 1992, 1534–1547.

A. Orlitsky and A. El-Gamal, "Communication with Secrecy Constraints," *Proc. of 16th ACM Symposium on Theory of Computing*, 1984, 217–224.

A. Orlitsky and A. El-Gamal, "Communication Complexity," in *Complexity in Information Theory*, Y. S. Abu-Mostafa, Ed., Springer: New York, 1988, 16–61.

G. Owen, "Game Theory," Academic Press: New York, Second edition, 1982.

K. F. Pang and A. El-Gamal, "Communication Complexity of Computing the Hamming Distance," *SIAM J. Computing* **15**(4), 1986, 932–947.

C. H. Papadimitriou, "Computational Complexity," Addison Wesley: Reading, Mass., 1994.

C. Papadimitriou and M. Sipser, "Communication Complexity," *Journal of Computer and System Sciences* **28**(2), 1984, 260–269. (Early version in *Proc. of 14th ACM Symposium on Theory of Computing*, 1982, 196–200.)

R. Paturi and J. Simon, "Probabilistic Communication Complexity," *Journal of Computer and System Sciences* **33**(1), 1986, 106–123. (Early version in *Proc. of 25th IEEE Symposium on Foundations of Computer Science*, 1984, 118–126.)

P. Pudlák, "Unexpected Upper Bounds on the Complexity of Some Communication Games," *Proc. of 21st International Colloquium on Automata, Languages, and Programming*, Lecture Notes in Computer Science (Springer) 820, Springer: Berlin, 1994, 1–10.

P. Pudlák and V. Rödl, "Modified Ranks of Tensors and the Size of Circuits," *Proc. of 25th ACM Symposium on Theory of Computing*, 1993, 523–531.

P. Pudlák and J. Sgall, "An Upper Bound for a Communication Game Related to Time–Space Tradeoffs," ECCC Technical Report TR95-010, 1995.

S. Rajagopalan and L. J. Schulman, "A Coding Theorem for Distributed Computing," *Proc. of 26th ACM Symposium on Theory of Computing*, 1994, 790–799.

R. Raz, "Fourier Analysis for Probabilistic Communication Complexity," unpublished manuscript, 1993.

R. Raz and B. Spieker, "On the *log rank* Conjecture in Communication Complexity," *Combinatorica* **15**(4), 1995, 567–588. (Early version in *Proc. of 34th IEEE Symposium on Foundations of Computer Science*, 1993, 168–176.)

R. Raz and A. Wigderson, "Probabilistic Communication Complexity of Boolean Relations," *Proc. of 30th IEEE Symposium on Foundations of Computer Science*, 1989, 562–567.

R. Raz and A. Wigderson, "Monotone Circuits for Matching Require Linear Depth," *Journal of the ACM* **39**(3), 1992, 736–744. (Early version in *Proc. of 22nd ACM Symposium on Theory of Computing*, 1990, 287–292.)

A. A. Razborov, "On the Distributional Complexity of Disjointness," *Theoretical Computer Science* **106**(2), 1992, 385–390. (Early version in *Proc. of 17th International Colloquium on Automata, Languages, and Programming*, Lecture Notes in Computer Science (Springer) 443, Springer: Berlin, 1990a, 249–253.)

A. A. Razborov, "Applications of Matrix Methods to the Theory of Lower Bounds in Computational Complexity," *Combinatorica* **10**(1), 1990b, 81–93.

A. A. Razborov, "Lower Bounds for Deterministic and Nondeterministic Branching Program," *Proc. of 8th International Conference on Fundamentals of Computation Theory*, Lecture Notes in Computer Science (Springer) 529, Springer: Berlin, 1991, 47–60.

A. A. Razborov, "The Gap between the Chromatic Number of a Graph and the Rank of its Adjacency Matrix is Superlinear," *Discrete Mathematics* **108**, 1992, 393–396.

M. Rodeh, "Finding the Median Distributively," *Journal of Computer and System Sciences* **24**, 1982, 162–166.

V. P. Roychowdhury, A. Orlitsky, and K. Y. Siu, "Lower Bounds on Threshold and Related Circuits via Communication Complexity," *IEEE Transactions on Information Theory* **40**(2), 1994, 467–474.

M. Santha and U. V. Vazirani, "Generating Quasi-Random Sequences from Slightly-Random Sources," *Proc. of 25th IEEE Symposium on Foundations of Computer Science*, 1984, 434–440.

L. J. Schulman, "Communication on Noisy Channels: A Coding Theorem for Computation," *Proc. of 33rd IEEE Symposium on Foundations of Computer Science*, 1992, 724–733.

L. J. Schulman, "Deterministic Coding for Interactive Communication," *Proc. of 25th ACM Symposium on Theory of Computing*, 1993, 747–756.

C. E. Shannon, "A Mathematical Theory of Communication," *Bell System Technical J.* **27**, 1948, 379–423, 623–656.

K. Y. Siu, V. Roychowdhury, and T. Kailath, "Discrete Neural Computation – A Theoretical Foundation," Prentice Hall: Englewood Cliffs, New Jersey, 1995.

R. Smolensky, "On Interpolation by Analytic Functions with Special Properties and Some Weak Lower Bounds on the Size of Circuits with Symmetric Gates," *Proc. of 31st IEEE Symposium on Foundations of Computer Science*, 1990, 628–631.

M. Szegedy, "Functions with Bounded Symmetric Communication Complexity and Circuits with mod m Gates," *Proc. of 22nd ACM Symposium on Theory of Computing*, 1990, 278–286.

U. Tamm, "Communication Complexity of Sum-Type Functions Invariant under Translation," *Information and Computation* **116**(2), 1995, 162–173.

S. H. Teng, "Functional Inversion and Communication Complexity," *J. Cryptology* **7**(3), 1994, 153–170.

C. D. Thompson, "Area-Time Complexity for VLSI," *Proc. of 11th ACM Symposium on Theory of Computing*, 1979, 81–88.

P. Tiwari, "Lower Bounds on Communication Complexity in Distributed Computer Networks," *Journal of the ACM* **34**(4), 1987, 921–938. (Early version in *Proc. of 25th IEEE Symposium on Foundations of Computer Science*, 1984, 109–117.)

J. N. Tsitsiklis and Z. Q. Luo, "Communication Complexity of Convex Optimization," *J. Complexity* **3**, 1987, 231–243.

L. Valiant, "Graph Theoretic Arguments in Low-Level Complexity," Technical Report CS 13-77, University of Edinburgh, 1977.

U. V. Vazirani, "Towards a Strong Communication Complexity Theory or Generating Quasi-Random Sequences from Two Communicating Slightly-Random Sources," *Combinatorica* **7**(4), 1987, 375–392. (Early version in *Proc. of 17th ACM Symposium on Theory of Computing*, 1985, 366–378.)

J. von Neumann, "Various Techniques Used in Connection with Random Digits," notes by G. E. Forsythe, Applied Math. Series, Vol. 12, National Bureau of Standards, 1951, 36–38. Reprinted in *von Neumann's Collected Works*, Vol. 5, Pergamon: XXX, 1963, 768–770.

I. Wegener, "The Complexity of Boolean Functions," Wiley-Teubner Series in Computer Science: Stuttgart, 1987.

I. Wegener, "The Size of Reduced OBDDs and Optimal Read-Once Branching Programs for Almost all Boolean Functions," *Proc. of International Workshop on Graph-Theoretic Concepts in Computer Science*, Lecture Notes in Computer Science (Springer) 790, Springer: Berlin, 1993, 252–263.

A. Wigderson, "Information Theoretic Reasons for Computational Difficulty or Communication Complexity for Circuit Complexity," unpublished manuscript, 1993.

B. Xiao, "New Bounds in the Cell Probe Model," University of California, San Diego, 1992.

M. Yannakakis, "Expressing Combinatorial Optimization Problems by Linear Programs," *Journal of Computer and System Sciences* **43**(3), 1991, 441–466. (Early version in *Proc. of 20th ACM Symposium on Theory of Computing*, 1988, 223–228.)

A. C. Yao, "Some Complexity Questions Related to Distributed Computing," *Proc. of 11th ACM Symposium on Theory of Computing*, 1979, 209–213.

A. C. Yao, "The Entropic Limitations on VLSI Computations," *Proc. of 13th ACM Symposium on Theory of Computing*, 1981, 308–311.

A. C. Yao, "Lower Bounds by Probabilistic Arguments," *Proc. of 24th IEEE Symposium on Foundations of Computer Science*, 1983, 420–428.

A. C. Yao, "On ACC and Threshold Circuits," *Proc. of 31st IEEE Symposium on Foundations of Computer Science*, 1990, 619–627.

A. C. Yao, "Quantum Circuit Complexity," *Proc. of 34th IEEE Symposium on Foundations of Computer Science*, 1993, 352–361.

Z. Zhang and X. G. Xia, "Three Messages are not Optimal in Worst-Case Interactive Communication," *IEEE Transactions on Information Theory* **40**, 1994, 3–10.

D. Zuckerman, "Simulating BPP Using a General Weak Random Source," *Proc. of 32nd IEEE Symposium on Foundations of Computer Science*, 1991, 79–89.

Index